T0135684

 University of Paderborn

Faculty of Electrical Engineering, Computer
Science, and Mathematics
Department of Computer Science
Warburger Straße 100
D-33098 Paderborn

Model-Driven Engineering of Reconfigurable Mechatronic Systems

by

Sven Burmester

PhD thesis submitted in partial fulfillment
of the requirements for the degree of
Doctor of Natural Science (Dr. rer. nat.)

Schriftliche Arbeit
zur Erlangung des Grades
Doktor der Naturwissenschaften (Dr. rer. nat.)

Bibliografische Information Der Deutschen Bibliothek

Die Deutsche Bibliothek verzeichnet diese Publikation in der Deutschen
Nationalbibliografie; detaillierte bibliografische Daten sind im Internet über
http://dnb.ddb.de abrufbar.

ISBN 3-8325-1298-5

Logos Verlag Berlin
Comeniushof, Gubener Str. 47,
10243 Berlin
Tel.: +49 030 42 85 10 90
Fax: +49 030 42 85 10 92
INTERNET: http://www.logos-verlag.de

Abstract

The Unified Modeling Language (UML) and the model-driven engineering (MDE) approach became standard in software engineering. The recent development in the design of mechatronic systems, which combine technologies from mechanical and electrical engineering as well as from software engineering, applies increasingly UML and MDE. Nowadays, new trends in mechatronics like the integration of self-optimization lead to reconfigurating systems which require advanced engineering techniques: Reconfigurating systems change their structure at runtime. This includes the exchange of single modules and restructuring of the communication connections. Even the application of existing UML-based modeling techniques for such systems leads to complex models which are difficult to handle and hard to analyze.

Therefore, a new UML-based modeling technique is presented in this thesis. This modeling technique is used for the specification of reconfigurable systems which integrate behavior from the mechanical, electrical, and from the software engineering domain. To support the model-driven engineering approach, the new modeling approach is seamlessly integrated in an approach for the model-based specification and verification of real-time systems. As standard verification techniques are not feasible for complex systems, the specification of real-time communication protocols, real-time behavior, and reconfiguration is separated. Applying compositional real-time modelchecking and using the separation in combination with refinement relations reduces the effort to ensure that these specifications are not contradictive and that the specified real-time requirements hold.

In order to ensure that the verification results do not just hold for the models, but also for the implementation, a code generator is presented. The applications derived by this code generator integrate implementations of the models from the different engineering domains, guarantee to hold the specified and verified real-time requirements, and provide efficient implementations in spite of complex reconfiguration.

IV

Acknowledgements

I am truly grateful to Professor Dr. Wilhelm Schäfer for incorporating me in the software engineering group and for making this work possible. Special thanks go to Dr. Holger Giese for leading me to the right track. The ideas arisen from the discussions with him play an important role in this thesis. Further, I am thankful to Professor Dr. Franz Josef Rammig, Professor Dr. Joachim Lückel, and Professor Dr. habil. Ansgar Trächtler for their supervision and Professor Jeff Magee for reviewing my thesis.

I am really obliged to my colleagues for the innumerous discussions and for causing a comfortable working atmosphere. Namely, these are Björn Axenath, Dr. Matthias Gehrke, Jutta Haupt, Stefan Henkler, Martin Hirsch, Dr. Ekkart Kindler, Florian Klein, Jürgen Maniera, Ahmet Mehic, Matthias Meyer, Ulrich Nickel, Dr. Jörg Niere, Vladimir Rubin, Dr. Daniela Schilling, Matthias Tichy, Dr. Jörg Wadsack, Robert Wagner, and Lothar Wendehals.

In this context, I am also grateful to Alfonso Gambuzza, Thorsten Hestermeyer, Eckehard Münch, Oliver Oberschelp, and Henner Vöcking from the control engineering and mechatronics group –formerly known as Mechatronics Laboratory Paderborn (MLaP)– for helping me with all control engineering problems. I am also thankful to Dr. Rainer Feldmann for the support in mathematical and algorithmic problems.

I appreciate the developers of the Fujaba Tool Suite, especially the students who worked on the Fujaba Real-Time Tool Suite, namely Vadim Boiko, Margarete Kudak, Wladimir Pauls, Matthias Schwarz, Björn Schwerdtfeger, and Andreas Seibel. I thank everyone who was reading and checking parts of this thesis or parts of my publications.

I am deeply grateful to my parents Karin and Wolfgang Burmester. Going this way would not have been possible without them. Finally, I thank my girl-friend Irena Budzan. You gave me all the support and motivation I needed. Spending my spare time with you is the reward for all the nights of work.

Contents

Chapter 1

Introduction

Mechatronic Systems The recent development of mechanical systems has been strongly supported by integrated circuits, microprocessors, and software. This combination of electrical engineering, mechanical engineering, and software engineering is denoted by the term *mechatronics*. Due to the combination of the different domains, tasks which have traditionally been assigned to one of these domains are transferred to one of the other domains. Thus, the design of mechatronic products requires a tight cooperation between the engineers of the different domains: Feedback-controllers are one example, because they belong to the electrical and mechanical engineering domains, but nowadays they are often realized in software. The advantage is that software is technically easier to maintain and to exchange than hardware – although the development and implementation of the concepts for the exchange of software is as extensive as for hardware.

Mechatronic systems have been intruded into daily life. Aircrafts, cars, and satellites are just some examples for mechatronic systems. They combine the three mechatronics disciplines for example to control engines, to control a car body, etc. Due to their application domain, mechatronic systems are usually safety-critical, embedded, hybrid real-time systems. The meaning of these terms is described in the following:

In a *real-time* system, it is not just important that the functional behavior is correct, which means that the system always reacts like expected. Additional, the time that is required to finish the reaction has to be predictable and must be guaranteed by the system. For example, the airbag of a car must not just be opened as soon as possible – it must be guaranteed to be finished within a certain time.

A *hybrid* system integrates *continuous* and *discrete* systems. A continuous system processes continuous input signals and produces continuous output signals (e.g. a feedback-controller controlling the velocity of a vehicle). A discrete system consists of different discrete modes. When a system switches between different discrete control-modes which are associated with different continuous systems (e.g. in order to apply different strategies to control the velocity), it is called *hybrid system*.

In *embedded* systems, a micro controller is embedded into a mechanical or an electrical product. The controller's software has to interact with the hardware (the electrical or mechanical modules) of the system. For economic reasons, the resources of embedded systems are usually drastically restricted: To produce these systems low priced, they have only a restricted amount of memory and limited computational power. In the design of classical software like for example office applications, it is usually assumed that sufficient memory and computational power is available, but in embedded systems' design, these limitations have to be respected and are relevant during the design process.

The important characteristic of a *safety-critical* system is that malfunctions can have fatal consequences. These consequences can be threatening of life caused for example by malfunctions in airplanes or cars, but also high economic losses for example caused by the demolition of a satellite.

Self-optimization and Reconfiguration   A new area of research concentrates on self-optimization in mechatronic systems. The aim of self-optimization is to improve the system behavior at run-time. This is done by recurrently (i) analyzing the current situation (inclusive the current state of the system and past experiences), (ii) determining new objectives of the system, and (iii) adapting the system behavior [FGK+04].

When a self-optimizing mechatronic system is part of a networked system, the past experiences, which are used to analyze the current situation, may partially be delivered from other parts of the networked system, e.g. they can be sent from other mechatronic systems by communication.   Such an interchange of information leads to a database which provides sufficient knowledge to make the self-optimization effective. Therefore, communication is often an essential prerequisite for effective self-optimization in such systems.

Different possibilities exist to adapt the system behavior: parameter adaptation, reconfiguration, and compositional adaptation. Reconfiguration and compositional adaptation constitute the concept of structural adaptation [FGK+04]:

Parameter adaptation is used if the behavior has to be changed, but does not require a change of the system's structure. In complex, mechatronic systems, the adaptation of the behavior often requires to exchange complex parts of the architecture or to change the system structure (*structural adaptation*). In this case, parameter adaptation can only be applied to switch parts of the system on and off by changing parameters. In complex, mechatronic systems with limited resources, this is usually not possible, because the available resources are just sufficient to run the required parts of the system. Then, it is required to exchange the respective parts of the system which includes an exchange of modules and a change of the system structure. If in structural adaptation the number of possible *configurations* of a system is finite and these configurations are known at design-time, i.e. all possible structures of the system are known, the adaptation is called *reconfiguration* otherwise, it is called *compositional adaptation* [FGK+04].

Currently, many approaches exist which support parameter adaptation in static structures. Some approaches support the adaptation of the behavior by exchanging modules, but structural modifications can only be modeled by workarounds which lead to a high visual complexity of the models and which are hard to analyze. Therefore, a technique is required to design complex, structural adapting mechatronic systems which reduces visual complexity and which leads to models that are analyzable with less effort. As compositional adaptation is an extensive enhancement of reconfiguration, first a sophisticated approach to model reconfiguration is required, which will be the basis for an approach to model compositional adaptation.

Due to the safety-critical character of mechatronic systems, the design process has to integrate methods for verification and validation to detect possible faults in the model. Therefore, advanced analysis techniques have to be applied. These analysis techniques have to deal with the complexity, with the real-time requirements, with hybrid behavior, with resource restrictions, they have to consider communication, and they have to ensure that the reconfiguration does not conflict with any of the other requirements.

Model-Driven Engineering   A software engineering approach to design complex systems is *model-driven engineering (MDE)* [Ken02]. Among others, MDE consists of the following three parts: (i) *modeling* the system, (ii) *verifying* the model, and (iii) *synthesizing* source code from the models.

Models are used to cope with the complexity. They reduce the complexity by abstracting from the implementation details and from the details of the target platform. Useful models contain all domain-specific details, which are required to provide an implementation when the capabilities of the target platform are known.

In order to support the software design for the domain of mechatronic systems, models should be used which allow specifying hybrid, real-time behavior, resource restrictions, communication, reconfiguration and which allow the application of analysis techniques to verify correctness. The syntax and semantics of the (domain-specific) models should be defined formally to avoid ambiguities.

An implementation of the model of the mechatronic system has to respect the model's semantics and it has to implement it accordingly for the target platform. Due to the complexity of an implementation, the manual mapping of a model to source code is usually error-prone. Thus, automatic code synthesis is necessary.

To achieve correct systems, verification techniques, e.g. modelchecking, and validation techniques, e.g. simulation and testing, are applied. The disadvantage of systems with a huge state space is that they cannot be simulated or tested completely, as it is not feasible to simulate or to test all possible scenarios. Then, verification techniques need to be applied in combination with advanced methods that enable verification even of systems with huge state spaces. As verification and simulation require a model of the plant, and as this model is always an abstraction of the reality, testing needs to be applied even after successful modelchecking. Therefore, verification, simulation, and testing need to be combined.

Currently, plenty of approaches exist to model real-time or hybrid systems (e.g. [SPP01, Sta01, Hen00, ADE$^+$01, FdO99, FGHL04, EKRNS00]). Some of them allow the application of modelchecking, but they do not scale for complex systems or they are based on semantics which are not realizable on real physical microprocessors, because of the assumption that the system acts or reacts infinitely fast. Other approaches do not focus on the verification or provide implementations which do not respect the real-time requirements appropriately. These approaches are discussed in detail in Chapter 6.

As mentioned above, all existing approaches have in common, that they provide no or just limited support for modeling reconfiguration. We will see that modeling reconfiguration with current approaches leads to a complexity which is difficult to comprehend and difficult to analyze when the modeled system is large. One common approach to reduce visual complexity is to introduce high-level constructs. Due to the extensive complexity of reconfigurable mechatronic systems, advanced modeling technologies are required introducing new high-level concepts to deal with the complexity. A verification approach is required that is even feasible for complex models. The design should be modular, component-based and it should support reconfiguration. Its semantics must be defined formally in order to apply efficient analysis and verification techniques and the semantics –inclusive the real-time behavior– must be implementable.

1.1   Objective & Conception

The aim of this work is to present a new design technique and a corresponding implementation which uses new concepts to specify and verify reconfigurable, mechatronic systems in consideration of hybrid and real-time behavior and resource-restrictions. Instead of *reinventing the wheel*, and providing just another modeling technique, our approach will refine existing approaches –namely the *Unified Modeling Language* (*UML*) and *block diagrams*– in order to facilitate an easy use of the new modeling technique. Automatic code synthesis guarantees an implementation conformant to the semantics of the model, and the functional and temporal correctness of the models is ensured by the integration with compositional verification techniques.

Modeling   As the Unified Modeling Language (UML) [Obj05b] is the standard in software engineering to specify architecture and behavior, we refine UML component diagrams by defining hybrid components, which integrate continuous and discrete behavior, and integrate them with extended UML state machines. The continuous behavior is specified by block diagrams, discrete behavior is specified by state machines. The basic idea to model reconfiguration by this integration is to relate component instance diagrams which specify the inner structure of a component to the component's discrete states. The tight integration of structure and behavior reduces complexity and allows simple checks to ensure that the specified behavior of the hybrid components is consistent with the specified real-time behavior without expensive exploration of the state space as for example required by modelchecking.

Implementation   The automatic code generation synthesizes software for real-time target platforms. The generated code integrates discrete and continuous behavior and it has a modular structure. With the modular structure, we provide an efficient implementation of the reconfiguration (replacing parts of the system and changing the system structure at run-time). The implementation respects all real-time requirements which are specified in the model, and it guarantees to work with restricted resources.

Verification Even when the high-level modeling constructs reduce the visual complexity, which supports the engineers in comprehension of a model, the reachable state space is not reduced by the applied modeling language. Therefore, the high-level constructs of the models do not always reduce the costs for analysis techniques like modelchecking. We provide a verification approach that exploits the new high-level modeling constructs to reduce analysis cost: In order to apply modelchecking even for complex mechatronic systems, a compositional approach is followed, where functional and temporal correctness must just be ensured for small subsystems. Refinement relations ensure that the composition of the small parts to the whole system still guarantees the verification results. Further refinement relations and consistency checks are used to ensure that the integration of hybrid subsystems does not invalidate the verified real-time behavior.

1.2 Application Example

In the remainder of this thesis, we demonstrate foundations and the new design technique by means of an application example. The concrete example, which has been described in [BGT05], stems from the RailCab research project (see Figure 1.1)[1] which aims at using a passive track system with intelligent, autonomous shuttles that operate individually and make independent and decentralized operational decisions. The vision of the RailCab project is to provide the comfort of individual traffic concerning scheduling and on-demand availability of transportation as well as individually equipped cars on the one hand and the cost and resource efficiency of public transport on the other hand.

Figure 1.1: Shuttles from the RailCab research project

The modular railway system combines modern chassis control with the advantages of the linear drive technology as employed in the Transrapid[2] to increase the passengers' comfort while still enabling high speed transportation. In contrast to the Transrapid, the shuttles from the RailCab project reuse the existing railway tracks. One particular problem is how to coordinate the autonomously operating shuttles in such a way that they build convoys whenever possible to reduce the air resistance and thus the energy consumption. Such

---

[1]http://www-nbp.upb.de/en
[2]http://www.transrapid.de/en

convoys are built on-demand and require a small distance between the different shuttles such that a high reduction of energy consumption is achieved.

When building or breaking a convoy, the speed control units of the shuttles need to be coordinated, which is a safety-critical issue and results in a number of hard real-time constraints. The behavior of a speed control unit is dependent on whether the shuttle is part of a convoy at all and it depends on the position within the convoy. The overall aim of the whole convoy is to drive with a reduced distance and to keep it on a constant level. This might be achieved by adjusting the velocity appropriately and –after reaching the required distance– holding all velocities on a constant value. This could be done by parameter adaptation (see above).

But even when all shuttles of a convoy apply a controller which holds the velocity on the same constant level, just small drifts between the controllers could cause rear-end collisions: Assume a front shuttle, driving 159.99 km/h, and a rear shuttle, driving in a distance of 100 mm behind the front shuttle at a velocity of 160 km/h. In this case the shuttles would collide after only 36 sec.

Therefore, the behavior of the rear shuttles is changed by replacing the velocity controller by a controller that holds the distance on a constant level. Obviously, such a feedback-controller requires different input signals, provided by different sensors, which leads to a reconfiguration of a larger part of the system instead of just exchanging one feedback-controller. Multiple possibilities exist to achieve this goal: In one solution, all shuttles hold the distance to their front shuttle on the same constant value. In another solution each shuttle holds an individual distance to the first shuttle of the convoy.

Further, the building of convoys causes a shuttle to change the behavior of braking: When another shuttle drives in a short distance behind, it has to reduce the intensity of braking to avoid a rear-end collision.

This example demonstrates that a shuttle dynamically (at run-time) reconfigures by changing the parts of the system which control its acceleration. This reconfiguration is coordinated with other shuttles by wireless communication. As the time, when the reconfiguration takes place, has crucial impact on the safety of the system, the coordination as well as the reconfiguration have to fulfill safety critical and real-time requirements.

1.3 Structure

In the next chapter, basics about model-based software engineering and our approach for the specification and verification of real-time systems are presented. Further, the fundamentals of feedback-controller design and implementation are introduced.

In Chapter 3, we present our refinement of UML 2.0 component diagrams to adapt them to the domain of mechatronic systems. In this chapter, we introduce hybrid components and describe our modular, component-based approach to specify the behavior of hybrid reconfigurable systems by our notion of hybrid reconfiguration charts. Further, we show that our modeling technique is easily integrated with the verification approach presented in Chapter 2.

Chapter 4 describes how to derive an efficient implementation of the models for real-time systems automatically. Chapter 5 presents how an existing CAE tool has been integrated with an existing CASE tool in order to support our modeling approach. The application example, which was presented in Section 1.2, is evaluated. Chapter 6 discusses related work and finally in Chapter 7, we draw a conclusion and give an outlook on future work.

Chapter 2

Foundations

In this chapter, we present the foundations that are required for the comprehension of the rest of this work. The chapter starts with an introduction about model-based engineering and points up the benefits that stem from model-based specification, automatic code synthesis, and model-based analysis. Then, our approach to specify real-time systems is presented. We give an overview about the compositional real-time modelchecking approach that is enabled by our modular models. The chapter closes with an introduction to control engineering and a discussion how the models for the specification of real-time systems should integrate the control engineering approaches.

2.1 Model-based Software Engineering with UML

Model-based software engineering is applied in order to cope with the complexity of software systems and to enable efficient analyses. The *Unified Modeling Language* (*UML*) provides a collection of notations which became the standard in model-based software engineering. In this section, the principles of model-driven software engineering are introduced first. This is followed by an overview about the subset of UML that is used in this thesis. Then, we introduce real-time systems and a UML extension for real-time systems.

2.1.1 Model-driven Engineering and Model-driven Architecture

Model-driven engineering (*MDE*) [Ken02] and *model-driven architecture* (*MDA*) [CUT02, Obj03a] describe approaches for the model-based software development. MDA describes a detailed and structured approach to derive an implementation from a specification. Among others, MDE additionally constitutes to apply verification techniques, which is not respected in MDA. Note that MDA and MDE both focus on architecture as well as on behavior, which is not implied by the name model-driven *architecture*.

As mentioned in Chapter 1, *model-driven engineering* is a key concept to design complex systems. In MDE, the system's architecture and its behavior are specified by a model. The model abstracts from the implementation details and from the details of the target platform(s) which leads to an important reduction of complexity. Formal techniques for analysis are applied to verify correctness of the model.

Besides verification, the implementation is a major concern in MDE. *Model-driven architecture* describes an approach to derive an implementation from a model. Since the model, which specifies the system's architecture and behavior, abstracts from the details of the target platform, it is called *platform independent model (PIM)* in MDA terminology.

Instead of mapping the PIM directly to source code, an intermediate model called *platform specific model (PSM)* is generated. This intermediate model contains more details about the implementation. Usually, information about the target platform is required to derive an appropriate PSM. Thus, we propose to use a *platform model (PM)* that provides this information when deriving the PSM similar to the approach described in [TBA04]. As different target platforms usually lead to different PSMs, multiple different PSMs exist for each PIM. Even when the PIM has been verified, the platform specific model may be subject to further analyses.

An abstract example for a PIM is a model that describes structure, behavior, and (real-time) requirements of an application, but abstracts from the realization. The PSM describes how the structure and the behavior are implemented to meet the requirements. For example the PSM describes how the application is partitioned into threads and which deadlines, priorities etc. they obtain. Of course, the result of this partitioning depends on worst-case execution times or on the scheduler available in the target system. Such information is part of the platform model. After deriving the PSM, a scheduling analysis can be performed for example to check if an implementation of the model is schedulable with other applications.

The final step in the MDA approach is to map the PSM to source code of a target language. In [CUT02] this is called *Enterprise Deployment Model (EDM)*. The benefit which stems from the mapping to the intermediate platform specific model is that this mapping describes the *concepts* for the implementation which are independent of the target language. When the PSM has been derived, it can be mapped to source code of multiple different target languages.

Figure 2.1 depicts the integration of MDE steps, outlined above, with MDA. The (platform independent) model is verified, which is either successful or provides a counter example. Then, the model is mapped to source code (EDM) by the implementation. This is done by an intermediate mapping to a PSM which requires a platform description in form of the PM.

The standard in software engineering to describe the PIM is the Unified Modeling Language (UML) [Obj05b]. We use the UML profile for Schedulability, Performance, and Time Specification [Obj05c] as PSM. C/C++, Ada, and in recent developments Real-Time Java [BBF+00] are used in the embedded and real-time domain as target languages. An overview about the subset of UML and the subset of the UML profile for Schedulability, Performance, and Time Specification that are used in this work is given in the next sections.

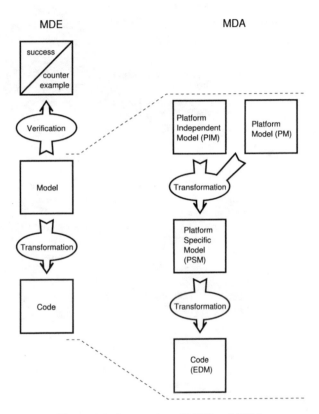

Figure 2.1: Integration of MDE and MDA

2.1.2   Unified Modeling Language

The standard description language in software engineering to describe PIMs is the *Unified Modeling Language* (*UML*) [Obj05b]. The UML consists of multiple diagram types to specify architecture and behavior. Component and class diagrams are used to specify the architecture (the structure) of a system, state machines and activity diagrams are used to specify the behavior. This section will give a brief overview about these diagrams.

Component diagrams

Complex systems are usually designed in a modular manner in order to manage the complexity. Using UML, the modular structure is specified by *component diagrams*. In a component diagram, multiple different *component types* are defined. A component type consists of *required* and *provided interfaces*. Each interface describes some features or obligations, e.g. the obligation to accept and process messages or requests. Multiple interfaces are grouped in *ports*.

When modeling the structure of the shuttle system, presented in Section 1.2, each shuttle is modeled as a component. In order to enable other shuttles to request the building of a convoy, it provides an interface that accepts such request messages. Vice versa, it requires a corresponding interface in order to send requests to build convoys as well. Figure 2.2 shows the component type Shuttle that realizes two interfaces: The required interface is visualized by a half-circle (socket) that is connected via a solid line with its port. The port is visualized as a square at the border of the component. The provided interface is visualized as a circle (ball) which is connected with its port. The ports obtain names, which are not visualized in Figure 2.2. In our example, the port of the required interface is called front, the other one is called rear. The features and obligations, which are described by an interface, are not visible in the UML component diagram. They can be specified by UML protocol state machines (see below).

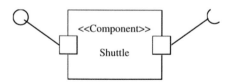

Figure 2.2: Specification of a component type

Besides specifying different component types, a component diagram is used to show the instance view as well. Figure 2.3 shows two instances s1 and s2 of the type Shuttle. In this situation, they established a communication link by plugging together the required and the provided interface. This communication link is called *connector*. The participating components of a communication need to be denoted explicitly by the notion of connectors, as the specification of broadcast is not directly possible and requires workarounds [KPSB04].

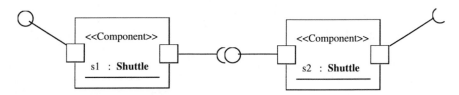

Figure 2.3: Components' instance view

The elements, shown in Figure 2.2 make up the *external (black-box) view* of the component type. This view describes the external visible behavior, i.e. the provided and required interfaces. The details about the internal structure of the component or how the interfaces are realized is not visible in the external view. This information is included in the *internal (white-box) view* and in the behavioral description.

A component's internal structure is specified by combining the type specification with the instance view, as shown in Figure 2.4: The type Shuttle consists of an instance dt of a DriveTrain component and one instance labeled lmb of a linear motor and brake component (LMB).

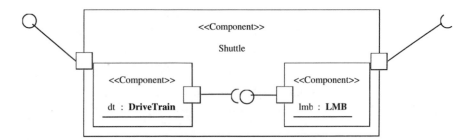

Figure 2.4: Component's internal structure

The concrete behavior of each component, which realizes among other things the component's interfaces, is not specified in a component diagram. For this purpose usually UML state machines are used (see below).

Even when the system and the component's internals are structured by component diagrams, as shown in Figures 2.3 and 2.4, a component often consists of further internals that are usually not understood as components (e.g. data structures applied within the components). UML proposes to use *class diagrams* to describe these internals which are local for a component.

Class diagrams

Class diagrams are used to describe the internal architecture of components. They describe the structure that is required to realize the component's behavior, or they model the data structures which are required within the component.

Figure 2.5 shows a cut-out of the data structure of the Shuttle component. This class diagram describes the environment of the shuttle. It represents the shuttle's view or its *knowledge* about the environment. The environment consists of tracks, shuttles and entities which we call *registries*. A registry is responsible for supervising a section, consisting of multiple tracks. Some tracks belong to multiple registries (as the track sections overlap). One or multiple shuttles are located on a track. A standard track has another track as successor and a further track as predecessor. If the track is a switch, it has two successors (splitting switch) or it has two predecessors (joining switch). Before a shuttle enters a track section, it has to register at the section's registry. This registration is not done implicitly by entering a track that belongs to the new entered registry. So the shuttle has to register at the registry explicitly to become one of multiple supervised shuttles.

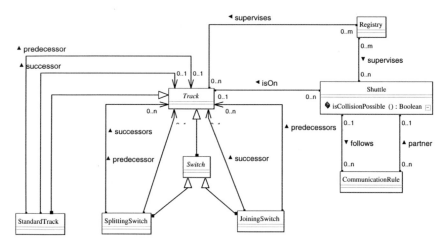

Figure 2.5: Class diagram representing the shuttle's view of the system

In Figure 2.5, the types of the environment are defined by the *classes* Shuttle, Registry, Track, StandardTrack, Switch, SplittingSwitch, and JoiningSwitch. Track is called *super class* of StandardTrack and of Switch, Switch is a super class of SplittingSwitch and JoiningSwitch. Track and Switch are *abstract classes* which is visualized by the cursive class names. The interrelationships between the classes is modeled by *associations*. Their *multiplicities* express for example that one shuttle is on 0 or 1 track and that a track hosts multiple (n) shuttles. The successor-association from StandardTrack to Track models that each standard track has a successor track. Notes about the association's semantics are expressed by the names of the associations (e.g. isOn and supervises in Figure 2.5).

The class Shuttle declares a method isCollisionPossible() that returns true if the current situation of the environment depicts a dangerous situation, false otherwise. After calling this method and dependent on the result, the shuttle starts a communication to coordinate the situation. This is represented in the shuttle's view by instantiating class CommunicationRule.

Class diagrams and component diagrams are both used for the architectural specification. Above in this section, it was shown that a component type, whose external view of the structure is just specified by the interface, can be linked to any component, which provides or requires the corresponding complement of the interface. This leads to a flexible use of the components as the communication partner is not fixed. In contrast to components, a class is linked to a specific other class by an association.

In the remainder of this section, diagrams are presented, which are used to specify the behavior of components as well as the behavior of classes. A class obtains just a behavior if it is an active one.

UML state machines

The UML 2.0 specification proposes two kinds of state machines: A *protocol state machine* to specify the communication protocol of a port or the obligations and features of an interface and a *behavioral state machine* to specify the reactive behavior of e.g. a class or a component.

UML state machines are extensions of finite automata (e.g. [Leu98]). Like automata models, UML state machines consist of multiple discrete states and transitions between the states. In contrast to automata, multiple discrete states can be active due to hierarchical or orthogonal states.

It is possible to specify temporal behavior by using either the after or the when construct as trigger for transitions. They specify points in time when a transition has to fire, relative to the entrance of the current state or in relation to a global clock.

UML state machines consist of high-level constructs such as hierarchical and orthogonal states and deep and shallow history mechanisms. These concepts are approaches to handle complexity. A detailed description of the syntax and an informal description of the semantics can be found in [Obj05b].

Protocol state machines   A *protocol state machine* specifies a communication protocol. Therefore, it is associated with an interface or a port. In contrast to behavioral state machines, the protocol state machine does not specify the operations or side-effects that are executed as reactions to signals. Instead, they specify possible sequences of occurring triggers similar to interface automata as defined in [dAH01]. Thus, it specifies in fact the features and obligations of an interface or a port.

Figures 2.6a and 2.6b specify a simple protocol for the communication between the ports front and rear from Figure 2.2. The *call trigger* callFront.startConvoy is associated with an operation that sends the signal startConvoy via the port front. Due to the self-transition on state noConvoy in Figure 2.6a, the state machine either stays in state noConvoy (for an unspecified number of steps) or switches to state noConvoy by sending the signal via port front. Figure 2.6b specifies, that rear has to switch from state noConvoy to convoy when it receives the signal startConvoy via port rear.

The example clarifies that a required interface (or its protocol state machine respectively) has to be consistent with the provided interface, it is connected to.

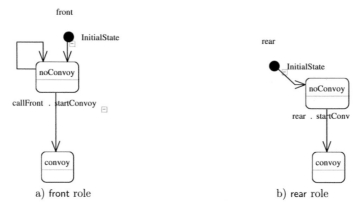

Figure 2.6: Simple communication protocol

Behavioral state machines In contrast to protocol state machines, a behavioral state machine specifies reactive behavior. It defines how a component or a class reacts to signal triggers or to a change of attributes. A transition is associated with a *trigger* (e.g. a *signal*), a boolean *guard*, and an *activity*. A transition, which leads from an active state to a target state, fires when the corresponding signal is raised and its guard evaluates to true. It executes an *activity* as *effect* or *side-effect* which consists of multiple *actions*. An action operates for example on the internal structure or sends signals to other components.[1] States are associated with entry, do, and exit activities. They are executed on entrance or exit of the corresponding state, or they are executed while residing in the corresponding state. If a component consists of ports and interfaces whose features are specified by a protocol state machine, the behavioral state machine realizing the reactive behavior of the component has to implement the protocols, specified by the protocol state machines.

Figure 2.7 shows a first attempt to specify the behavior of the DriveTrain component from Figure 2.4. The state machine consists of the two (discrete) states Vel and Pos. The component switches its states when the signal toPos, or toVel respectively, is raised. The activity initVelocityController() is executed when state Vel is entered. On entrance of state

---

[1]Note that *signals* are often called *events*.

Pos, the activity initPositionController() is executed. While the system resides in this state, the activity sendPosition() is executed. The state machine will be refined within this thesis to confer with real-time requirements and to include hybrid behavior.

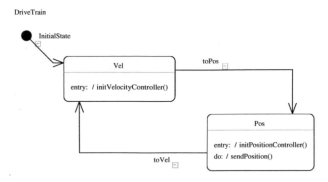

Figure 2.7: UML state machine

Activities

An *activity* coordinates the execution of lower-level actions. It is specified by an *activity diagram* which again consists of activities and of nodes and edges that define the control flow. Within the execution of an activity, usually no interaction takes place like in state machines.

Figure 2.8 shows an abstract example for an activity diagram, consisting of three sub-activity. The behavior of these sub-activity is specified by source code of a programming language. Diamonds visualize forks of the control flow. Transitions, visualized as arrows, are associated with boolean guards ([g] in the example). They direct the control flow to the corresponding sub-activities. Circles around black-filled circles denote the end of the activity. They can be associated with a return value, if the activity diagram specifies the behavior of a method with a corresponding return type.

2.1.3 UML Profile for Schedulability, Performance, and Time Specification

With the UML Profile for Schedulability, Performance, and Time Specification (SPT profile) [Obj05c] the OMG[2] introduces support for modeling resources, time, concurrency, schedulability, and performance. The model extensions are integrated with UML by the concepts of tagged values and stereotypes. With the profile, capabilities of real-time systems

---

[2]http://www.omg.org

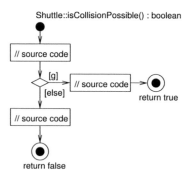

Figure 2.8: Activity diagram

are specified like tasks with their periods, deadlines, and priorities, WCETs and other properties of the model. Thereby, platform specific information, like WCETs, is mixed up with platform independent information, like deadlines. Further, the profile provides advanced possibilities to express time (e.g. clocks, timer), but it does not define how to integrate this with behavioral models like state machines.

Therefore, we will use just a subset of the SPT profile in order to describe the platform specific model. We will derive WCETs, memory consumption, resource requirements, and tasks with their periods, deadlines, and priorities from the platform independent model (see Chapter 4).

2.1.4   Real-Time Target Platforms

In the previous sections, some UML diagrams and the SPT profile as a UML extension have been described, which are used as platform independent and platform specific models. As described in Section 2.1.1, the platform specific model and finally the code are dependent on the target platform. Possible target platforms for real-time systems are introduced in this section.

Common target systems for real-time systems consist of a processor board and a *real-time operating system* (*RTOS*). The RTOS enables multithreading applications. These tasks are scheduled by a real-time scheduler, e.g. a priority scheduler [But97, BR99]. Often, the RTOS offers further services in addition to the real-time scheduler. Such services can be priority servers [But97, BR99] or a flexible resource management system [BO04] (see below).

As RTOS differ in the services they provide, standards have been created. They are classified by the POSIX standard [BW01]. For real-time systems four POSIX profiles exist: *Minimal real-time system profile* (*PSE50*), *real-time controller system profile* (*PSE51*), *dedicated real-time system profile* (*PSE52*), and *multi-purpose real-time system profile* (*PSE53*). The profiles PSE51 - PSE53 are extensions of the base profile PSE50. To fulfill this profile, the RTOS has to provide, among others, a priority scheduler and support for multithreading. As the flexible resource management system, which is introduced below, has been developed after the definition of these standards, it is obviously not part of any of these standards.

Flexible Resource Management

Especially applications for safety-critical systems allocate all resources which are required for worst case scenarios already during initialization. This ensures that problems due to missing resources occur –if at all– at initialization time and not during run-time. The drawback is that this leads often to bad resource utilization, as the resources that are required for rare occurring worst-case scenarios are not used in the rest of the time.

To overcome this problem, the *profile framework* as part of the RTOS service called *flexible resource management (FRM)* is introduced in [BO04]. It is realized in the RTOS Dreams [Dit99] that fulfills the POSIX PSE50 standard. Using the profile framework, an application just announces its worst-case resource requirements, but the resources are not assigned, yet. The FRM guarantees to assign resources to the application up to the announced maximum within a fixed worst-case time.

Thus, another application may use these resources while they are unused. In order to fulfill requests for resources within the guaranteed amount of time, this application has to free these resources in time. To ensure that the application frees the resources, it is implemented in different modi and the FRM can switch the application from one modus to another one that requires less resources. Each modus of an application is described by a *profile*. A profile is defined by its maximal and minimal *resource requirement*, the maximal allowed *assignment delay* when requesting resources, switching conditions describing how long it takes to *enter* and to *leave* the profile respectively, and its *quality*.

Each possible combination of the profiles of the system's applications is called a *configuration* in terms of the profile framework. An optimization algorithm of the FRM uses the profile's qualities to find optimal configurations. As this is an NP-complete problem, the search for a better configuration is done in the idle time of the system only under soft real-time constraints. So the worst-case – if no better solution is found – is as bad as if the FRM is not used. For flexibility, the optimization algorithm in the FRM framework is exchangeable, so heuristics can be used. If a better configuration of profiles is found, the FRM causes the applications to switch the profiles, so that each one reaches the corresponding profile.

A *profile reachability graph* is derived from the profile definitions. It describes all possible profile combinations for the active applications and the time restrictions how to switch between them.

Table 2.1 shows as example the profiles of an application AccelerationControl and the ones of an application BodyControl. AccelerationControl consists of the profiles Standard and Advanced, BodyControl of Robust, Comfort1, and Comfort2. The first application and its profiles are discussed in Chapters 3 and 4, the latter application is taken from [BGGO04a]. The Standard profile has a quality of 0.6, a minimal memory requirement of 2140 kByte, and a maximal memory requirement of 2150 kByte. Requests for more memory may be delayed up to $11\mu sec$. Entering the profile has a duration of $1\mu sec$, leaving takes $2\mu sec$.

Task	Profile					
	Profile name	Quality q	Memory in kb	Delay	WCET Enter	Leave
AccelerationControl	Standard	0.6	2140-2150	$11\mu sec$	$1\mu sec$	$2\mu sec$
	Advanced	1.0	2140-2156	$11\mu sec$	$2\mu sec$	$4\mu sec$
BodyControl	Robust	0.1	200-200	$10\mu sec$	$1\mu sec$	$2\mu sec$
	Comfort1	0.4	200-550	$12\mu sec$	$3\mu sec$	$3\mu sec$
	Comfort2	0.9	200-850	$10\mu sec$	$5\mu sec$	$7\mu sec$

Table 2.1: Profile definitions

Figure 2.9 shows the profile reachability graph of the two applications from Table 2.1. Each node of the graph denotes a *configuration of profiles*. If all worst case resource requirements of all applications can be granted, the configuration is called *guaranteed allocation state*. If the sum of all worst case resources is bigger than the system's available resources, it is called *over-allocation state*. The directed edges with their annotated time attribute describe the time required to switch from the edge's source to its target configuration. The times of the switches from over-allocation states to guaranteed allocation states must be compliant (i.e. they must be less or equal) with the corresponding allocation delay. Over-allocation states are visualized with double surroundings.

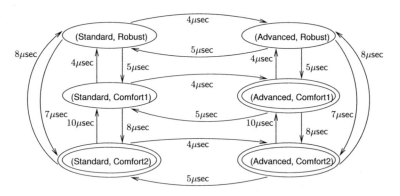

Figure 2.9: Profile reachability graph

2.1.5 Discussion

This section gave an overview about model-based software engineering, about UML, and about real-time platforms. The integral part of MDE is the model, which is the base for analyses and code synthesis. Standard models for the specification of structure are component diagrams and class diagrams. Behavior is modeled by state machines and activities.

Especially the component diagrams provide advanced support for the specification of the architecture of complex, distributed systems. As UML was not designed for the development of embedded, real-time systems, it lacks of description techniques for the specification of such behavior:

The only possibility to specify temporal behavior for state machines are the after and when constructs. They allow the specification of points in time when a transition has to fire, but the existing semantics for these constructs assume the transition to be fired immediately without delay and to fire without consumption of time. This *zero execution time* assumption is not implementable on real physical machines as it requires an *infinitely fast* execution of parts of the implementation to detect activated transitions without delay or to fire transitions without consumption of time. Especially when a transition is associated with an activity as side-effect with a significant *worst-case execution time* (*WCET*), the specified behavior differs a lot from the behavior of a realistic implementation.

The SPT profile is an attempt to introduce real-time extensions to UML. It lacks of the distinction between platform specific information and platform independent information demanded by the MDA approach. Further, it provides a set of tagged values that can be annotated to UML models in nearly all imaginable variants. For the specification of real-time systems and in order to define a formal semantics, a strict syntax is required that defines which information is specified in which diagram by which annotation. The introduction of a time model inclusive timers, clocks, etc. just extends the modeling possibilities. It does not solve the problems arising from the zero execution time assumption.

Similar problems occur in the specification of communication of complex, distributed, real-time systems. A connector which delivers signals without delay does not exist. Thus, a realistic model has to respect quality of service (QoS) capabilities like delays.

As it is not realistic to specify that a transition has to fire *infinitely fast* or that a communication has to be *infinitely fast*, it is required to specify *how fast* it has to be. Even if UML supported such specifications, it would additionally be required that the WCETs of the activities are well-known or that they can be derived from the model in order to analyze if the specified values are reasonable.

It is not trivial to determine the WCETs of activities. Even when the source code would be analyzed step by step, it is not possible to determine the *worst-case number of iterations* (*WCNIS*) of loops, which is essential for WCET determinations [Erp00]. Without knowledge of the WCETs, the activities are just applicable in no-real-time systems.

Different implementations for applications for real-time systems are possible, dependent on the applied target platform. If no operating system is applied, the application has to consist of exactly one thread. The application of a POSIX PSE50 conform RTOS enables multithreading. Using the RTOS Dreams, which offers additionally the flexible resource management, leads to optimized resource utilization if the models are implemented appropriately. By allowing delays for the resource allocation, all applications of a system run even when not the sum of all maximal required resources is available. At least the minimal required resources must always be guaranteed.

When following the MDE approach to model and to implement mechatronic systems and when implementing the models for a target platform that supports flexible resource management, the models should contain sufficient information to synthesize profiles and to implement them for the target platform.

2.2 Specification of Real-Time Systems

In Section 2.1, it was shown that UML is a useful model-based description language to design behavior and architecture of software. On the other hand, standard UML was not constructed to design mechatronic systems, since there is no support to specify real-time or hybrid behavior and there is no possibility to respect restricted resources in the models. Further, UML provides just modeling support. It does not propose verification approaches.

Therefore, we refined or extended some UML diagrams to achieve support for the specification of real-time systems. This approach is presented in this section. Our verification approach is presented in Section 2.3. Similar to the UML approach, we specify the whole real-time system by an architectural model (see Section 2.2.1), the communication behavior (see Section 2.2.2), and the components' behavior (see Section 2.2.3). This separation is used in Section 2.3 for the verification of the system by compositional real-time modelchecking.

2.2.1 Architecture

We use UML component diagrams, as introduced in Section 2.1.2, to specify the system structure and the components' internal architecture. We distinguish between the black box and white box view and we distinguish between component types and component instances as well. The internals of a component, like data structures representing the component's system view, are modeled by UML class diagrams as described in Section 2.1.2.

The signals which can be received or sent by the port are associated with the port's required and provided interfaces. Instead of protocol state machines, we apply our notion of *real-time statecharts* (see below). Associating the real-time statecharts with the single interfaces would separate the protocols for sending and for receiving. As we will use the models –among other things– for the verification of the *bidirectional* communication protocol, we associate them just with ports and not with interfaces which is a refinement of the UML approach.

Further, we introduce an arrow as syntactical short-cut for the visualization of connectors: The arrow begins at the port that hosts the required interface and ends at the port that hosts the provided interface. A bidirectional arrow indicates communication in both directions. Figure 2.10 shows our visualization of two shuttle instances and their bidirectional communication channel.

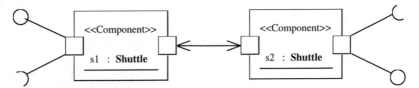

Figure 2.10: Short-cut for the visualization of connectors

One major requirement when communicating messages in a safety-critical context, e.g. messages about failed components or about a component's position, is that it needs to be ensured that each receiver receives these messages. Applying a network system with low failure rate or high fault tolerance, so that it is legitimate to assume that no message losses occur (e.g. CAN[3]), this requirement is fulfilled. But when the network is unreliable, a communication protocol needs to be applied that guarantees safety even in case of failures like message losses. This protocol needs to be applied between the sender and all receivers. Therefore, the number of receivers obviously needs to be well-known. As the sender has to ensure communication with all receivers, it is more accurate to apply one unique protocol multiple times instead of designing one protocol for a fixed number of participants. Therefore, communication is usually peer-to-peer in the domain of networked mechatronic systems and thus, it does not matter that we adopt the UML approach that does not allow specifying broadcasts.

2.2.2 Communication

When modeling communication and when defining communication protocols in real-time systems, signal propagation delays have to be respected and response times have to be guaranteed. Therefore, we specify a communication protocol by means of our *real-time coordination patterns* [GTB+03].[4] Such a pattern consists of

- the members that participate in the communication which we call *roles*,

- the behaviors of the roles,

- the connectors between the roles,

- the behaviors of the connectors,

- an invariant for each role,

---

[3]http://www.can.bosch.com
[4]Note that we do not refer to the patterns from [GHJV95].

- and the pattern constraint.

The behavior of a role specifies the *external* communication, i.e. the communication protocol, of the participant. Automata models can be applied to specify all possible valid orders of sending and receiving signals. For our real-time coordination patterns, we apply real-time statecharts for the specification of a role's real-time behavior.

The connectors specify communication links between the participants of the communication. They specify to which destination a signal is delivered or from which source it may be received. The behavior of a connector, i.e. its quality of service capabilities like reliability or delay, is also specified by a real-time statechart.

The role invariant describes properties that are guaranteed by the participant. The pattern constraint specifies a requirement that needs to be fulfilled by the pattern. It can be verified for example by modelchecking based on the roles' and connectors' behaviors and the role invariants (see Section 2.3).

Note that the statecharts, that describe the behavior of the roles, do not specify the concrete behavior of a component. Instead, they abstract from the components' internals and specify just the *external* communication. In order to be able to participate in a communication, a concrete component has to *realize* the corresponding role(s), i.e.

- it has to realize the external communication, specified by the role behavior, but it may not add additional external communication, and

- it has to fulfill the role invariant.

Thus, a component realization may just add additional *internal* behavior to the realized role behaviors. Dependent on the communications in which a component participates and dependent on the roles it incurs in each communication, it realizes different roles from different coordination patterns.

Due to the abstraction between component behavior and role behavior, a pattern can be reused in different systems or it can be used in one system multiple times (see Section 2.2.4). This enables the developer to construct the system structure by choosing patterns from a set of available patterns and plugging them together like building blocks of a construction kit [BGT05]. Further, separating the specification of real-time coordination and component behavior has advantages which are exploited in the verification of the system, as described in Section 2.3.

Figure 2.11 shows the specification of the ConvoyCoordination pattern. It defines that the ConvoyCoordination pattern consists of the roles front and rear and the bidirectional connector between them. The pattern constraint consists of the two conjunctive elements A[] not deadlock and A[] not (rear.convoy and (front.noConvoy or front.answer)). The first element describes that no deadlock may occur in the communication, e.g. both roles waiting for the reception of a signal. The second element is described below, as it refers to the roles' behaviors, which are described in the following.

As mentioned in Section 1.2, a shuttle that is the front shuttle of a convoy has to brake with reduced force to avoid rear-end collisions if another shuttle follows with a reduced

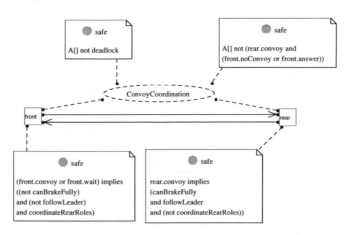

Figure 2.11: ConvoyCoordination pattern

distance behind. Further, it has to coordinate its rear shuttles. This is expressed by the role invariant (front.convoy || front.wait) implies ((not canBrakeFully) and (not followLeader) and coordinateRearRoles). If it is at the rear end of the convoy, it may brake with full intensity: rear.convoy implies (canBrakeFully and followLeader and (not coordinateRearRoles)). convoy and wait are states from the behavior of the rear role resp. the front role (see below). canBreakFully, followLeader, and coordinateRearRoles are (abstract) properties which describe if a shuttle may bake with full intensity, has to follow a leading shuttle, or if it has to coordinate other following shuttle.

Therefore, the shuttles have to be coordinated when they build convoys to avoid that the front shuttle is in no-convoy mode (and thus brakes with full intensity) and the rear shuttle is in convoy mode (reducing the distance). This requirement is expressed by the second conjunctive element of the pattern constraint (cf. Figure 2.11).

In order to meet the requirements, the coordination protocol from Figure 2.6 needs to be extended: Besides adding time constraints which specify the maximal allowed delay, caused for example by the connector, the protocol should also respect possible message losses and it has to include not only the possibility to build convoys, but also to break them [GTB+03, BGH+05c].

As mentioned above, role behavior and the behavior of connectors are specified by a formalism called *real-time statecharts*. Their syntax and semantics are informally described in the following section and the example real-time statecharts for the ConvoyCoordination pattern are given. The formalization can be found in [GB03] or in Appendix A.

Real-Time Statecharts

Real-time statecharts (*RTSCs*) [BGS05, BG03, GB03] combine the advantages of UML state machines and hierarchical timed automata [DMY02, DM01] and extend them with additional constructs. In real-time statecharts, transitions are not assumed to fire *infinitely fast*, which is unrealistic on real physical devices, especially when considering the execution of the actions attached to the transitions. Instead, it is possible to specify *how fast* transitions have to be fired or executed. This is done by adding deadlines to the transitions in form of intervals. These time constants specify a relative point in time, defining the minimum time and the maximum time which may be spent from actually triggering the transition until the execution of the action has to be finished.

Like in timed automata [HNSY92, LPY97], our approach also defines clocks that can be reset when a transition fires. As the firing consumes time, we defined that these clocks are reset at the point in time when the transition is triggered.

Using these clocks, time invariants are specified for a state, defining the point in time, when the state has to be left via a transition. To trigger transitions dependent on a specific point in time, time guards are specified. Deadlines can either be relative to the triggering of the transition or relative to a clock.

Transitions are triggered when the time guard becomes true, the associated event is available, and a guard, consisting of a boolean expression over different variables or methods, is also true. In real-time statecharts, we distinguish between *non-urgent* transitions, visualized as dashed arrows and *urgent transitions* visualized as solid arrows. Urgent transitions fire immediately when they are triggered. Non-urgent transitions may delay firing when the temporal specifications of the model would still allow a later firing, i.e. even a non-urgent transition has to fire before a time invariant becomes invalidated.

To achieve determinism in case of multiple urgent transitions ready to fire, each transition gets a priority attached. The after-construct (known from UML state machines) is mapped to a time guard and a time invariant and thus gets a semantic definition which makes it possible to generate code from this definition.

Although the use of multiple clocks requires more modeling effort than using the after-construct, it has the advantage that the points in time, when transitions are triggered, cannot only be defined relative to the point of entrance of the current state, but also relative to the point of triggering of any previously fired transition or the point of entrance or exit of any previously entered state, because clock-resets can be associated even to the entries or exits of the states.

The form of the time guards is limited to $\wedge_{t_i \in C}(a_i \leq t_i \leq b_i)$, $a_i \in \mathbb{N}$, $b_i \in \mathbb{N} \cup \{\infty\}$, where C is the set of clocks. The form of time invariants is limited to $\wedge_{t_i \in C}(t_i \leq T_i)$, $T_i \in \mathbb{N} \cup \{\infty\}$. In our experience, this limitation, i.e. the exclusions of arbitrary logic expressions and arithmetic operations on different clock times, does not hamper the modeling of realistic systems and makes it easier for the model developer to build intuitive models rather than very complicated ones.

The semantics definition of real-time statecharts does not have the usual macrostep and run-to-completion semantics of standard statecharts [HP98, HPSS87], because the zero execution time for intermediate steps is not realistic in our application domain. As the run-to-completion semantics would cause the system to react to an external trigger and to all further triggers that are caused by this reaction till a stable state is reached, the system cannot react to new external triggers during this sequence of reactions. The run-to-completion semantics is applicable in non-real-time systems or in soft real-time systems with short side-effect, but it is not applicable any more in hard real-time systems when each reaction has a significant *worst-case execution time (WCET)*. We define our semantics formally, as given in [GB03] or in Appendix A by a mapping of real-time statecharts to a subset of an extended version of hierarchical timed automata as defined in [DMY02, DM01].

This semantics, which respects that side-effect have WCETs greater than zero, enables a mapping to a platform specific model and partitioning the application into threads so that all specified deadlines are met. Other approaches (e.g. [LQV01, BlLM02, Har98, KP92, PAS94, DM01, DMY02, HNSY92, LPY97]) that focus mainly on formal analyses assume transitions to fire infinitely fast. Even when the formal analysis of such a model is successful, its behavior is not realizable as no real physical machine exists that reacts infinitely fast.

In order to still be able to describe the required local synchronization between multiple orthogonal states of a single real-time statechart within a single step, synchronous communication via synchronization-signals and -channels, similar to the mechanism described in [LPY97], is also supported.

Apart from the extensions mentioned above, which are partly adapted from timed automata, features from UML state machines, like hierarchy, parallelism and history as well as entry()-, exit()- and do()-operations for states are of course provided further on for modeling. The do()-operation of a state has to be executed at least once before the state is left. To perform temporal analysis, WCETs are also required for these operations. While a specific state is active, its do()-operation is executed periodically. The user may specify a time interval for this period. Note also that actions are not limited to integer assignments (like in timed automata), but that they can be complex method calls in the object-oriented model.

Real-time statecharts combine the advantages of UML state machines and of timed automata and extend them by additional annotations. These annotations enable to generate code for real-time platforms on the one hand and offer constructs to model complex temporal behavior on the other hand. The main differences to UML state machines are that they (i) support to model the time consumption of transition execution and (ii) have a realistic semantic definition based on a subset of timed automata mirroring appropriately the application domain.

As mentioned above, the behavior of the roles of the ConvoyCoordination pattern is specified by our notion of real-time statecharts. Figures 2.12a and 2.12b show the behaviors of the two roles, as described for example in [BGH+05c].

The rear role non-deterministically sends a convoyProposal signal via the rear role and the connector to front role (cf. Figure 2.11). The non-determinism is indicated by the non-urgent transition, visualized by the dashed arrow. The front role replies either by rejecting (event convoyProposalRejected) or by accepting the proposal (event startConvoy). Note that a raised event rolename.eventname denotes sending event eventname via role rolename to the role which

ConvoyCoordination.front

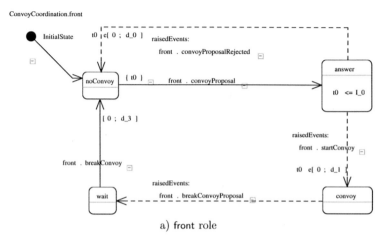

a) front role

ConvoyCoordination.rear

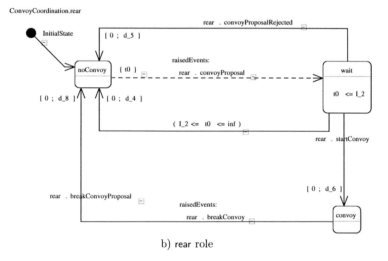

b) rear role

Figure 2.12: Role behaviors of front role and rear role

is connected with rolename. An event trigger rolename.eventname denotes receiving event eventname via role rolename from the role, which is connected with rolename. In this example, t_0 indicates a clock, which is reset to zero, when the transition to state answer is fired (visualized by the annotation {t0}). In state answer, the time invariant $t_0 \leq I_0$ is specified which describes how long the RTSC may reside in this state.

Note that the behavior of real-time systems is usually urgent behavior, but in the specification of coordination patterns, non-urgent transitions are frequently used. For example in Figure 2.12b, it is used to specify that the convoyProposal signal can be sent at any point in time, when state noConvoy is active. In Figure 2.12a, the non-urgent transitions specify that the state answer has to be left at the latest the time specified by I_0 after the point in time when convoyProposal was received.

The *deadlines* $t_0 \in [0; d_0]$ and $t_0 \in [0; d_1]$ in Figure 2.12a specify that the firing of the transitions from answer to noConvoy and to convoy resp. have to be finished at the latest the time d_0 or d_1 respectively after the transition from noConvoy to answer has been fired, which set the clock t_0 to zero. After receiving the approval signal startConvoy, rear role switches to convoy mode. The deadline $[0; d_6]$ models that the firing of the transition has to be finished at the latest the time d_6 after it has been triggered, i.e. after event startConvoy has been received.

Assume that delivering a signal between the two roles takes the time d_c in the worst case. The time from deciding to request for building a convoy till reaching state convoy takes for rear role in the worst case $I_2 + d_6$: I_2 till it leaves state wait plus d_6 for switching from state wait to convoy. front role reaches state convoy in the worst case at the latest $d_c + d_1$ after rear role sent the request for building a convoy: d_c for the delivery of the signal plus d_1 for reacting to it.

When front role sends the startConvoy event to rear role, it switches to convoy mode. This protocol has the advantage that even in case of message loss the aforementioned pattern constraint is never violated: If startConvoy message is lost, the front role is in state convoy and will brake with reduced power, and the rear role will be in no-convoy mode, holding a large distance. Although both shuttles are in different modes, safety is still guaranteed. This is verified by modelchecking (see Section 2.3). Breaking the convoy is done similarly.

The behavior of the connectors is specified by real-time statecharts as well. They model the realistic behavior that signals are forwarded into both directions under the assumption that some of them get lost. Figure 2.13 shows the behavior of the connector from rear role to front role. It contains a boolean attribute active, used as guard at some transitions to model that messages are lost when the attribute is false. The deadlines model a delay of up to d_c in the delivery of the signals.

Role Behavior & Component Behavior

Recall that the statecharts, that describe the behavior of the roles, do not specify the concrete behavior of the shuttle component and that they abstract from the component's internals, instead. So, in Figure 2.12a, it is specified that the participant of the communication, realizing the front role, may receive a convoyProposal signal (as long as front role is in

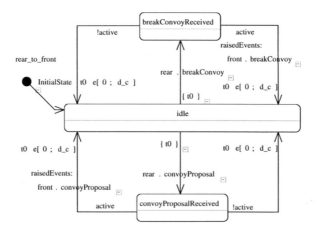

Figure 2.13: Behavior of the connector from rear role to front role

state noConvoy). It has two possibilities to react to the reception of this signal: either by sending the signal convoyProposalRejected back or by answering with startConvoy. In the role behaviors, it is not specified which internal reactions are initiated by the reception of this event (e.g. exchanging a controller to reduce the distance) or how to decide which event to send back. This does not belong to the communication protocol, but it is part of the component's behavior that is described in Section 2.2.3. Therefore, the transitions of a RTSC, specifying role behavior, never have side-effects – except a list of raised signals. Also, the states of a role behavior are never associated with entry()-, do()-, and exit()-activities. This is similar to the distinction between UML protocol state machines and UML behavioral state machines.

As mentioned above, a concrete component has to *realize* the roles of a coordination pattern in order to participate in the communication. If the component has for example the part of the front role in this communication, it has to *refine* the front role behavior (see Section 2.2.3). If it should be possible to additionally incur the part of the rear role (concurrently or not), it has to refine this behavior, too.

2.2.3   Component Behavior

In the previous section, it was explained how to use real-time statecharts to specify role behavior of real-time coordination patterns. Real-time statecharts are also used to specify the component behavior. In contrast to the real-time statecharts that specify role behavior, they contain complex activities as effects and entry()-, do()-, and exit-activities. This section describes the reactive behavior, specified by real-time statecharts first and then presents a model-based approach to specify activities.

Reactive Behavior

As mentioned in Section 2.2.2, the real-time behavior of a component is specified by a real-time statechart, as well. The behavior, specified by this RTSC, has to *refine* the behaviors of the roles of the coordination patterns, which are associated with the component's ports. This refinement is exploited in the system's verification (see Section 2.3).

As a *valid* refinement has to guarantee the behavior, specified by the roles, and may not add possible external behavior, the refinement usually resolves the non-determinism, specified in the role behavior. Although the component's behavior may not consist of additional external communication behavior, it may add internal behavior. Therefore, in contrast to real-time statecharts specifying role behavior, the real-time statecharts which specify component behavior may be associated with effects. Of course deadlines, specified in the role behavior have to be met in spite of the effects.

Figure 2.14 shows the relation between patterns and components: The front role of an instance of the ConvoyCoordination pattern is associated with the front port of the component and the rear role is associated with the rear port (note that port names are not visualized). Because of these associations, the component has to realize and thus it has to refine the role behaviors, specified in Figures 2.12a and 2.12b. For example, when it sent a breakConvoyProposal, it may not accept a convoyProposal signal before receiving a breakConvoy signal. The component may add internal behavior, e.g. it may execute internal actions when switching from state answer to convoy to exchange feedback-controllers.

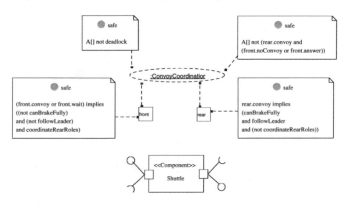

Figure 2.14: Instantiation of the ConvoyCoordination pattern

Figure 2.15 shows the behavior of the Shuttle component realizing both roles from Figure 2.12.[5] It consists of three orthogonal states: The upper orthogonal state refines the front role behavior, the lower orthogonal state refines the rear role behavior, and the orthogonal state

---

[5]Note that in our CASE tool Fujaba (http://www.fujaba.de) the dashed lines between orthogonal states are not visualized.

in the middle synchronizes the roles. The latter one initiates the building and the breaking of the convoys, dependent on the boolean value delivered by the method isCollisionPossible(), which is described below. Further, it ensures that a shuttle does not act as front role and as rear role at the same time and keeps track if the shuttle is currently in a convoy at all, if it is the front shuttle or if it is the rear shuttle of a convoy. This enables just convoys consisting of at most two shuttles. In Section 2.2.4, it is demonstrated how to reuse the ConvoyCoordination pattern to build convoys of realistic length. When the upper orthogonal state changes its substate, internal modifications are performed. In Figure 2.15, these modifications are specified by the activity internalModifications(). An advanced and more precise specification technique for such modifications will be presented in Chapter 3.

Note that the refined roles realize the same external communication behavior like the corresponding roles from Figure 2.12. They add internal behavior in the form of synchronous signals for the synchronization with the orthogonal state in the middle. The non-determinism from the role behaviors is resolved by this internal, synchronous communication: In the front role behavior, it was specified that a convoyProposal message is either answered by a convoyProposalRejected message or by a startConvoy message. In the component behavior, it is specified in detail when the shuttle answers with which message. The deadlines of the synchronized transitions of the middle orthogonal state have to be consistent with the deadlines of the corresponding transitions of the refined roles.

Activities and Side-Effects

Besides communicating between components and controlling the internal states of components, a real-time system usually has to execute side-effects as reactions to state changes or actions, because of the current state. Such actions are internalModifications() or isCollision-Possible() in Figure 2.15, which is periodically called as guard when the middle orthogonal state is in substate noConvoy in order to check if the corresponding transition is triggered.

We specify the application flow of a method by *story diagrams* [Zün02] which are a refinement of UML activity diagrams (see Section 2.1.2). In story diagrams, the behavior of each activity is specified by a *story pattern*. A story pattern consists of an instance diagram that may exist during run-time. The instance diagram is based on a data structure specified by a class diagram (see Section 2.1.2). If the instance diagram exists when the story pattern is evaluated, i.e. if all instances and references are successfully *matched*, this currently existing data structure is modified conform to modification rules which are also specified in the story pattern: New instances and references may be created and existing ones may be destroyed.

Figure 2.16 shows the story diagram of the activity isCollisionPossible(). It consists of just one activity that is specified by a story pattern. It is based on the data structure from Figure 2.5. It is evaluated if the shuttle (this) is on a track (t0) which is part of the track system, supervised by the registry reg, as modeled by this object diagram. If the situation occurs that another shuttle is on the track labeled in the pattern with t1, both shuttles will reach the switch (switch) at about the same time which is a conflict as they might collide. Thus, they need to be coordinated. This is represented by creating an

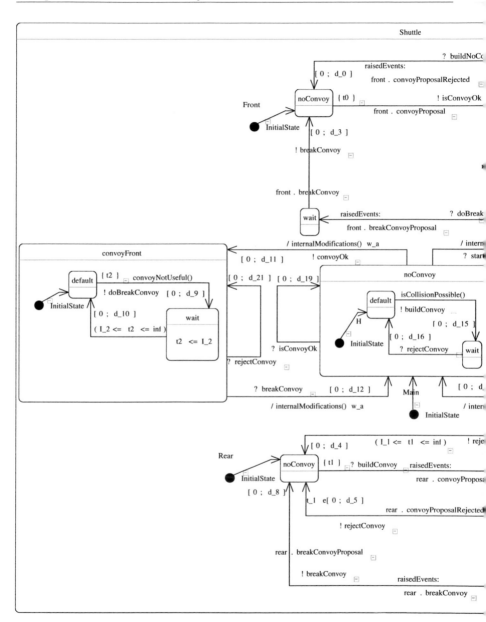

Figure 2.15: Behavior of the Shuttle component

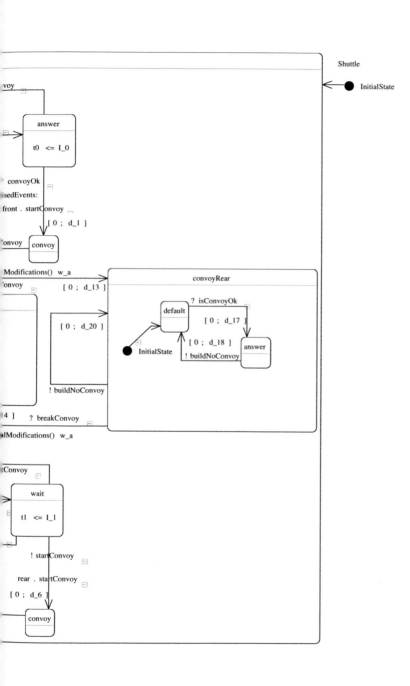

Shuttle

InitialState

voy

answer

t0   <=   I_0

° convoyOk

sedEvents:
front . startConvoy

[0 ; d_1]

onvoy   convoy

Modifications()   w_a

onvoy

[0 ; d_13]

convoyRear

? isConvoyOk

default

[0 ; d_17]

[0 ; d_20]

[0 ; d_18]

! buildNoConvoy

InitialState

answer

! buildNoConvoy

4]   ? breakConvoy

Modifications()   w_a

Convoy

wait

t1   <=   I_1

! startConvoy

rear . startConvoy

[0 ; d_6]

convoy

instance of CommunicationRule and referring it to both shuttle instances. One possibility to solve the conflict is to build a convoy. The action isCollisionPossible() returns true if this situation occurs, false otherwise. true will trigger the transition from Main:noConvoy:default to Main:noConvoy:wait and initiate the convoy building process. Obvious, this is just one example, as plenty of other possibilities exist, when coordination is required for safety-critical reasons or when it is just useful to build convoys to maximize energy efficiency.

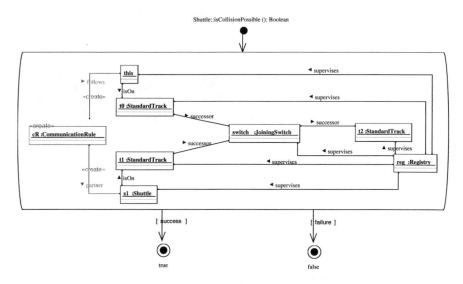

Figure 2.16: Action isCollisionPossible()

To specify complex modifications, high-level constructs are applicable: Links or instances that are specified to be *negative* in the story pattern may not be existent for a successful matching of the story pattern. *Optional* links or instances may be existent or non-existent. Further, conditions, assignments, or method calls can be associated with the instances. Constraints about properties of multiple instances can also be specified. A detailed description can be found in [Zün02, KNNZ00, NSZ03].

In order to guarantee safety, the upper bounds for the execution-times of the activities, like isCollisionPossible() need to be known. This is important, because without a *worst-case execution time (WCET)* the real-time behavior is not predictable. It would not be possible to predict the latest point in time when the test for activation of the transition will be finished, which is essential for real-time systems. As the execution of the method requires searches in data structures which are unbound (recall that some associations in Figure 2.5 have a multiplicity of 0..n), an upper bound for these searches does not exist. Therefore, our approach to model data structures for real-time systems requires specifying only finite multiplicities or a bound number of instances for each class [BGST05]. Figure 2.17 shows the modified data structure. In our example, further coordination patterns are used to ensure that the data structure is up to date except for some delay.

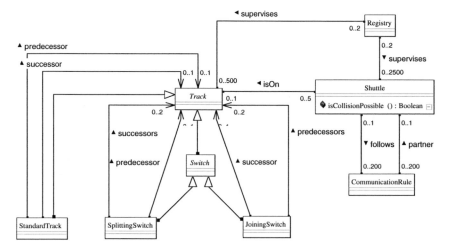

Figure 2.17: Shuttle's system view with finite multiplicities

2.2.4   System Construction

In the previous sections, it was presented how to design components for real-time systems and how to design the real-time coordination between components. In this section, we demonstrate how to construct a system by plugging together multiple instances of components which realize multiple instances of coordination patterns. Often, it reduces development costs to reuse components and patterns multiple times instead of designing one superordinated component or pattern. Further, this is the basis for compositional verification (see Section 2.3).

In our example, we specified real-time behavior and coordination for two Shuttle instances, forming a convoy. In a realistic application, it is desirable to form much longer convoys. Therefore, we instantiate the ConvoyCoordination pattern multiple times instead of designing different patterns with more complex roles for more complex scenarios.

Multiple architectures exist that reuse the presented real-time coordination pattern. Their advantages and disadvantages are presented and discussed in this section.

Chain Design

Figure 2.18 shows a convoy, consisting of 4 shuttles. A ConvoyCoordination pattern has been instantiated between the first and the second shuttle, between the second and the third shuttle and so on. As intended, this design reuses the pattern multiple times.

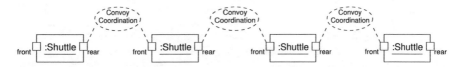

Figure 2.18: First approach to reuse the ConvoyCoordination pattern

Nevertheless, this architecture has a crucial disadvantage: Communication within the convoy has a delay that depends on the distance between the two communicating shuttles. When, for example, a new shuttle joins the convoy at an arbitrary position, the propagation of this information is delayed and requires multiple steps till it receives the shuttles at the end of the convoy. The same problem arises when a shuttle communicates with the first shuttle, for example to receive information about the front shuttle's current position or velocity.

Master-Slave Design

Another design is presented in Figure 2.19. The first shuttle of the convoy becomes the master that coordinates all other shuttles. Each communication is done via the master shuttle that collects all required information and sends them to all other shuttles if required. Therefore, the communication delay is at most two steps.

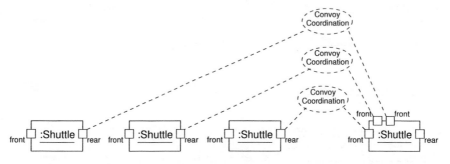

Figure 2.19: Advanced design of convoys reusing ConvoyCoordination pattern

To realize the design, a shuttle has to instantiate the pattern roles multiple times. The synchronization statechart still consists of the three states as shown in Figure 2.15:

being the master shuttle (convoyFront), being in a convoy, but being not the master shuttle (convoyRear), and not being in a convoy at all (noConvoy). It just has to be extended so that the shuttle accepts multiple requests to build a convoy.

When merging two convoys approching a switch (conf. Figure 2.20a) another advantage of the master-slave architecture becomes obvious: After the application of further coordination patterns to decide if the shuttles are merged into one convoy and to negotiate about the order of the resulting convoy, the situation may be as depicted in Figure 2.20b. Although the convoy is not merged yet (which obviously cannot happen before the shuttles passed the switch), the shuttles adjust already the distances to the master shuttle. The required information to hold the distance is sent by the master shuttle. Actually, the master shuttle sends a trajectory that describes the required position for the shuttle and thus defines the distance implicitly. This adjustment leads to a smooth, safe merging at the switch.

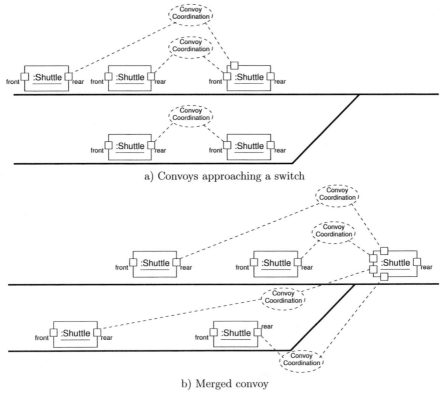

a) Convoys approaching a switch

b) Merged convoy

Figure 2.20: Merging convoys at a switch

Two disadvantages of this design become obvious in Figure 2.19: (i) To enable building convoys consisting of n shuttles, a shuttle must realize n instances of front role and (ii) as the number of realized roles is always finite, the length of the convoys is restricted, as well. To overcome even these drawbacks, we propose the layered master-slave design.

Layered Master-Slave Design

The indicated problems are solved by a layered architecture as it is depicted in Figure 2.21. The figure depicts two *sub-convoys*: the first one consisting of the shuttle s1, s2, s3, and s4, the second one consisting of the shuttle s4, s5, and s6. Note, s1 coordinates the second convoy as well, by sending coordination instructions to s4, which is member of the first convoy and master of the second convoy.

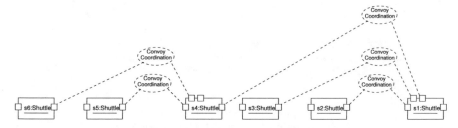

Figure 2.21: Layered convoy architecture

This structure can be applied multiple times to construct an arbitrary number of layers, which leads in principle to arbitrary long convoys. Of course, each shuttle can become the leader of a sub-convoy. As each layer increases the communication delay, the length of the whole convoy is just restricted by an upper bound for the maximal allowed communication delay.

Assume each shuttle realizes r front role instances. On the first layer, one shuttle coordinates r shuttles, which leads to a convoys consisting of $1 + r$ shuttles (1 master and r shuttles on the first layer). On the second layer, each shuttle from the first layer coordinates r shuttles, which leads to r^2 shuttles on the second layer and to $1 + r + r^2$ shuttles in the whole convoy. Following this architecture, the n-th layer consists of r^n shuttles and the overall convoy consists of $\sum_{i=0}^{n} r^i = (r^{n+1} - 1)/(r - 1)$ shuttles.

To realize the design, each shuttle has to instantiate one instance of rear role and multiple (r) instances of front role. Note, that the roles do not need to be changed in the different designs for the convoy. The only extension has to be done in the synchronization statechart: An additional state subConvoyFront is introduced which represents that the shuttle is leader of a sub-convoy, but not the leader of the overall convoy.

2.2.5   Discussion

In this Section 2.2, we demonstrated that UML 2.0 component diagrams are useful to specify the architecture of real-time systems. In order to specify real-time communication protocols and the component's real-time behavior, the UML state machine model has been extended to the model of real-time statecharts. By letting off from the *zero execution time* assumption (cf. Section 2.1.5), the specified behavior is implementable.

The whole real-time coordination between components, including constraints, role invariants, role behaviors and the behavior of the connectors, is specified by real-time coordination patterns, which can be instantiated multiple times between different components. The behavior of a component realizes the corresponding roles of the real-time communication(s), by refining the role behaviors that are associated with its ports.

An open issue that is not discussed in this work is when to instantiate the real-time coordination patterns: As it is practically impossible to instantiate patterns between all existing component instances and as these patterns are not always required (e.g. just when the shuttles are in certain closeness), resources can be saved by dynamically instantiating and deinstantiating the patterns. For example, the orthogonal states from Figure 2.15, realizing the corresponding role behavior, do not need to be active if no other shuttle is around. When instantiating patterns dynamically, it has to be ensured that the required patterns are instantiated in certain (safety-critical) situations. In [Sch06, GS04], a model-based approach to describe the dynamic instantiation of patterns is presented. The patterns are instantiated dependent on certain states of the environment which is described by data structures like the one from Figure 2.17. These instantiation rules are described by story diagrams. Modifications of the environmental information are specified by story diagrams, too.

[Sch06, GS04] benefits from the model-based specification of environment, instantiation rules (to instantiate communication patterns), and modification rules (to modify the data structures describing the environment) for the verification of the correct instantiation of patterns. Obviously, all possible modifications of the environment must be well-known to perform verification. Thus, the modification of the environmental representation must be specified by story diagrams. In order to enable an integration of this approach with our approach for the specification of mechatronic systems, we require all methods which modify the shuttle's system view to be specified by story diagrams. In our approach, these methods are side-effects in real-time statecharts which are executed as reaction to some events. In combination with data structures, specified by class diagrams with bound multiplicities, their worst-case execution times are derivable.

When for example a shuttle receives a signal that provides new information about the environment, the real-time statechart that processes this signal executes a story diagram as side-effect and thus updates the environment. Integration with [Sch06, GS04] will lead to dynamic instantiation of real-time coordination patterns if needed.

Although our approach overcomes the drawbacks of UML for the design of real-time systems, support for the design of hybrid systems is still required. In the example, the controller software has been specified so that the component's current state denotes if the shuttle is in convoy mode or not. The model still lacks of the information how to operate while being in the corresponding discrete states, i.e. for example how to hold the distance to the front shuttle on a constant level or how to ensure that an emergency brake will not be done with full intensity. Such continuous behavior is usually specified by feedback-controllers. As introduced in Chapter 1, the integration of discrete and continuous behavior is called *hybrid* behavior.

Therefore, the internal reconfiguration of the shuttle (exchange of feedback-controllers or change of their structure), which takes place when the component changes its current discrete state, needs to be described in more details. To enable or simplify model verification and analysis, a model-based approach is required.

A new, appropriate modeling approach is described in Chapter 3. In the next section, it is shown how to exploit the separated description of communication behavior and component behavior for the verification of the overall real-time system.

2.3 Verification by Compositional Real-Time Modelchecking

In Section 2.2.2, real-time coordination patterns have been introduced for the specification of communication. In Section 2.2.3, it has been described that a component usually realizes different roles of different patterns. The behavior of the component has to refine the behavior of the roles it realizes. The separation of communication behavior and component behavior leads to a compositional model which is exploited for verification:

The basic idea is to verify in a first step, if each pattern is correct. In a second step, it is checked if each component is correct and if it refines the roles it realizes. When both verification steps are successful for all patterns and components, a syntactically correct composed system, consisting of multiple pattern and component instances, is also correct [GTB+03]. An additional verification step to verify the composed system is not necessary.

This approach for compositional verification is sketched in more details in Sections 2.3.1 – 2.3.3. It is formalized in Appendix A.

2.3.1 Pattern Correctness

As described in Section 2.2.2, the behavior of a pattern is composed by the behavior of the roles and by the behavior of the connectors. A pattern is correct, if its pattern constraint holds and if it is free from deadlocks [GTB+03]. To verify the constraint and the deadlock freedom, an overall RTSC is constructed, combining the RTSCs of the roles and connectors in orthogonal states.

For modelchecking, the existing modelchecker Uppaal is applied. The RTSC model is mapped to the hierarchical HUppaal [DM01, DMY02] model as described in [BGHS04]. Then, it is translated to Uppaal [LPY97], which allows the application of the modelchecker. This verification approach has been followed in [Sch05a] in a similar manner: There,

UPPAAL is also used to verify consistency between interface specifications described by timed automata.

2.3.2   Component Correctness

A component has to fulfill 4 items:

1. User defined properties have to be fulfilled,

2. the component may not contain deadlocks,

3. it has to fulfill the invariants of the roles, it realizes, and

4. it has to refine the roles, it realizes,

Items 1, 2, and 3 are verified again by translating the real-time statechart to the Uppaal model and by applying the real-time modelchecker. If the role invariants contain abstract properties, these properties need to be mapped (manually) to states, i.e. the set of states have to be identified where each property holds. Item 4 does not need to be verified, as we ensure the component to be *correct-by-construction*: When building the component behavior by refining role behavior, it is only allowed to add states and transitions for internal synchronization and internal modifications. They have to preserve the guaranteed external communication behavior and may not add additional external communication behavior [GH06]. The formalization of refinement is provided in Appendix A.

2.3.3   System Correctness

A system consists of multiple component instances and of multiple pattern instances. When for each pattern, the pattern constraint holds and each component refines the roles, it realizes, and fulfills their role invariants, a composed system fulfills also all pattern constraints and role invariants. An additional verification step to verify the composed system is not necessary.

The reason, why this additional verification step is not necessary, is that the verified patterns provide some non-determinism within their roles. As the component just resolves this non-determinism in its behavior and does not add additional behavior, it just refines the role behavior and thus preserves the verified pattern constraint. The formal proof can be found in Appendix A and in [GTB+03].

2.3.4   Discussion

The compositional modelchecking, enabled by the compositional design, does not only reduce modelchecking costs, it makes the verification of huge systems feasible. This is due to the fact that each pattern type and each component type just needs to be checked *once* and they can be checked before the whole system has been constructued. For example, to verify correctness of the system from Figure 2.21 from Section 2.2.4, just the ConvoyCoordination pattern and the Shuttle component need to be checked. There is no need to verify the whole system, consisting of 6 component instances and 5 pattern instances.

When extending the modeling approach for the specification of reconfiguration and of hybrid behavior, as mentioned in Section 2.2.5, the resulting modeling approach should be integrated with this compositional verification approach.

2.4 Control Engineering

Systems, like for example a shuttle, are permanent subject to excitations and disturbances. Reasons for such excitations are for example unevennesses of the tracks, wind, etc. Feedback-controllers are applied to minimize the difference between a specific input and the current output or to hold the output on a constant level dependent on the input. This is achieved by a closed loop control system, as depicted in Figure 2.22. The figure shows a block diagram (see Section 2.4.1) with the system under control which is called *plant*, the *feedback-controller*, the *reference input* $r(t)$, the disturbance $n(t)$, and the plant's output $y(t)$ which is fed back to the controller.

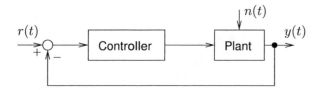

Figure 2.22: Closed loop control system

A feedback-controller has to be designed properly, so that excitations and disturbances do not lead to oscillations which can lead to catastrophes like collision or derailment in the RailCab example. If a feedback-controller holds the output of the plant on the desired value and restores the desired value after an excitation or disturbance, the whole system is called *stable*.

2.4.1 Block Diagrams

A common technique for the specification of feedback-controllers that is widely-used in different CAE (Computer-Aided Engineering) tools is the notion of hierarchical block diagrams. Block diagrams generally consist of *basic blocks*, specifying behavior and *hierarchy blocks* that group basic and other hierarchy blocks and thus lead to a reduction of the visual complexity. Figure 2.23 shows a block diagram consisting of the basic blocks BB1, ..., BB5 and the hierarchy blocks HB1 and HB2.

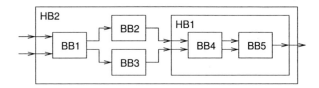

Figure 2.23: Block diagram

Each block has input and output signals. The unidirectional interconnections between the blocks describe the transfer of information, for example the output signal of basic block BB2 is fed as input signal into hierarchy block HB1.

The behavior of basic blocks is usually specified by differential equations, specifying the relationship between the block's inputs and outputs. A simple example for such a differential equation is shown in Equation 2.1 describing a feedback-controller that we call PDT_1 controller.[6] It consists of the input signal $u(t)$ and it provides the output signal $y(t)$. T_1, k_1, and k_2 are constants.

$$y(t) + T_1\dot{y}(t) = k_1 u(t) + k_2 \dot{u}(t) \tag{2.1}$$

2.4.2 LaPlace Transformation & Transfer Functions

The differential equation from Equation 2.1 describes the output $y(t)$ dependent on the input $u(t)$. Another mathematical description of the system's input-output relation, is given by the system's *impulse response* $g(t)$, which is characteristically for each system and which can unambiguously be derived from the differential equation [Oga02]. Using the impulse response, the output is derived from the input as described by Equation 2.2.[7]

$$y(t) = g(t) * u(t) \tag{2.2}$$

Solving the convolution integral is usually not trivial. A standard approach is to exploit the properties of the *LaPlace transformation*: Each function $f(t)$ has an unambiguously derivable LaPlace transform $F(s)$. $f(t)$ is called the *inverse LaPlace transform* of $F(s)$. One property of LaPlace transforms is that *the LaPlace transform of the convolution of two functions is the product of the LaPlace transforms of these functions*. Formally, this property is expressed in Equation 2.3 with respect to Equation 2.2.

$$Y(s) = G(s)U(s) \tag{2.3}$$

---

[6]Note that the dot above a variable denotes the variable's derivative with respect to the time t: $\dot{y}(t) := d/dt\, y(t)$.

[7]Note that $*$ does not denote *multiplication*, but *convolution* which is defined as $f(t) * g(t) := \int_0^t f(t - \tau)g(\tau)d\tau$.

In practice, the derivation of LaPlace transforms and their inverses is straightforward [Oga02]. Thus, the standard process to determine an output signal $y(t)$, dependent on an input signal $u(t)$, is

1. to determine the LaPlace transforms of the input signal $U(s)$ and of the impulse response $G(s)$,

2. to multiply the LaPlace transforms to obtain $Y(s)$, and

3. to determine the inverse LaPlace transform $y(t)$ of the product.

Therefore, a common representation of a block's behavior is its *transfer function* $G(s)$ which is the LaPlace transform of the impulse response $g(t)$.

In order to derive the transfer function for a system, described by a differential equation, another property described in Equation 2.4 of the LaPlace transform is exploited: If $F(s)$ is the LaPlace transform of $f(t)$, the LaPlace transform of $\dot{f}(t)$ is $sF(s) - f(0)$ with $f(0)$ the zero initial value of $f(t)$.

$$g(t) = \dot{f}(t) \Leftrightarrow G(s) = sF(s) - f(0) \tag{2.4}$$

In practice, the system's zero initial values are usually zero, i.e. $f(0) = 0$. Under this assumption, transforming both sides of Equation 2.1 leads to equation 2.5 for the transfer function.

$$Y(s) + T_1 sY(s) = k_1 U(s) + k_2 sU(s)$$
$$\Leftrightarrow \tag{2.5}$$
$$G(s) := \frac{Y(s)}{U(s)} = \frac{k_1 + k_2 s}{1 + T_1 s}$$

2.4.3 Implementation

Feedback-controllers are realized either time-continuous or time-discrete. A time-continuous realization is usually implemented in hardware for example by connecting different electrical modules like resistors, capacitors, or inductors. For time-discrete realizations, multiple possibilities exist: One possibility is to generate VHDL code to program a Field Programmable Gate Array (FPGA). Another possibility is to implement a feedback-controller in software.

This work is based on components that are realized in software and thus, we regard time-discrete feedback-controller implementations in software. As each computation step requires a non-zero amount of time (cf. Section 2.1.5) which leads to delays when executing the implementation, the time continuous description of the feedback-controller (cf. Equation 2.1) needs to be discretized.

For a time-discrete implementation of a feedback-controller specification, the choice of the *integration algorithm* is important. Each integration algorithm describes a different strategy for discrete integration. These strategies are also applied for discretization. Well-known algorithms are Euler-Cauchy (Adams-Moulton 1-point), Euler (Adams-Bashforth 1-point),

Tutin (Adams-Moulton 2-point), Adams-Moulton 3-point/4-point, Adams-Bashforth 2-point/3-point, Simpson's 2 Strip, or Simpson's Half of 2 Strip. Each integration algorithm has advantages and disadvantages with respect to stability, magnitude gain, phase lag, and computational complexity [Oga87].

Transforming a feedback-controller block to a time-discrete implementation requires three steps:

1. choosing an integration algorithm,

2. using the integration algorithm to transform the LaPlace transformation to a discretized description called *z transform* [Oga87], and

3. deriving an iterative description of the input-output relation from the z transform of the controller block.

Each integration algorithm is characterized by its z transform, e.g. the Euler-Cauchy integration algorithm is described by $F(z) = Tz/(z-1)$ with T the *sampling rate* or *period*. To derive the z transform of the block, described by Equation 2.5, all occurrences of s are eliminated by replacing $1/s$ by Euler-Cauchy's term $Tz/(z-1)$. The result is shown in Equation 2.6.

$$\frac{Y(z)}{U(z)} = \frac{k_1 + k_2\frac{z-1}{Tz}}{1 + T_1\frac{z-1}{Tz}} = \frac{(k_1T + k_2)z - k_2}{(T + T_1)z - T_1} \tag{2.6}$$

To derive an iterative description, simply $z^{-n}Y(z)$ needs to be replaced by y_{k-n} ($U(z)$ similar) [Oga87].[8] Thus, we converse Equation 2.6 to Equation 2.7 and make the replacement whose result is shown in Equation 2.8

$$(T + T_1)zY(z) - T_1Y(z) = (k_1T + k_2)zU(z) - k_2U(z)$$
$$\Leftrightarrow$$
$$(T + T_1)Y(z) - T_1z^{-1}Y(z) = (k_1T + k_2)U(z) - k_2z^{-1}U(z) \tag{2.7}$$
$$\Leftrightarrow$$
$$Y(z) = \frac{1}{T+T_1}(T_1z^{-1}Y(z) + (k_1T + k_2)U(z) - k_2z^{-1}U(z))$$

$$y_k = \frac{1}{T + T_1}(T_1y_{k-1} + (k_1T + k_2)u_k - k_2u_{k-1}) \tag{2.8}$$

Equation 2.8 describes the iterative form of the PDT_1 controller with T the sampling rate, y_k the output y at point of time kT, k_1, k_2, and T_1 the controller parameters, u_k the input at point of time kT (the *current* input), and u_{k-1} the input at point of time $(k-1)T$ (the *previous* input). This is a description that just requires to be evaluated at discrete points in time. Thus, this description is implementable in software.

The choice of the sampling rate T is an important issues as it affects stability massively. As too large periods lead to instability, a feedback-controller's sampling rate has to be below a system-specific upper bound.

---

[8]Note that $z^{-n} = \frac{1}{z^n}$

The LaPlace transform is a specification of a controller block in the continuous time domain. The z transform and the iterative form are a description in the discretized time domain. To distinguish these discrete controller descriptions from discrete signals or events, sent or received for example by state machines, the z and the iterative description are usually called *quasi-continuous*. The term *quasi* expresses that the sampling rate T is usually very small compared with the periods of discrete systems, like state machines. In the remainder of this thesis, we do not regard systems that are continuous in the sense explained above. Therefore, we call components *continuous* even when we refer to *quasi-continuous* components.

2.4.4 Abstraction from Implementation Details

In order to reduce computational complexity, additional variables may be introduced as substitutions in a controller implementation. In such implementations, a new issue has to be respected: the *dependency relations*. When a variable y depends on another variable x, in each computation cycle y may not be evaluated before x has been evaluated. Thus, we combine all equations of a controller block implementation that have a fixed ordering into a *node*. The resulting nodes and the dependency relations, describing which nodes require the results of which other nodes, build the *reduced graph* of the feedback-controller block. The representation of a continuous component by its reduced graph is an *abstraction* of its internal behavior [OGBG04, BGGO04b].

We visualize the reduced graph as shown in Figure 2.24 for an abstract example controller with two inputs (u_1 and u_2) and 3 outputs (y_1, y_2, and y_3). n_{d0}, n_{d1}, n_{d2}, and n_{s0} denote the nodes containing the equations. The latter one denotes the node that keeps track of the component's internal *continuous state*, e.g. the previous inputs.

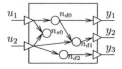

Figure 2.24: Reduced graph of a feedback-controller block consisting of four nodes

This example demonstrates that different kinds of nodes exist: Generally, a continuous block consists of one node that contains only expressions which influence just the inner continuous state and no outputs of the controller. In [OGBG04, BGGO04b] this evaluation node is denoted as *state node (S)*. As no particular evaluation order is required for these expressions, at most one state node exists per controller block. Furthermore, at most one evaluation node is created that determines outputs which depend just on the internal continuous state and not on the current inputs (*non-direct link node (ND)*). Only the expressions whose outputs depend on the inputs (*direct link nodes (D)*) are partitioned into multiple evaluation nodes.

As mentioned before, no particular order about the evaluation of n_{d0}, n_{d1}, and n_{d2} exists. This depends on the configuration in which the controller block is embedded. The configuration specifies the external couplings of the block: If two instances of the block from Figure 2.24 are connected as shown in Figure 2.25a, they build an overall hierarchical block with 2 inputs and 4 outputs and there are still no further dependency relations except that the nodes of controller c2 have to be evaluated after the nodes of controller c1. When connecting the controller blocks as depicted in Figure 2.25b, the number of inputs, the number of outputs, the dependency relations, and thus the evaluation order changes: When input u_1 is available, only node n_{d2} of c1 can be evaluated, as the inputs for the other nodes are not available. After evaluating this node, only n_{d2} of c2 can be evaluated and so on. This results in the evaluation order: c1:n_{d2}, c2:n_{d2}, c1:n_{d0}, c1:n_{d1}, c2:n_{d0}, c2:n_{d1}. The state nodes are always evaluated at the end of each evaluation cycle.

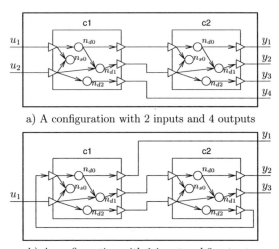

a) A configuration with 2 inputs and 4 outputs

b) A configuration with 1 input and 3 outputs

Figure 2.25: External couplings determine evaluation order

This example demonstrates that the evaluation order of a controller block's nodes depends on the external couplings. Further, it is easy to construct models that contain loops that lead to deadlocks (e.g. connecting y_3 in Figure 2.24 with u_2). Thus, we require for each configuration not to contain loops.

2.4.5   Switching

In reconfigurating systems, it is often required to exchange feedback-controller structures. When applying different feedback-controllers, they may produce different output signals. In this case, a switch between them will lead to a (discrete) jump in the output signal. Such jumps lead to additional, unintended oscillations.

To avoid or to reduce these oscillations, *output cross-fading* is applied as described in [Vöc03] and applied in [BGO06, GBSO04].[9] Output cross-fading fades the output of the old controller (the one that is to be replaced) out while the output of the new controller is faded in. It is specified by a *fading function* $f_{fade}(t)$ and an additional parameter t_{end} which determines the duration of the cross-fading (see Figure 2.26).

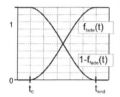

Figure 2.26: Fading function

The fading function describes how the old feedback-controller is weighted during the fading (the weight changes dependent on the time). $1 - f_{fade}(t)$ describes the weight of the new controller. Thus, the overall output is described by $y(t) = f_{fade}(t)y_{old}(t) + (1 - f_{fade}(t))y_{new}(t)$. Note that during the fading process both feedback-controllers and an additional fading block are active.

2.4.6 Example Feedback-Controllers

Further feedback-controller blocks that will be used in the application example besides the PDT_1 controller are a P controller block and a block that describes the inverse shuttle dynamics. The transfer function of the P block is $G_P(s) := K$. The transfer function that describes the inverse shuttle dynamics is $G_{Shuttle}^{-1} := \frac{s(1+T_1 s)}{(1+T_w s)^2}$. K, T_1, and T_w are constants.

Figure 2.27 shows the controller blocks which will be used in the remainder of this work: Figure 2.27a depicts the *velocity controller*. It gets the required velocity v_{req} and the current velocity v_{cur} as input and feeds their difference into the mentioned P controller block. The output is the acceleration a which is required to reach or to hold the required velocity. In our shuttle scenario, this output is fed into the linear motor and brake module that sets up this acceleration. The reduced graph of the velocity controller consists of one D node. The position control block (Figure 2.27b) gets two input signals: the required position x_{req} and the current position x_{cur}. Their difference is fed into a PDT_1 controller block. It produces the velocity v as output which is required to reach or hold the required position. Its reduced graph consists of a D node and an S node. The pilot control block also gets the current and the required position as input, but it feeds the difference of these input signals into the $G_{Shuttle}^{-1}$ controller block. The reduced graph consists of two nodes,

---

[9][BGO06] is also known as [BGO04b]

similar to the one of the position control block, but the internals of the nodes, i.e. their equations, differ in both cases.

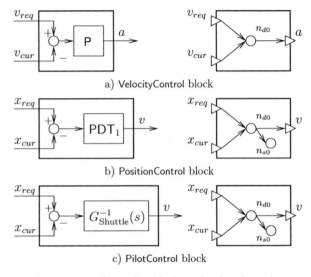

a) VelocityControl block

b) PositionControl block

c) PilotControl block

Figure 2.27: Controller blocks and reduced graphs

Besides the velocity controller, we will apply two different kinds of position controllers for the shuttle example. The latter ones are built by the introduced controller blocks from Figure 2.27: Figure 2.28a shows the *position controller*. It is realized by the position control block from Figure 2.27b. Its output is fed into the velocity controller from Figure 2.27a.

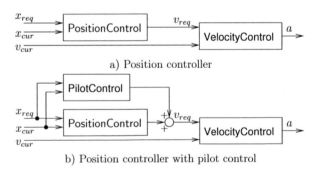

a) Position controller

b) Position controller with pilot control

Figure 2.28: Position controllers

In Figure 2.28b, the *position controller with pilot control* is depicted. It applies additionally the pilot control block from Figure 2.27c [HVB+05]. This controller structure leads to a faster convergence to the required position.

2.4.7 Discussion

In this section, we gave an overview about the foundations of control engineering. A feedback-controller is specified by a block diagram, a differential equation, or a transfer function. Such a continuous model is transformed into a discrete model by choosing an integration algorithm. This discretization enables an implementation in software. The notion of nodes provides an abstraction from the implementation details.

Feedback-controllers are pure continuous systems. Therefore, we call a feedback-controller component *basic continuous component*. Basic continuous components have a static structure which does not permit to model structural adaptations [ILM92]. Thus, their behavior can just be changed by parameter adaptation. Complex, mechatronic systems often require structural adaptation, which is exemplified by the feedback-controller examples from Section 2.4.6: Exchanging the velocity controller, the position controller, and the position controller with pilot control by parameter adaptation would lead to one complex, monolithic controller, that changes parameters to switch single outputs of the system on or off. Due to the complexity of such a model, it would be hard to analyze. An implementation would be inefficient with respect to resources, as all parts of the system would be active.

Thus, there is the need to support reconfiguration (as first part of structural adaptation) which integrates architecture, discrete real-time behavior, and discrete real-time communication as presented in Section 2.2 with continuous behavior as presented in this section.

2.5 Conclusion

In this chapter, we introduced model-based software engineering which consists of the three parts modeling, verification, and code generation. We introduced our UML-based modeling approach for cooperative real-time systems and the existing verification approach. Due to the compositionality, the verification is even applicable for complex systems. As mechatronic systems usually apply continuous feedback-controllers, we introduced continuous models.

For the specification of hybrid, reconfigurable, embedded, real-time systems, there is need for an integration of discrete real-time systems with continuous feedback-controllers. As exemplified and discussed in the previous section, mechatronic systems often require a change of the control structures at run-time. Therefore, the integration does not only have to support the exchange of feedback-controllers, but also reconfiguration. In order to avoid wasting resources, the models have to enable an implementation that respects restricted resources. The resulting modeling approach must be integrated with the presented compositional verification approach.

We will present our approach to model hybrid reconfigurable mechatronic real-time systems in the next chapter. Existing approaches for this integration are discussed in Chapter 6.

Chapter 3

Modeling and Analysis of Reconfigurable Mechatronic Systems

In the approaches described in Sections 2.2, and 2.4, the design of discrete real-time software engineering components and continuous control engineering components is separated. In order to specify hybrid behavior, there is need for an integration. In this chapter, we present a new approach for the specification of hybrid behavior, supporting even reconfiguration. We will see that our approach –compared to current state of the art approaches– leads to models which require reduced effort for analyzes and which thus enable ruling the complexity of mechatronic systems. The models of our approach respect that the resources of embedded systems are usually limited. Thus, they enable implementations that free resources when parts of the system become inactive.

In order to clarify the need for the integration, we consider again the application example: We specified the behavior of Shuttle by the real-time statechart from Figure 2.15 in Section 2.2.3. This behavior is a refinement of the roles from the ConvoyCoordination pattern, described in Section 2.2.2 and thus, this behavior coordinates building and breaking of convoys. When running a shuttle, it is not just sufficient to ensure a correct coordination and a correct change of the discrete states. Further, the shuttle's behavior needs to be changed dependent on the current discrete state: As described in Section 1.2, the strategy to control the velocity and the behavior when performing an emergency brake change. This change of the shuttle's behavior is expressed by the pattern role invariants from Figure 2.11: (front.convoy or front.wait) implies ((not canBrakeFully) and (not followLeader) and coordinateRearRoles).

These role invariants –which are requirements for the component realization– must be realized by the internal behavior of the Shuttle component, e.g. by integrating feedback-controllers like the ones introduced in Section 2.4.6.[1] This *internal behavior* may not be contradictory to the component's external communication behavior, ensured by the roles, i.e. changing the behavior to control the velocity may not influence the coordination process

---

[1]Obviously, it is not possible to automatically derive an appropriate feedback-controller from a role invariant specification. Rather, the component's requirements, which result from the realized roles, guide the engineers to find an appropriate solution.

when building or breaking convoys. This is achieved by our design approach. The following paragraphs give a brief overview about the design steps and their relations:

Overview about the Design Steps

Section 2.3 described how to verify real-time system specifications by compositional real-time modelchecking. In this chapter, we present an advanced modeling technique to design reconfigurable mechatronic systems and to integrate behaviors of structurally embedded basic continuous and hybrid components. Obviously, embedding components changes the behavior of the superordinated component. We have to ensure that this embedding will not invalidate the results of the real-time modelchecking.

Figure 3.1 shows an overview about our design and verification approach extending Figure 2.14 in an abstract way. The upper part of the figure shows an abstract real-time coordination pattern, consisting of the role behaviors $M_1, \ldots, M_n$ and the connector behavior M^P. The pattern has to fulfill the pattern constraint ϕ. As described in Section 2.3 and presented in [GTB$^+$03], we verify by modelchecking that the parallel composition of $M_1, \ldots, M_n$ and M^P fulfills ϕ and that this parallel composition does not contain deadlocks. This is formally expressed by $(M_1\|\ldots\|M_n)\|M^P \models \phi \wedge \neg\delta$ in Figure 3.1. This notation is taken from the formalization and is explained in Appendix A.

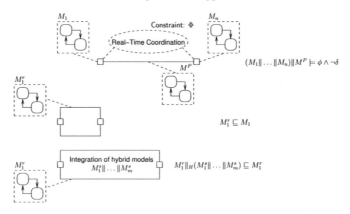

Figure 3.1: Overview about our verification approach

Further, we explained that a component with a behavior M_1^r that realizes the role with the behavior M_1 has to refine this behavior ($M_1^r \sqsubseteq M_1$). If it realizes also another role with behavior M_j ($j \neq i$), it also has to refine its behavior ($M_1^r \sqsubseteq M_j$). M_1^r may describe a real-time behavior – like the behavior introduced in Section 2.2.3. M_1^r has to ensure that the invariants of the realized roles hold. Then, we apply modelchecking to verify user-defined properties of this component, deadlock freedom, and role invariants. When we integrate further components (e.g. feedback-controller components) in such a behavior, the composition of all components –which we call *hierarchical parallel composition* (see Section 3.2.1)– may not add additional external behavior and thus, it has to be a refinement of the component realization $(M_1^r \|_H (M_1^s \| \ldots \| M_m^s) \sqsubseteq M_I^r)$. As this implies that it is also a refinement of the pattern's role behaviors, the hierarchical parallel composition does not invalidate verification results.

Outline

In the remainder of this chapter, we will first introduce our advanced specification technique and then, we will show that this technique simplifies analyses to ensure the refinement relations described above. This reduces effort in the verification as indicated above. The example feedback-controller structures demonstrate that it is not always required to exchange complete controller structures, but that it can be required to reconfigure the structure of the applied feedback-controller (e.g. by adding or removing a pilot control block). Therefore, we focus on reconfigurating controller structures instead of just exchanging continuous models.

First, we present how to specify the structure of the reconfigurable system in Section 3.1. Then, Section 3.2 deals with modeling the reconfiguration taking into account limited computational power and other limited resources (e.g. memory). Further, we present how to integrate this modeling approach with compositional real-time modelchecking. We close this chapter with a conclusion in Section 3.3.

3.1 Architecture

Hierarchical component structures enable a structural separation of components that realize internal behavior from components realizing external behavior. Figure 2.4 in Section 2.1.2 depicts a first version of such a hierarchical component structure: The shuttle component, realizing the external coordination, embeds an instance of the DriveTrain component, which is responsible to fulfill the followLeader requirement, and one instance of the linear motor and brake (LMB) component. This component diagram does not respect that there are different kinds of data, in hybrid systems. There are

- discrete signals that cause changes of the discrete state, like the events used for coordinating convoys and

- quasi-continuous signals, like the inputs and outputs of feedback-controllers.

As the engineer usually requires the separation of these different kinds of data on the modeling level, we refine the UML port concept and distinguish between *discrete ports*, sending discrete signals and *continuous ports*, sending (quasi-) continuous variables. Figure 3.2 shows the internal structure of Shuttle as a refinement of Figure 2.4. The ports of the internal components are refined to continuous ports, visualized as triangles. Further, we explicitly provide the notion of hybrid ports, combining multiple discrete and continuous ports as syntactic construct to reduce visual complexity (hybrid ports are not applied in this example).

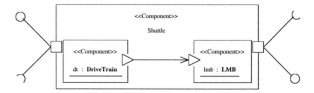

Figure 3.2: Structure with continuous and discrete ports

Similar to the Shuttle component, which is composed of multiple other component instances, the types of these subordinated instances are defined by further compositions. This leads to an architectural description of Shuttle, consisting of multiple layers.

Figure 3.3 shows for example that the DriveTrain component is composed of instances of the components AccelerationControl, PosSensor, VelSensor, Storage, and ReferenceSpeed. The instance ac:AccelerationControl determines the required acceleration which is delegated to the output of the superordinated DriveTrain component. To determine this output, it obtains the current position from ps:PosSensor, the current velocity from vs:VelSensor, the required position from st:Storage where the required trajectory is stored, and the required velocity from the rs:ReferenceSpeed instance which determines the required velocity based on optimizations e.g. for fast traveling or for slow low cost traveling. Thus, DriveTrain encapsulates ac:AccelerationControl and the components that provide the input signals.

We will see that not all instances, embedded in DriveTrain, are needed simultaneously at run-time. Therefore, the component diagram shows the superposition of all instance situations possible at run-time.

AccelerationControl embeds again five further instances (see Figure 3.4). Recall that we introduced in Chapter 2 *basic discrete components* whose behavior is specified by real-time statecharts and *basic continuous components* whose behavior is specified by block-diagrams, differential equations, or transfer functions. In this chapter, we will introduce a modeling language to specify hybrid behavior. Thus, we call all components *hybrid components* in general and see basic discrete and basic continuous components as special cases. We adapt the UML notation for components and component instances even for basic continuous components: To denote for example a P controller type, we simply use P. To denote two different instances of that type, we use for example p1:P and p2:P, and we refer to them later simply by p1 and p2.

This notation is used to specify the internal structure of AccelerationControl. It embeds the component instances velCtrl:VelocityControl, posCtrl:PositionControl, pilCtrl:PilotControl, sum:Sum, and fade:Fading. velCtrl:VelocityControl, posCtrl:PositionControl, and pilCtrl:PilotControl are the velocity controller, the position control block, and the pilot control block respectively from Figure 2.27. The blocks pilCtrl:PilotControl and sum:Sum are used to build a configuration that realizes the position controller with and without pilot control as shown in Figure 2.28.

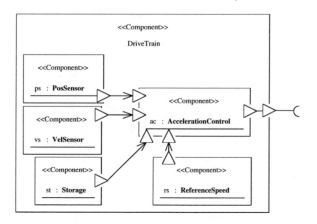

Figure 3.3: Structure of the DriveTrain component

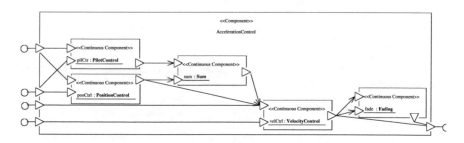

Figure 3.4: Structure of the AccelerationControl component

The block fade:Fading implements cross-fading as explained in Section 2.4.5. The inputs of AccelerationControl can be connected to the inputs of the embedded component instances as shown by the connectors in Figure 3.4. The output is provided either by velCtrl or by fade. Note again, that the component diagram does not show a static instance situation, but the superposition of all instance situations possible at run-time.

3.2   Behavior

As we require discrete switching between the different presented continuous configurations to control the acceleration, AccelerationControl is a component that shows hybrid behavior. We do not use classical or current approaches –like for example [SPP01, Sta01, Hen00, ADE+01, FdO99, FGHL04, EKRNS00]– to specify hybrid behavior, as they have several limitations (see also Chapter 6): One serious limitation is due to the fact that the continuous part of each state (*location* in the terminology of hybrid systems) has to have the same set of required input and output variables, which complicates consistency analyses. Further, reconfiguration is limited to architectures with low hierarchy, the models of complex systems become difficult to handle, and the approaches lack of efficient methods for model analysis. To overcome these drawbacks, we introduce our modeling technique called *hybrid reconfiguration charts*[2] [GBSO04, BGO06, BGT05] as advanced behavioral description language for the specification of hybrid behavior.

3.2.1   Hybrid Reconfiguration Charts

The hybrid reconfiguration chart model is an extension of the real-time statechart model. In a hybrid reconfiguration chart that describes the behavior of a component that embeds instances of other components, each discrete state is associated with a *configuration* of subordinated components. Thus, each state defines which subordinated components are used while residing in this state and how their inputs and outputs are connected. If the subordinated components show hybrid or discrete behavior themselves, i.e. if they can reside in different discrete states as well, the configurations even contain the discrete state which the corresponding component has to adopt in this configuration. The behavior of the embedded components executes concurrently to the superordinated component, while the components' output signals are delivered to the targets, specified by the connections of the active configuration. As this is a parallel (concurrent) execution of hierarchical embedded components, we denote this to be a *hierarchical parallel composition* of hybrid components.

Recall, that one serious limitation of related approaches is that they have static interfaces. Therefore, we define a set of required input and output variables *per state*. Each state has to define the delegations from the state's required in- and outputs to the components of its associated configuration.

When the superordinated component changes its state, this state change *implies* a change of the configuration of the component's embedded component structure, as specified

---

[2]formerly known as *hybrid statecharts*

by the configuration of the target state. Further, the state change of the superordinated component *implies* a state change of the subordinated components which show discrete or hybrid behavior themselves. If these subordinated components embed further components, the implied state changes may lead to further state changes on the hierarchical layer below. These state changes may imply further state changes and so on. This adaptation of structure and states is called *reconfiguration* (see Chapter 1).

Figure 3.5 shows a hybrid reconfiguration chart that describes the behavior of the AccelerationControl component (see Figure 3.4).[3] It consists of five discrete states: The states VelocityControl, PositionControl, or PositionControlWithPilotControl are associated with the continuous controller component configurations which have been described in Section 2.4.6. The states FadeVelocityControlPositionControl and FadeVelocityControlPositionControlWithPilotControl are introduced to realize output cross-fading between the VelocityControl-configuration and the PositionControl- or PositionControlWithPilotControl-configuration (cf. Section 2.4.5). When for example residing in state VelocityControl, state PositionControl can only be reached via the *fading state* (or *fading location*) FadeVelocityControlPositionControl. This intermediate state is associated with the configuration of state VelocityControl (which consists just of velCtrl), the configuration of state PositionControl (which consists of posCtrl and velCtrl), and a component fade:Fading realizing the fading. Note that velCtrl is part of both the source and the target configuration. Thus, a second instance (tmpVelCtrl:VelocityControl) needs to be instantiated and initialized properly. Further, note that in this example all embedded components are basic continuous components that do not show discrete or hybrid behavior. A clock t0 (a continuous variable whose flow is in every state $\dot{t0} = 1$) is introduced to specify invariants and time guards that guarantee fading durations $t^i_{fade} \in [l^i_{ac}; d^i_{ac}]$.

Figure 3.5 demonstrates that fading locations lead to a high visual complexity. Thus, we introduce a syntactical high-level construct called *fading transition* which is an extension of the time consuming transition from the real-time statechart model (see Section 2.2.2). Recall that these transitions are associated with deadlines, indicating a time interval when firing the transition has to be finished at the earliest and at the latest. A fading transition is additionally associated with a *fading function* that describes how to fade from the source configuration to the target configuration and –in case of multiple outputs– which output of the source configuration is faded to which output of the target configuration. The deadline interval describes the minimal and the maximal fading duration.

These fading transitions reduce massively the visual complexity of the models as shown in Figure 3.6 which shows a hybrid reconfiguration chart that uses fading transitions and that specifies the same behavior like the hybrid reconfiguration chart from Figure 3.5. Fading transitions are visualized as thick arrows. The fading function f_{fade} refers to the controller block fade.

Recall, that the structural view from Figure 3.4 specifies all *possible* connections between a component's input and output ports and its subordinated components. The example shows that some connections are not established in some situations and some subordinated

---

[3]Actually, it shows a restricted kind of a hybrid reconfiguration chart: a *hybrid reconfiguration automaton* (cf. formalization in Appendix A).

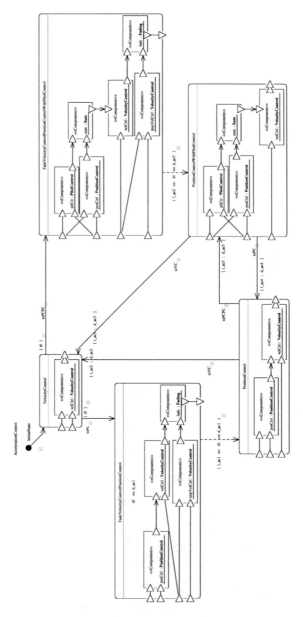

Figure 3.5: Hybrid reconfiguration chart of AccelerationControl

components are not required in some situations and thus they are not active the whole
run-time.

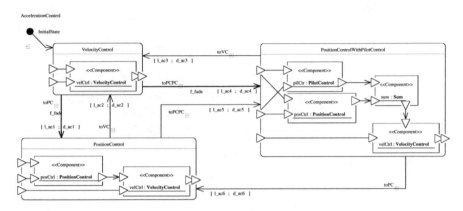

Figure 3.6: Hybrid reconfiguration chart of AccelerationControl with fading transitions

Similar to the semantics definition of real-time statecharts, the semantics definition of
hybrid reconfiguration charts does not have the macrostep and run-to-completion semantics.
A formal definition of the semantics is given in Appendix A.

3.2.2 Automatic Abstraction of Configurations

We explained in Section 2.4.3, that each continuous component consists of at most one S
node, at most one ND node, and possibly multiple D nodes. The evaluation order *within* each
node is static and independent of the configuration in which the component is embedded,
but the evaluation order of the nodes themselves depends on the component's external
couplings, i.e. the configuration in which it is embedded. Respecting these couplings, it is
possible to derive a reduced graph even for a configuration.

When building the reduced graph of a configuration, the nodes of the configuration's
components that have a static evaluation order are grouped (*partitioned*) again into
superordinated S, ND, and D nodes. *Partitioning* the nodes into superordinated nodes
reduces the number of nodes which leads to an efficient management of the configuration's
nodes and its possible evaluation orders. Especially, when the architecture consists of
multiple hierarchical levels, partitioning the nodes reduces the effort for managing the
evaluation orders massively.

Thus, we have to derive the reduced graph of every state's configuration. Although for
complexity reasons, it is desired to obtain as few nodes as possible, it is not expedient to
group all nodes into one superordinated node: If such a node influences multiple output
ports and if this node requires further inputs, the whole evaluation would be blocked till all

input signals are available. Due to loops in the external coupling, as exemplified in Figure 3.7, deadlocks can be caused: Figure 3.7a shows an abstract configuration consisting of the five nodes $n_{d0}, \ldots, n_{d4}$. If these nodes are partitioned into one node n_{d5} as depicted in Figure 3.7b, the shown external coupling would cause a cycle and thus a deadlock, as n_{d5} requires its output as input. A partitioning as shown in Figure 3.7c that groups just nodes n_{d1}, n_{d2}, and n_{d4} into a superordinated node n_{d8} (n_{d0} becomes n_{d6} and n_{d3} becomes n_{d7}) avoids this deadlock. Obviously, also the other inputs and outputs of the component need to be connected in a well-formed manner, i.e. without cycles that lead to deadlocks.

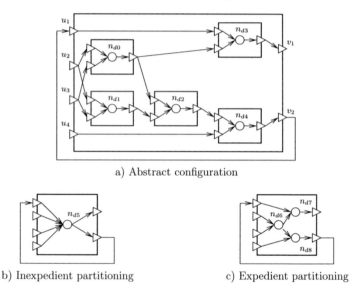

a) Abstract configuration

b) Inexpedient partitioning   c) Expedient partitioning

Figure 3.7: Abstract partitioning examples

As deadlocks occur only due to cyclic couplings of nodes whose outputs are directly influenced by their inputs, we distinguish (as in Section 2.4.3) between state nodes (S), non-direct link nodes (ND), and direct link nodes (D) and partition a configuration into maximal one S node, maximal one ND node and possibly multiple D nodes.

Our partitioning algorithm, as first presented in [OGBG04] and then extended in [BGGO04b], determines in a first step for each block on which inputs and on which state nodes its output depends. In a second step, it is determined for each block which outputs and which state nodes are influenced by the node's output. A node is assigned to the superordinated S node if its output influences exclusively S nodes. It is assigned to the superordinated ND-block, if its output depends exclusively on state nodes. The remaining nodes build the superordinated D nodes:

To partition the D nodes, it is considered again for each node which outputs of the configuration it influences. Then, it is considered on which inputs these outputs depend. Then, the algorithm determines for each node the inputs that are required by *each* of its influenced outputs. All nodes for which these input sets are identical are grouped into the same D node.

This algorithm is exemplified by the abstract example from Figure 3.7a. Figure 3.8a shows the nodes from the example, the in- and outputs, and their dependencies. As mentioned above, we first determine the input dependencies, labeled D_{in}. n_{d0}, n_{d1}, and n_{d2} depend on the inputs u_2 and u_3. n_{d3} depends on u_1, u_2, and u_3 and n_{d4} depends on u_2, u_3, and u_4. In a second step, we determine which outputs are influenced by each node. This set of outputs is labeled I_{out}. As shown by the annotations in Figure 3.8a, n_{d0} influences both outputs v_1 and v_2; n_{d1}, n_{d2}, and n_{d4} influence v_2; and n_{d3} influences v_1. The third step is to determine for each node the inputs that are required by *each* of its influenced outputs which is labeled with L: As seen above, n_{d0} influences v_1 and v_2. v_1 requires u_1, u_2, and u_3 while v_2 requires u_2, u_3, and u_4. Thus, u_2 and u_3 are the inputs that are required by each of n_{d0}'s influenced outputs. Determining L for the other nodes is simpler, because they influence just one output. Thus, L for the nodes n_{d1}, n_{d2}, and n_{d4} is equal to D_{in} from n_{d4} and for node n_{d3}, L is equal to its set D_{in}. As the labels L of n_{d1}, n_{d2}, and n_{d4} are similar, they are grouped into one superordinated node (visualized by the grey background in Figure 3.8b). The other two nodes are not grouped together.

The example shows the advantage of this grouping of the D nodes: Each intermediate result that is required by multiple outputs can be determined whenever its required inputs are available (node n_{d6} in the abstract example from Figure 3.7c). Thus, this intermediate result can be used to determine each output when the other required inputs are available. On the other hand, this partitioning has the advantage that nodes requiring different inputs are grouped when their result can only be used if all of their input signals are available. This reduces the number of superordinated nodes.

The last step required to obtain the reduced graph of the configuration is to derive the dependencies between the new derived superordinated nodes: Two superordinated nodes depend on each other iff at least one dependency exists between their subordinated nodes. This leads to the reduced graph, shown in Figure 3.7c.

A formal description of the partitioning algorithm is presented in Appendix B. The partitioning results of the three configurations of component AccelerationControl are visualized in Figure 3.9.

3.2.3 Component Interface

The partitioning algorithm, outlined in the previous section, leads to an abstraction of a configuration's external visible structure. We use a configuration's abstraction to derive an abstract black box view of a whole component. When showing the black box view of a component –for example to embed instances in further configurations– just the *external visible behavior* (or just *external behavior*) is relevant. It abstracts from the component's detailed internal structure and from details about its behavior. Such abstraction will lead

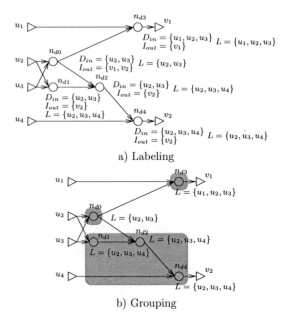

a) Labeling

b) Grouping

Figure 3.8: Partitioning algorithm

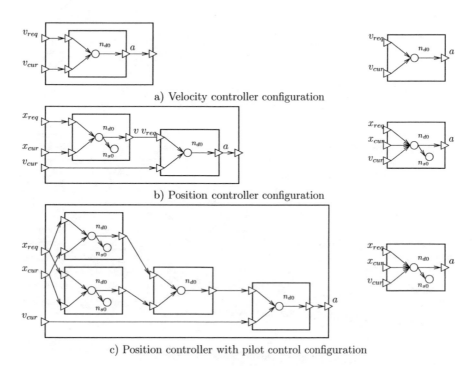

a) Velocity controller configuration

b) Position controller configuration

c) Position controller with pilot control configuration

Figure 3.9: Configurations and reduced graphs of AccelerationControl

to reduced complexity when using the component in further models or when analyzing such models. We specify a component's external visible behavior by an abstraction called *interface state charts*. An interface state chart consists of

- the external visible states,

- the timing constraints, describing how to switch between the external visible states,

- the state dependent in- and output signals,

- the reduced graph of each state's configuration, and

- properties of the external visible states.

If multiple states of a component's realization show the same interface, i.e. they have the same in- and output signals, the same reduced graph, and the same properties, they build just one *external visible state* (or simply *external state*). In such cases, the number of external visible states of a component is less than the number of states of the component's realization. Especially when a large number of states coincide to the same external state, the abstraction, provided by the interface state chart, reduces complexity massively.

We will see in Section 3.2.6 that the state-dependent in- und output signals help to ensure *consistent configurations* when embedding components in other components, e.g. to ensure that all required input signals and further used output signals are available. The timing constraints ensure *consistent reconfiguration*, and the dependency relations enable an evaluation of the nodes in the correct order when the component is embedded in other configurations. The properties are optional for the interface description. If they are specified, they provide an abstract description of the properties of the internally applied configurations, or –in a top down design– they describe requirements for the realization of the component.

As mentioned above, an interface state chart abstracts from details about its internal realization: There is no information about the active subordinated components or about the structure they build. Further, an interface state chart abstracts from the applied fading transition and thus focuses just on the real-time properties that describe how to switch between the external visible states. How to automatically derive an interface state chart from a hybrid reconfiguration chart and how to check if an interface state chart is consistent with its hybrid reconfiguration chart is discussed in [Kud05].

The interface state chart of the hybrid reconfiguration chart from Figure 3.6 is depicted in Figure 3.10. Note that it consists of just two external visible states, as states PositionControl and PositionControlWithPilotControl show the same external behavior: They require the same input signals, produce the same output signals, their configurations consist of the same reduced graph, and both are not associated with a property. The reduced graph is not visualized in the interface state chart – for the external state VC, it was shown in Figure 3.9a, for PC, it was shown in Figures 3.9b and 3.9c.

The interface state chart shows that AccelerationControl requires v_{cur} and v_{req} as input signals and provides a as output signal when residing in the external state VC. Residing in

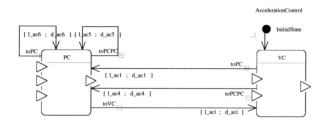

Figure 3.10: Interface state chart of AccelerationControl

the external state PC, it requires v_{cur}, x_{cur}, and x_{req} as input signals to provide a as output signal.

The state PC in the interface state chart groups the two states PositionControl and PositionControlWithPilotControl from the concrete realization. The transitions from VC to PC obtain the deadline intervals from the corresponding transitions from the realization. The transition from PC to VC groups both corresponding transitions from the realization. This is only possible, because both transitions are associated with the same event, guard and time guard. It obtains the deadline $[l_{aci}, d_{aci}] := [min(l_{ac2}, l_{ac3}), max(d_{ac2}, d_{ac3})]$ which is an abstraction of the two transitions from the realization.

Using the notion of interface state charts leads to a significant reduction of complexity, but they still show the external visible real-time behavior, which is necessary for example to ensure consistent reconfiguration when embedding the component into further configurations. This issue is exemplified in the next section.

3.2.4 Integration of Architecture and Behavior

In the previous sections, it was introduced that a component embeds other components on different hierarchical layers. As behavior is specified for each component, the behaviors of the hierarchical parallel embedded components need to be integrated. The integration of basic continuous components has been described in the previous sections and it has been demonstrated by the component AccelerationControl and its subordinated components. The integration of the behaviors of hybrid components, which also has been explained in the previous section and works similar, is exemplified in this section by means of the DriveTrain component and by means of the Shuttle component.

DriveTrain

In our example, an instance of the hybrid component AccelerationControl is embedded in the DriveTrain component. We apply our hybrid reconfiguration charts to integrate the behaviors of structural embedded hybrid components. In Section 3.2.1, it was described that each state of a hybrid reconfiguration chart is associated with a configuration of embedded components, which may show hybrid behavior as well. In Section 3.2.3, it was mentioned that just the external visible behavior of a component, described by our notion of interface state charts, is required when embedding component instances in further configurations. We exemplify this by means of component DriveTrain.

We define two states for component DriveTrain (see Figure 3.11): Vel which represents the system being under velocity control and Pos which represents that the system is under position control.

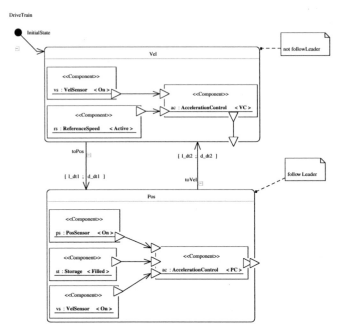

Figure 3.11: Hybrid reconfiguration chart of DriveTrain reconfigurating its embedded components

In substate Vel, DriveTrain's configuration consists of the instance ac, and of the instances vs and rs (cf. Figure 3.11), which are connected with two inputs of ac. In this configuration, ac is required to be in state VC, indicated by the angular brackets. When DriveTrain switches to state Pos, it reconfigures as follows: The state change of DriveTrain *implies* a state change of ac from VC to PC. Due to this *implied state change*, ac's interface changes so that it requires –in addition to v_{cur}– x_{cur} and x_{req} instead of v_{req} as input signals (cf. AccelerationControl's interface state chart from Figure 3.10). To feed the input signals correctly, we specified that they are connected with the outputs of ps, st, and vs.

Note that the same instance of AccelerationControl occurs in both states and note that the notion of interface state charts is applied: It is just specified that ac has to be in the state PC of its interface state chart – if this results in state PositionControl or in state PositionControlWithPilotControl is not specified on this level of abstraction.

Further, we have to integrate an instance of DriveTrain with the Shuttle component. Recall, that we require the Shuttle component to fulfill the requirement followLeader when it is in substate convoyRear and to fulfill not followLeader when it is in the substates convoyFront or noConvoy. Thus, we specify properties for both states of DriveTrain. These properties describe capabilities of the associated configurations in an abstract way. In order to simplify the integration of DriveTrain and Shuttle, we define the attributes, required by Shuttle, as properties of the two states of DriveTrain (see Figure 3.11). These properties lead to an abstract understanding of the behavior without detailed knowledge about the associated configurations.

In order to further embed instances of DriveTrain into other configurations especially in order to integrate its behavior with the behavior of component Shuttle, we derive DriveTrain's interface state chart as depicted in Figure 3.12. The deadline intervals are the same as the ones from its realization. The reduced graphs are determined by the algorithm described in Section 3.2.2. The results are visualized in Figure 3.13. Although both states of DriveTrain contain the same external interface concerning the in- and outputs, the according interface state chart consists of two states, as the states' properties and the reduced graphs are different.

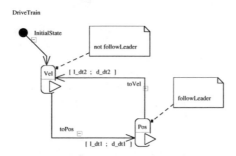

Figure 3.12: Interface state chart of DriveTrain

Shuttle

Figure 3.14 shows the hybrid reconfiguration chart that specifies the behavior of Shuttle. It is a refinement of the real-time statechart from Figure 2.15. Here, the middle orthogonal state is associated with different configurations.

All substates of the Main substate are associated with the instances dt:DriveTrain and lmb:LMB. While Shuttle is in the substates convoyFront or noConvoy, dt has to reside in state

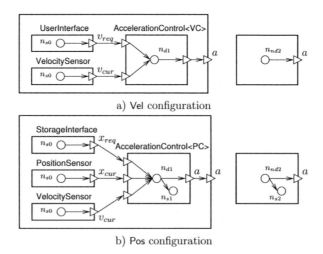

a) Vel configuration

b) Pos configuration

Figure 3.13: Configurations and reduced graphs of DriveTrain

Vel; in substate convoyRear, dt has to reside in state Pos. If Shuttle switches for example from noConvoy to convoyRear, this switch implies a state change of its subordinated dt component from Vel to Pos. As dt shows hybrid behavior itself, this implies a further state change of its subordinated components: ac:AccelerationControl will switch, due to this from VC to PC which leads to reconfiguration on all architectural levels.

Thus, hybrid reconfiguration charts are a modeling approach to specify reconfiguration, i.e. they specify when to change the structure of the subordinated components and how to change this structure. By associating configurations to discrete states, an integration of architecture and behavior is achieved. The concept of the implied state changes leads to reconfiguration via multiple hierarchical levels.

When specifying the different configurations, consistency needs to be ensured, for example so that all inputs of all components are fed with the required input signals. When specifying reconfiguration by associating different configurations with the discrete states, consistency needs to be ensured as well. In this case consistency means for example that the subordinated components allow the implied state changes. Details about consistency for reconfiguration and for configurations and how to exploit the notion of interface state charts to achieve consistency are shown in Section 3.2.6.

3.2.5   Extended Models

Sometimes, it is desirable to specify different kinds of non-determinism. One possibility to specify non-determinism has been introduced in Section 2.2.2 in form of non-urgent transitions. Additionally, we introduce non-deterministic transitions that we call *blockable*

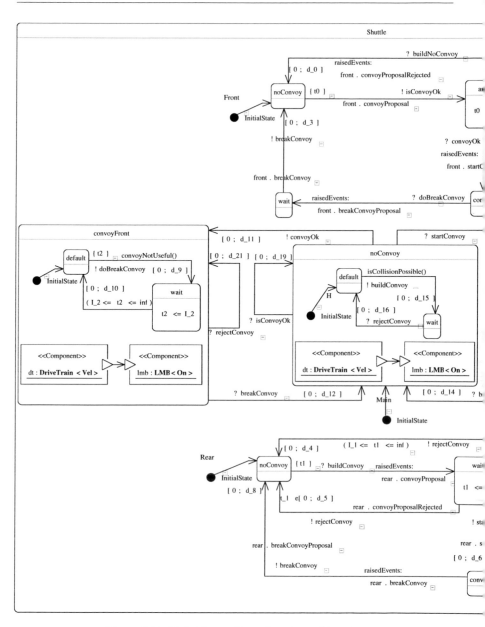

Figure 3.14: Hybrid reconfiguration chart of Shuttle

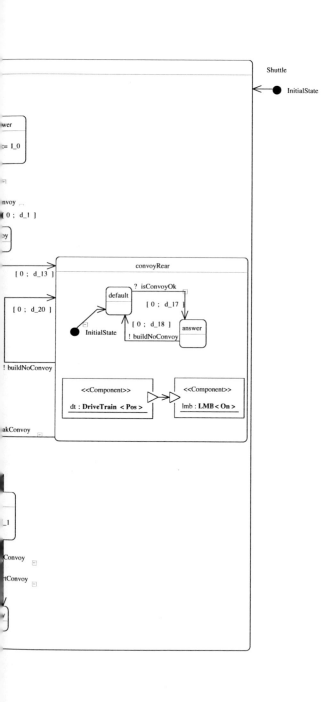

wer

$:= I\_0$

nvoy

[0 ; d_1]

oy

Shuttle

● InitialState

convoyRear

[0 ; d_13]

default

? isConvoyOk

[0 ; d_17]

[0 ; d_20]

[0 ; d_18]

answer

● InitialState

! buildNoConvoy

! buildNoConvoy

<<Component>>

dt : **DriveTrain** < **Pos** >

<<Component>>

lmb : **LMB** < **On** >

akConvoy

_1

Convoy

rtConvoy

or *enforceable*. If a transition is marked to be blockable and if guard and time guard evaluate to true and the according event is available, it is decided non-deterministically if the transition is activated like a standard transition in this case or if the transition is not activated. A transition that is not blockable, is called *required*. If a transition is marked to be enforceable and if guard or time guard evaluate to false or the according event is not available, it is decided non-deterministically if the transition is activated nevertheless or if the transition is not activated like a standard transition in this case.

As non-deterministic models lead to degrees of freedom when refining or implementing them, blockable or enforceable transitions can be implemented like standard transitions. However, it is also possible to block or to enforce the marked transitions. We exploit this degree of freedom when implementing hybrid reconfiguration charts and hybrid components for different target platforms (see Chapter 4): If the target platform supports flexible resource management (see Section 2.1.4), we exploit the semantics of blockable and enforceable transitions to realize different profiles. Otherwise, we implement the blockable and enforceable transitions like standard transitions.

In order to avoid that the system is reconfigurating continual via enforceable transitions and to provide the possibility to fire even non-enforceable transitions, a constant called *minimal inter enforceable time* T^{MIET} is specified: At least this time has to elapse between two enforcements of enforceable transitions. Further, we define *qualities* for every state, indicating the quality of the associated configuration.

Figure 3.15 shows the hybrid reconfiguration chart from Figure 3.6 enriched with qualities and blockable, required, and enforceable attributes. The idea is that the system can be in state PositionControl instead of state PositionControlWithPilotControl and work proper nevertheless. Therefore, the transitions to PositionControlWithPilotControl are blockable, the transition from PositionControlWithPilotControl to PositionControl is enforceable. PositionControlWithPilotControl has the highest quality, PositionControl and VelocityControl have the same qualities.

3.2.6 Integration with compositional Real-Time Modelchecking

In the introduction of this chapter, we explained that a component's realization must be a refinement of its external communication behavior in order to avoid invalidating the results of the real-time modelchecking. Then, we presented how to design reconfigurable mechatronic systems with the advanced modeling technique of hybrid components and hybrid reconfiguration charts. In particular, it was presented how to integrate the behaviors of structural embedded components. Obviously, embedding components changes the behavior of the superordinated component. In this section, we will discuss how the specification of component's behavior by hybrid reconfiguration charts supports proving a refinement relation to be valid.

Figure 3.16 shows the overview about our verification approach from Figure 3.1 in a more detailed manner. The upper part of the figure shows the abstract real-time coordination pattern, and a component behavior M_1^r realizing one of the pattern's roles. The lower part of the figure depicts this component with its internal structure and its embedded

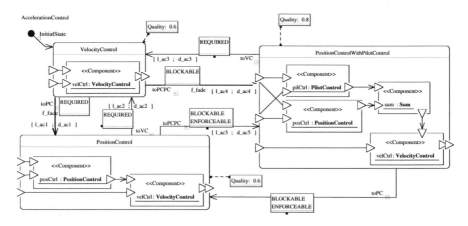

Figure 3.15: Extended hybrid reconfiguration chart of AccelerationControl

components. The behavior, resulting from this hierarchical parallel composition of the subordinated components $M_1^s, \ldots, M_m^s$, their interconnections and the hierarchical parallel composition with M_1^r (denoted by $M_1^r \|_H (M_1^s \| \ldots \| M_m^s)$) has to refine the behavior M_1^r. This has the advantage that the hierarchical parallel composition does not add additional external behavior. Thus, the verification results, which ensure the correctness of the pattern and the correctness of a component's real-time behavior are still valid as well as the correct refinement between component realization and role behavior.

In order to verify that the component fulfills the invariants of the roles it realizes, each property of a role invariant and its negation is mapped to some states: We have to identify the states in which the properties hold and the ones in which they do not hold. Obviously, this identification is supported by the properties we add to the states of subordinated components and to the states of their interface state charts. Then, the roles' constraints are adapted by replacing the properties by the corresponding states. Then, we obtain a formula that is checked by the applied real-time modelchecker.

Further, we stated in Section 3.2.3 that a realization of an interface description is only correct, if the realization *refines* the interface specification. Vice versa, an interface state chart has to be an *abstraction* of the component's realization (*abstraction* is the opposite of *refinement*). We will prove in Appendix A that refinement is *transitive*, i.e. if model C refines model B and if model B refines model A, C refines also A. Thus, it is sufficient to use the interface state charts for the refinement checks: If $M_1^s, \ldots, M_m^s$ are interface state charts that abstract the concrete behaviors $M_1^c, \ldots, M_m^c$ and if we prove that $M_1^r \|_H (M_1^s \| \ldots \| M_m^s) \sqsubseteq M_1^r$, it follows that $M_1^r \|_H (M_1^c \| \ldots \| M_m^c) \sqsubseteq M_1^r$, too. Using the interface state charts instead of the detailed behavior, the complexity of the proofs of refinement is significantly reduced.

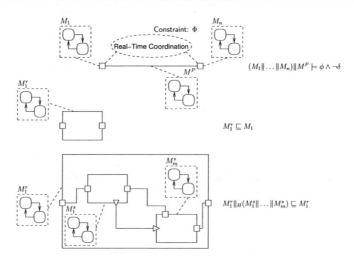

Figure 3.16: Refined overview about our verification approach

Further, transitiveness for refinement has the advantage that the proofs of the refinement relations just need to be performed via one hierarchical level: In our example, Shuttle embeds DriveTrain and DriveTrain embeds AccelerationControl. The proofs of the refinement relations just need to be performed between Shuttle and DriveTrain and between DriveTrain and AccelerationControl. There is no need to perform this check between Shuttle and AccelerationControl.

In Section 3.2.4, we introduced that there is need for the notion of consistent configurations. One basic requirement for our models is that the configurations have to be consistent. Only if they are consistent, further analyses are meaningful. Thus, we discuss the notion of consistency for configurations in the next part of this section. Then, we show how to exploit our modeling approach to identify refinement relation with adequate effort. Further, we introduce the notion of consistency for reconfiguration and show how this is related to the refinement relations.

Consistent Configurations

As mentioned before, the components' dynamic interfaces lead to the notion of *consistency*. A configuration that is associated with a state is consistent if

1. all discrete, continuous, and hybrid ports (all ports that are declared to be visible in the state and the external visible ports of the embedded components) are connected,

2. the dependency relations resulting from the connections contain no cycles, and

3. the requirements that are associated with the discrete state are fulfilled by the associated configuration.

In our example, the configurations are consistent as in each configuration all ports are connected and the reduced graphs contain no cycles. The requirements, specified for the states of component Shuttle (A[] not followLeader and A[] followLeader) are fulfilled by the corresponding states of the subordinated DriveTrain component.

Note that in the model of component AccelerationControl, it is specified that for example the input signal v_{req} is not required in state PositionControl. This information is part of the interface state chart. Thus, the interface state chart reflects that our concrete instance ac:AccelerationControl will be fully functional in state PositionControl even when component vs:VelocitySensor fails. In classical or current approaches that do not support dynamic interfaces, v_{cur} would be part of the component's static interface and thus no conclusion about the components functionality, dependent on the available input signals, is possible without a detailed analysis of the component's behavior.

Consistent Reconfiguration

The remainder of this section presents two ways to proof that the reconfiguration behavior, specified for a hierarchical parallel composed component, is a refinement of the non-composed component: First, we present a syntactic check which is applicable in many cases. If this check is not applicable, we apply modelchecking to proof the refinement.

Syntactic Checks   Checking the refinement relation simply requires answering the following three questions:

1. Are the *implied state changes* possible, i.e. exists a transition from the source state of the subordinated component to the target state?

2. Do the temporal requirements of this transition not contradict the temporal requirements of the superordinated component?

3. Can the transition of the subordinated component become triggered simply by raising events?

The answer of question 3 determines if the syntactic checks are applicable: If the transition of the subordinated component is simply associated with a signal and if guard and time guard are constantly true, the reconfiguration is simply executed by raising the appropriate signal. Otherwise, a complex analysis is required to determine if raising the signal will lead to a correct reconfiguration in all cases. This analysis is done by modelchecking as presented below.

Obviously, the first question is answered positively if the third question is answered positively. In order to prove that the temporal specifications are not contradictory, simply the deadlines need to be regarded: The deadline interval d_{sub} of the subordinated component needs to be a subset of the deadline interval d_{sup} of the superordinated component: $d_{sub} \subseteq d_{sup}$.

In the hybrid reconfiguration chart from Figure 3.14, modeling the behavior of component Shuttle, it is specified that a switch from state noConvoy to state convoyRear has to be finished at the latest the time d_{13} after being triggered. Further, this state change implies a state change of dt from Vel to Pos. Figure 3.12 reflects that this state change has a minimal duration of l_{dt1} and a maximal duration of d_{dt1}. These constants guarantee a smooth and stable fading. In order to guarantee that the hybrid component is just refined by embedding a further component, the temporal behavior of DriveTrain must be included in the temporal behavior of Shuttle. We require: $[l_{dt1}; d_{dt1}] \subseteq [0; d_{13}]$. As the transition can be enabled, simply by raising signal toPos, the implied state change is executable. If this state change of dt is specified to be finished at the earliest l_{dt1} after initiation with $l_{dt1} > d_{13}$, this would be contradictory to the Shuttle's real-time requirements. These relations between the deadline intervals are shown in Figure 3.17 by the dashed arrows.

Modelchecking The modelchecking has to prove if a parallel composition of the components may lead to undefined state combination. As we first apply the syntactic checks where possible, modelchecking just needs to be applied if complex analysis is required to obtain the information if a transition of a subordinated component can be triggered just by raising the corresponding signal.

As the interface state charts are regarded on this level of abstraction instead of the detailed behavior, specified by the corresponding hybrid reconfiguration chart, the complexity of this verification step is significantly reduced.

3.2.7   Discussion

Hybrid reconfiguration charts provide concise support for the specification of reconfiguration by integrating architecture and behavior. Due to the association of one configuration of embedded components to each discrete state, hybrid reconfiguration charts lead to clearly arranged models: It is obvious which configurations exist, when which subordinated components and connections are active, and when which components are in which states. This information is derivable straight forward from the model without complex reachability analyses. The same holds for the reachable global state space: A consistent model contains the information which combinations of the single components' states are reachable and which ones are not reachable.

The different configurations allow dynamically changing connectors. Thus, the components are reused in the different configurations, but they are connected in different ways. Using traditional approaches to specify the exchange of two configurations that are (partly) built by similar components (e.g. PositionControl and PositionControlWithPilotControl) requires a self-contained model for each configuration. Our approach allows the reuse of the components that arise in both configurations and requires just modeling the new parts of the new configuration (e.g. the same instance of the VelocityControl component is used in all three configurations). This reduces modeling effort.

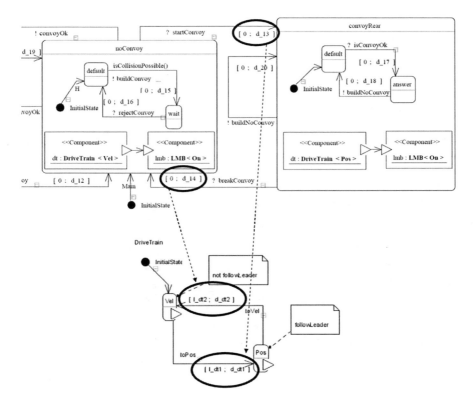

Figure 3.17: Ensuring consistent reconfiguration by syntactic checks

The components that are reconfigured are not restricted to basic continuous components; they may also show hybrid behavior, as well. This leads to the concept of the implied state changes. The implied state changes do not only lead to concise models, they also enable reconfiguration via multiple hierarchical levels as implied state changes in the embedded components may lead to further implied state changes in the components, embedded on the lower hierarchical levels.

To point out these advantages of modeling reconfiguration with hybrid reconfiguration charts, we present the behavioral models of Shuttle, DriveTrain, and AccelerationControl from our example modeled with traditional hybrid automata in Figure 3.18.[4] Similar to the approach, presented in [HKW04], the reconfiguration is modeled by firing transitions which send events that lead to state changes. These events are implied in our approach: Here, the signals toPos and toVel from Shuttle to DriveTrain and the signals toPC and toVC from DriveTrain to AccelerationControl explicitly need to be denoted. Thus, the global reachable state space and the existing configurations are not derivable in a straight forward manner and their determination requires further analysis. Due to static interfaces, all continuous models, associated with the states of AccelerationControl, have four inputs although just two or three of them are used at the same time. The information that the components PositionControl and PositionControlWithPilotControl use similar subcomponents is neither visible in the model nor exploited during design. Therefore, these subcomponents are usually modeled and implemented multiple times, e.g. VelocityControl is part of all three continuous models in Figure 3.18c.

The structure of such a model, specified by a traditional approach, looks like the structures depicted in Figures 3.2 and 3.3. The difference is that the structure is static and does not change during run-time. In our reconfigurable case, the component diagrams show all *possible* configurations, but the communication links are not established during the whole run-time and the instances do not exist during the whole run-time. As we do not require each component the whole run-time, the system is even able to operate when a sensor like PosSensor fails. Other approaches to specify reconfiguration, e.g. by self-organizing software architectures as presented in [GMK02], are not applicable in the domain of mechatronic systems. Such approaches usually do not consider real-time or hybrid behavior, the components are restricted to static interfaces, and communication is based on reliable broadcast and virtual synchrony which is unrealistic in the domain, considered in this thesis.

The specification of reconfiguration with hybrid reconfiguration charts requires consistent models. Ensuring consistency is supported by the notion of the interface state charts. They show the externally visible behavior of a component by abstracting from the component's details. On the one hand, their information about dynamic interfaces leads to consistent configurations, on the other hand, the information about the temporal restrictions when changing the dynamic interfaces leads to consistent reconfiguration. The integration of architecture and behavior and the syntactic consistency checks ensure that

---

[4]We present in this model just how to model reconfiguration with traditional approaches. The problem how to model fading or realizable real-time requirements is omitted.

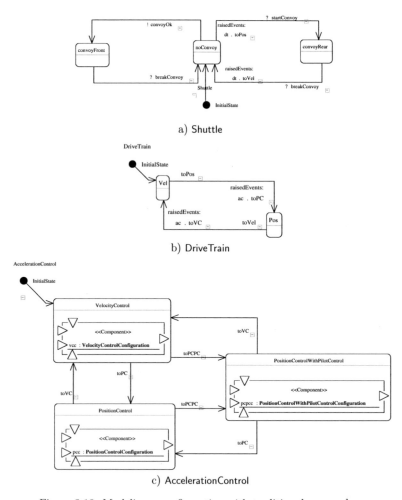

Figure 3.18: Modeling reconfiguration with traditional approaches

a component's inner structure and the behavior of the components of the inner structure are not contradictory to its real-time behavior: Embedding components in a consistent manner does not invalidate the verified real-time behavior of the superordinated component. Due to transitiveness of refinement, the checks for consistent reconfiguration just need to be performed via two hierarchical layers, although hybrid reconfiguration charts lead to reconfiguration via multiple hierarchical layers. The syntactic checks reduce the effort for analyses massively. Even when modelchecking has to be applied to check for consistent reconfiguration, the abstraction provided by the interface state charts has significant impact on the costs of this verification step.

The abstract description of the properties of a component in different external states supports identifying the states that fulfill a role's requirement's property. This is required to verify correctness of a component. Finally, the syntactical high-level construct of fading transitions helps massively to reduce the complexity of the models.

3.3 Conclusion

In this chapter, we presented a new modeling approach to specify reconfiguration of hybrid mechatronic systems. First, we provided an architectural design which refines standard UML diagrams. Based on state of the art approaches, we presented a UML-based specification technique to model the behavior. Our concept of associating configurations of embedded components to the discrete states of the superordinated component leads to a tight integration of architecture and behavior.

This integration even respects the communication between components, specified by patterns as described in Section 2.2.2. The integration of basic continuous components –or hybrid components in general– does not invalidate verification results.

As stated by Edward Lee et al. in [HLL+03], it is essential to formalize the semantics *if the diagrams are to be used for system specification and design.* Also, a formal semantics is required to enable formal analyses and automatic code generation. Therefore, the formal semantics of this new high-level modeling language –introduced informally in this chapter– is defined in Appendix A. The next chapter focuses on automatic code synthesis. Of course, the generated code has to respect the model's semantics.

Chapter 4

Automatic Implementation of Reconfigurable Mechatronic Systems

In this chapter, we derive an implementation from the specification, presented in Chapter 3. Following the MDA process, we first map the platform independent model (PIM), specified by hybrid component, class, and story diagrams and hybrid reconfiguration charts, to a platform specific model (PSM). This mapping requires knowledge about the properties of the target platform, specified by a platform model (PM). In a second step, we use the information from the PSM to synthesize code for the target platform.

We provide a run-time framework as part of the PSM to encapsulate structure, attributes, methods, and application flow that is common for all applications that are derived from our models. This has the advantage that just one implementation of the framework is required for each target platform and the code that is required for every application does not need to be generated for every application.

As mentioned in Chapter 2, we use the UML Profile for Schedulability, Performance, and Time Specification (SPT profile) [Obj05c] as PSM. Our PM description provides worst-case execution times and information about available schedulers: As the implementation scheme i.e. the strategy how our models are implemented is known, the WCETs of the code that *will* be generated can be determined *before* the code is generated. This requires just the knowledge of the WCETs of the elementary operations, like boolean-assignment, while-statement etc. Thus, our PM contains a table of the elementary operations, used by our code generation, and their WCETs. An overview about the used elementary operations and their WCETs for an example platform can be found in Appendix C.

Another capability of the target platform that is specified in the PM is the capability if schedulers are available and which schedulers are available. In this work, we provide an automatic implementation for target systems that are conform to the POSIX PSE50 standard (see Section 2.1.4) and thus provide a priority scheduler.

We first introduce the applied run-time framework IPANEMA in Section 4.1. Section 4.2 shows how to use the information of a PM and a PIM to derive a PSM that uses classes from the IPANEMA framework. Section 4.3 describes how to generate source code from the PSM.

4.1   The Run-Time Framework IPANEMA

We use the real-time run-time framework IPANEMA [Hon98] to execute hybrid component implementations which have to fulfill hard real-time constraints. IPANEMA was primarily developed for the execution, monitoring, and simulation of continuous components both to control the plant and with hardware-in-the-loop (HIL) simulation. It provides the integration algorithms that are required for the execution of feedback-controller implementations (cf. Section 2.4.3) and it ensures the periodic evaluation of the feedback-controller implementations.

To also support the execution of hybrid components inclusive their reconfiguration, IPANEMA has been extended.[1] One of the main extensions was to provide a modular structure that enables reconfiguration. Figure 4.1 shows a cut-out of the framework: The class diagram shows that the central class of the IPANEMA framework is the class Component. The subcomponent-association realizes embedding of other components. Each component has multiple continuous or discrete ports which are connected with each other (modeled by the connection associations). Reconfiguration is realized by dynamically instantiating and deinstantiating components, ports, and connections at run-time.

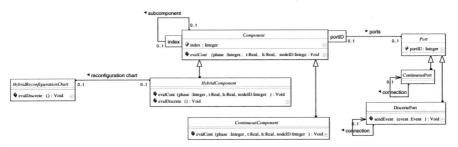

Figure 4.1: Class diagram (cut-out) of the IPANEMA framework

As the behavior of hybrid components is specified by hybrid reconfiguration charts, the abstract HybridComponent class is associated with the abstract HybridReconfigurationChart class. An implementation of the HybridReconfigurationChart class contains the logic of the component's hybrid reconfiguration chart. The logic of basic continuous components is implemented in classes that are derived from the abstract class ContinuousComponent. In contrast to hybrid components, a basic continuous component has no association to a hybrid reconfiguration chart.

The continuous behavior of a component is implemented by the evalCont method. It is called by the framework which sets its parameters accordingly. The discrete behavior,

---

[1]The extension has been realized in cooperation with the *control engineering and mechatronics* group (http://rtm.uni-paderborn.de) formerly known as *Mechatronics Laboratory Paderborn (MLaP)* from University of Paderborn. In particular the cooperation was with Vadim Boiko, Alfonso Gambuzza, and Oliver Oberschelp.

which is obviously not available for basic continuous components, is implemented by the evalDiscrete method.

An IPANEMA application consists of one periodic real-time thread which calls – dependent on the applied integration algorithm (see Section 2.4.3)– at least once per period the evalCont method followed by exactly one evaluation of the evalDiscrete method of one uniquely defined top-level component. This is visualized in Figure 4.2: The WCET of the continuous part is labeled w_c, the WCET of the discrete part is labeled w_d.

Figure 4.2: Periodic evaluation of the continuous and discrete system parts

We separate the discrete part from the continuous one and evaluate them sequentially, as the evaluation of the discrete part influences the continuous evaluation (see Section 4.2.2).[2] If the system consists of multiple structurally, hierarchically embedded hybrid components, the evaluation of evalCont or evalDiscrete respectively triggers the evaluation of these methods of the active subcomponents that are exactly one hierarchical level below. Their evaluation triggers again the evaluation of the evalCont or evalDiscrete methods cne more hierarchical level below and so on. This leads to an evaluation of the components in an order that corresponds to their hierarchy. To ensure that discrete changes in the superordinated components are propagated to the subordinated components within one execution cycle, the evaluation order of the discrete components has to be according to their hierarchy [BGGO04b].

4.2   From the Platform Independent Model to a Platform Specific Model

As explained in Section 2.1.1, different possibilities exist to implement a PIM for different target platforms, e.g. for a processor board without an operating system, for an operating system with a priority scheduler, for operating systems with other schedulers, or others (see Section 2.1.4). Obviously, the thread for the single-thread system without operating system requires other scheduling parameters than the threads of a multithreading system for a real-time operating system. These concepts for the implementation for the chosen target system –e.g. the partitioning into threads– is described by the mapping to the PSM. We describe the mapping to a PSM that offers the API (application programming interface) of the run-time framework IPANEMA in the remainder of this section. The mapping is

---

[2]In Section 4.2.4, we will disengage from the strict sequential evaluation and we will role out some parts into aperiodic threads to fulfill real-time requirements.

based on a PM that describes a POSIX PSE50 conform real-time operating system allowing multithreading and offering a priority scheduler.

In our implementation, an application, specified by hybrid components and hybrid reconfiguration charts as described in the previous chapter, is mapped to a couple of classes. Most of these classes are derived from the classes of the IPANEMA framework. On the one hand, these classes implement the system's structure and on the other hand, their methods implement the system's behavior. One of them is an *active class*, i.e. it is implemented as an own thread. We will see that it starts further threads. As we consider target platforms with priority schedulers, we have to derive the threads' scheduling parameters, i.e. their periods, deadlines, and priorities. Further, we have to derive properties like WCETs of the methods, memory consumption of the classes' instances and profile information if the target platform provides a flexible resource manager.

Thus, we describe how to map the system's architecture to the IPANEMA framework in Section 4.2.1, and how to implement the behavior and the reconfiguration in Section 4.2.2. In order to partition the system into multiple threads inclusive their real-time parameters, we require the knowledge of all WCETs. Thus, we first present how to determine the resource requirements like WCETs and memory in Section 4.2.3 and then describe our partitioning in Section 4.2.4. Finally, we show how to automatically derive profiles from the extended models (see Section 3.2.5) for the profile framework (see Section 2.1.4) in Section 4.2.5 and close this section about PSM derivation with a discussion in Section 4.2.6.

4.2.1   Implementation of Architecture of Hybrid Components

Due to the reconfiguration, not every component is part of every configuration. Therefore, a modular implementation supporting the dynamic exchange of components is required. As IPANEMA has been extended to provide such a modular architecture, we derive an implementation for the IPANEMA framework. When mapping the structure, specified by a component diagram, to a class diagram that uses this framework, we map each component to a class. The classes are annotated with tagged values as proposed by the SPT profile.

Our example structure, depicted in Figures 3.2, 3.3, and 3.4 is transformed to the class diagram shown in Figure 4.3. The hybrid components extend the framework class HybridComponent and the basic continuous components extend the framework class ContinuousComponent. For each hybrid component whose behavior is specified by a hybrid reconfiguration chart, a corresponding subclass of the framework class HybridReconfigurationChart is generated. The connections are instantiated by instantiating the connection association between instances of ContinuousPort or DiscretePort respectively. When reconfiguration takes place, the corresponding instances of the HybridComponent and HybridReconfigurationChart subclasses and the instances of the connection association are deinstantiated and other corresponding classes and associations are instantiated at run-time.

Further, the example class diagram shows a class Master which is generated as top-level thread for every application. Here, the Master component is realized as a real-time thread with a period and a deadline of 1 msec. and 1 as its priority. The WCETs of the methods are indicated by the offeredQoS worstCaseExecutionTime-tag. The Profiles-tag describes which

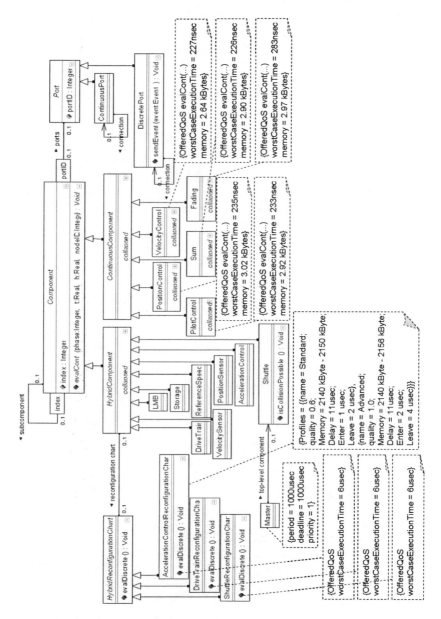

Figure 4.3: Realization of the example's architecture

profiles exist for the corresponding component and the profiles' resource requirements and attributes. How to determine the values of the tagged values is described in the remainder of this section.

Class diagrams, like the one from Figure 2.17, are added to this synthesized class diagram, which results in the structure shown in Figure 4.4. The instances of the Factory pattern that is based on the Abstract Factory pattern [GHJV95] ensure that all possible instances of the corresponding classes are created during initialization. This avoids dynamic instantiation and deinstantiation of these classes at run-time. The maximal possible number of instances is derived from the bound number of instances or from the finite multiplicities (cf. Section 2.2.3).

A cut-out of a possible instance situation at run-time is shown in Figure 4.5. The references labeled subcomponent describe that shuttle has lmb and dt as subcomponents, that dt has ac, vs, and rs as subcomponents, and that ac has vc as subcomponent. Except shuttle, each component has different continuous ports. Their connections are realized by the connection references. The instances of the Shuttle, DriveTrain, and AccelerationControl components, which show also discrete behavior, reference instances of their corresponding subclasses of the framework class HybridReconfigurationChart. These classes implement the discrete behavior.

4.2.2　Implementation of Behavior of Hybrid Components

Discrete Behavior

As shown in Figure 4.1, each implementation of a hybrid reconfiguration chart consists of a method evalDiscrete. This method is called periodically by the evalDiscrete method of the corresponding HybridComponent instance. It handles the execution of the discrete parts of the hybrid reconfiguration chart: It checks, dependent on the current state, which transitions are activated and it triggers the execution of the transition that was activated first (conform to the semantics, which was informally presented in Section 2.2.2 and which is formalized in Appendix A). In order to avoid that transitions that have just been activated for a time interval between two executions of evalDiscrete are ignored, it is determined which transitions have been activated since the last execution of evalDiscrete. The transition(s) activated first are fired. In case of discrete models with orthogonal AND states, the evaluation of multiple transitions can be triggered within one period.

As multiple discrete states can be active in a hybrid reconfiguration chart due to hierarchical or orthogonal states, we use a complex data structure, i.e. a list of lists that stores integer values, to encode the current states. The lists are separated corresponding to their orthogonal states. In order to support history, we associate such a data structure also with every discrete state to store the last relevant active substates when exiting the corresponding state [Bur02]. Altogether, firing a transition has the following effects:

1. Execution of the do methods of the current states iff they have not been evaluated, yet,

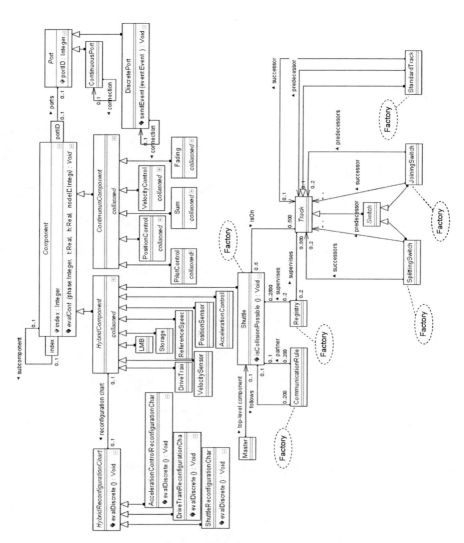

Figure 4.4: Enhancing the architecture with Shuttle's class diagram

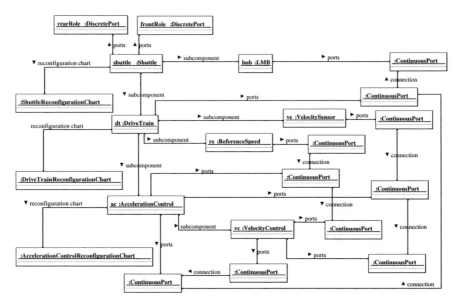

Figure 4.5: Possible instance situation at run-time

2. execution of the exit methods of the current states,

3. resets of the clocks associated with the firing transition,

4. raise of events,

5. adaptation of the current attribute to represent that the hybrid reconfiguration chart switched to the target state and storage of the relevant history information,

6. deinstantiation of the components and connections that are no further required in the target state,

7. instantiation and initialization of the components and connections required by the target configuration and which do not exist yet,

8. execution of the side-effect, and

9. execution of the entry methods of the new current states.

Note that the syntactical construct of the fading transitions is resolved in the implementation: Firing a fading transition leads to a switch to an intermediate fading location and after passing of the fading duration, a further switch to the target state is executed. Side-effects are just started when switching to the intermediate state. The switch to the target state does not initiate the execution of side-effects.

In Section 4.2.4, the order of the items is discussed and it is explained between which items this activity of firing may be interrupted.

Continuous Behavior

As explained in Section 4.1, each implementation of a feedback-controller and of a hybrid component in general provides an evalCont method, which is evaluated periodically. This method triggers the evaluation of the component's D, ND, and S nodes.

Due to reconfiguration, not all components and not all nodes of a component are evaluated and the evaluation order of the nodes changes (cf. Sections 3.2.2 and 2.4.4). Which components are evaluated at run-time and in which order their blocks are evaluated, depends on the configuration in which they are embedded. Thus, an implementation of a hybrid component must allow evaluating the nodes in different order. This is achieved by enhancing the method evalCont with the parameter nodeID. According to the parameter of the method, the corresponding node is evaluated [BGGO04b].

Figure 4.6 shows for example a cut-out of the implementation of the continuous Position-Control block as an activity diagram. The nodeIDs n_d0 and n_s0 correlate to the nodes n_{d0} and n_{s0} of the feedback-controller (see Figure 2.27b). The internals of the nodes (_q[0] = ...) are the mathematical equations that implement the behavior of the continuous component (similar to the implementation, presented in Section 2.4.3).[3]

---

[3] Note that this code was generated by the CAE-tool CAMeL-View (http://www.ixtronics.de). The implementation of basic continuous components has been described in [Hah99] and is not part of this work.

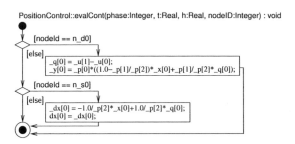

Figure 4.6: Activity diagram showing a cut-out of the PositionControl implementation

As the evaluation order of the nodes of hybrid components depends on the configuration in which they are embedded and thus on the discrete state of the superordinated component, exactly one evaluation order exists per global discrete state. Enhancing the top-level component with this information is usually not feasible as the number of global states is exponential in the number of components. Therefore, we benefit from the tree structure of the system, that results from the hierarchical component design and is reflected in the modular implementation, presented in Section 4.2.1 (e.g. Figures 4.4 and 4.5).

In this tree structure, where each hybrid component references its subordinated components via the subcomponent association, each superordinated component stores just the information which nodes of the components that are directly located one hierarchy-layer below have to be evaluated. In such an implementation, each hybrid component holds the information, necessary for correct evaluation, locally and thus, this information does not need to be stored globally in the top-level component which leads to efficient implementation of the reconfiguration [BGM+06]. The superordinated components have no knowledge about the implementation details of the individual blocks of the embedded components. They just evaluate the blocks in the appropriate evaluation order. Therefore, local reconfigurations within subordinated components which do not affect the superordinated components do not need to be propagated (see below).

Due to this evaluation scheme, the implementation of the evalCont method of a *hybrid hierarchical component*, i.e. a hybrid component that is neither a basic continuous nor a basic discrete component, differs from that of a basic continuous component. Its nodes do not contain mathematical expressions but state-dependent lists of continuous nodes of the embedded hybrid components [BGGO04b].

Figure 4.7 shows the content of the evalCont method of AccelerationControl. In dependency of the current discrete state, each node (n_{d1} and n_{s1}) consists of a different list of nodes of the embedded components. If, for example, the component is in state PositionControl, the node n_{d1} consists of two sequential calls of the nodes n_{d0} from component posCtrl and n_{d0} from component velCtrl. If the state changes to PositionControlWithPilotControl, the next evaluation of n_{d1} leads to sequential calls of node n_{d0} from component posCtrl, n_{d0} from pilCtrl, n_{d0} from sum, and n_{d0} from velCtrl.

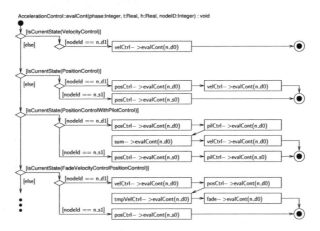

Figure 4.7: Activity diagram showing the evalCont method of AccelerationControl

Furthermore, the implementation of the *fading location* FadeVelocityControlPositionControl is shown in Figure 4.7. Note that in this case the node n_{d1} is similar to a concatenation of the according nodes of states VelocityControl and PositionControl. As the instance velCtrl:VelocityController is required in both configurations, a further instance tmpVelCtrl:VelocityController is used and initiated accordingly in this state (see Figure 3.5). The fade component realizes the fading.

Note that the partitioning, introduced in Section 3.2.2 and shown in Figure 3.9, determines which nodes of the subordinated components are evaluated when n_d1 or n_s1 is evaluated. These nodes of the subordinated components are the nodes from their corresponding reduced evaluation graphs. Thus, no knowledge about the internal structure of these nodes is required inside AccelerationControl.

Recall that in our example, the interface state chart of the AccelerationControl component consists of two discrete states although the component itself consists of three discrete states. The implementation of its evalCont method in Figure 4.7 exposes again that the component consists of exactly one D node and exactly one S node in both states PositionControl and PositionControlWithPilotControl. Further, it points out that the notion of nodes abstracts from the implementation details as in both states, the content of the nodes' lists is different.

Figures 4.8 and 4.9 show the implementation of the evalCont methods of DriveTrain and Shuttle. They call the corresponding evalCont methods of the components that are located exactly one hierarchical layer below. Note that due to the abstraction, provided by the notion of nodes, reconfiguration that is local within AccelerationControl (e.g. when the component switches from PositionControl to PositionControlWithPilotControl) does not affect the superordinated components: DriveTrain will still evaluate nodes n_d1 and n_s1 and will not notice the change of the structure, multiple hierarchical levels below.

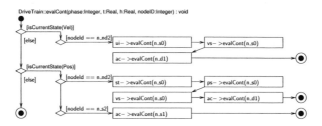

Figure 4.8: Activity diagram showing the evalCont method of DriveTrain

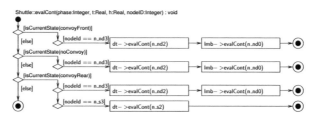

Figure 4.9: Activity diagram showing the evalCont method of Shuttle

If a hybrid component is *self-contained*, it does not need to be embedded into another context or configuration to become executable. Self-contained components usually do not have any continuous ports in their interface state chart and they consist of exactly one continuous block (which usually references multiple blocks of the subordinated components). Top-level components, like Shuttle in our example, are usually self-contained.

The implementation points out that changing the discrete state influences the evaluation of the continuous system part. Therefore, safety can only be guaranteed if one continuous evaluation cycle is not preempted by the evaluation of a discrete node that switches the current discrete state. Therefore, we separate the evaluation of the discrete nodes from the evaluation of the continuous nodes in time. This separation is guaranteed by the run-time framework IPANEMA (see Section 4.1). How to schedule the discrete nodes, if they have too long WCETs, is described in Section 4.2.4. Obviously, this scheduling requires knowledge about the WCETs. In the next section, it is described how to determine them.

4.2.3 Determination and Minimization of Resource Requirements

Worst-Case Execution Times

As mentioned in the previous sections, the worst-case execution times of the generated code need to be known. Current WCET analysis techniques are restricted to imperative programming languages. Dynamic, object-oriented programming languages are not addressed at all. Buttazzo even demands to avoid dynamic data structures in real-time systems [But97].

The standard approach in WCET analysis is to analyze the longest executable path, to map each instruction of this path to *elementary operations*, to determine the WCETs of these elementary operations and to sum up these WCETs for the longest executable path. The elementary operations can be for example assembler instructions like in [Erp00] or Java Byte Code instructions like in [BBW00].

In [Erp00], the WCET of a fragment of generated C code is determined by summing up the number of processor cycles each C instruction's corresponding assembler instructions require. For loops, the *worst-case number of iterations (WCNIs)* is derived from a statechart model to obtain the maximum number of executions of the loop-bodies.

[PB00] describes multiple existing approaches that use different annotations to specify the WCNIs and thus the longest executable path. All described approaches are restricted to imperative programming languages, that do not provide dynamic data structures. Further, the authors explain that an execution time analysis on the hardware level, which considers techniques like caching or pipelining, is required to avoid a too pessimistic estimation.

The WCETs of our generated code fragments are determined in a similar way, i.e. simply by summing up the WCETs of the elementary operations which are C++ code fragments in our case. This leads to WCETs for the items 3-7 from Section 4.2.2. The WCNIs for loops is given by the model, e.g. by the number of transitions, the number of orthogonal states, etc.

For the determination of the WCETs of the side-effects and the do, entry, and exit methods (items 1, 2, 8, and 9), the WCETs of the single activities are required. If an activity's behavior is specified by a story pattern (see Section 2.2.3), the standard approach is not applicable, as a story pattern operates on dynamic data structures (specified by a class diagram). The problem is that an implementation of a class diagram as for example shown in Figure 2.5 in Section 2.1.2 allows specifying unbound dynamic data structures. When for example searching in a data structure that implements a to many association, the WCNIs is not known a priori. Thus, a WCET for these searches cannot be determined.

Therefore, we specify *exact multiplicities*, as introduced in Section 2.2.3. These exact multiplicities are used as upper bounds for the data structures in an implementation and they lead to the WCNIs for searches in data structures and thus enable the determination of the WCET for a story pattern.

The WCET of a story pattern does not only depend on the WCETs of its single code fragments and on the WCNIs when searching in data structures. The problem of WCET determination for story patterns is more complicated, because the order in which the elements of a story pattern are matched has significant impact on the resulting WCET as (partly) nested iterations can occur:

Multiple different matching sequences that lead to different WCETs exist, because story patterns can contain bidirectional cycles. In the example story pattern from Figure 2.16, several bidirectional cycles exist. For example, if the only bound object is this, this $\rightarrow$ t0 $\rightarrow$ reg $\rightarrow$ this is a bidirectional cycle, because we also have the possibility to choose this $\rightarrow$ reg $\rightarrow$ t0 $\rightarrow$ this to match this part of the story pattern.

The reason why different matching sequences usually lead to different WCETs is that the two multiplicities of an association can be different. When, for example, a link between a

Registry and a Shuttle instance is specified in the story pattern, starting at the Registry object and binding the Shuttle object requires a search in a data structure with 2500 as upper bound. Binding the Registry object from the Shuttle object requires just a search in a data structure consisting maximal of 2 instances. In this case, the algorithm, which determines the matching sequence, has two possibilities that lead to the same instance matching but use different matching sequences.

Another reason why different matching sequences usually lead to different WCETs is that the matching process explores in the worst-case a path for each existing instance when binding an instance that is connected to a bound instance via a to-many association. To obtain an optimal WCET, the number of such paths has to be minimized. This is usually achieved by first respecting the path via associations with low multiplicities.

As we specified exact multiplicities and thus know the upper bounds of the corresponding data structures, we can determine the WCET of a matching sequence. As usually multiple matching sequences exist, we will determine one of the matching sequences that will lead to the optimal (i.e. minimal) WCET. In the remainder of this section, it is described how to determine the WCET for a matching sequence of a story pattern and how to find the optimal matching sequence during code generation.

WCET Determination   In order to calculate the WCET of a matching sequence for a story pattern and in order to determine a matching sequence that optimizes the WCET of a story pattern, we derive a graph called *story graph* from the story pattern [BGST05, Sei05] (see Appendix D for the formalization). The nodes from this story graph correlate to the nodes of the story pattern. The edges between the nodes of the story graph represent different kinds of checks that can be performed during matching. Usually, a story graph contains much more edges than its corresponding story pattern, as different kinds of checks are possible for each edge of the story pattern. Note that not all checks need to be performed, as some checks are mutually exclusive (see below). The story graph consists of edges representing all *possible* checks. The following kinds of edges exist in a story graph:

- BindNormal: If a reference between a source object that is bound and a target object that is unbound has to be checked, a BindNormal check determines if a target object exists that is referenced by the source object via the corresponding reference. We distinguish between links for to-one and for to-many associations.

- CheckLink: If a reference between a source object and a target object has to be checked and if both objects are bound, a CheckLink check is performed to determine if a reference exists between the objects.

- BindOptional: A reference that is marked to be optional is mapped to a BindOptional edge.

- CheckNegativeLink: These edges represent the check that a link must not be existent. We distinguish also between negative links for to-one and for to-many associations.

- CheckIsomorphism: In order to check, if two objects of the same type are different objects, a CheckIsomorphism edge is introduced between the nodes, representing the two objects.

- CheckAttribute: If an object is associated with an attribute which can be a condition, this condition needs to be checked. Thus, a CheckAttribute edge is introduced in the story graph.

- CheckConstraint: These edges are introduced in the story graph to check story pattern constraints.

- CheckNegativeNode: If a node is declared to be negative, the links to this node are mapped to CheckNegativeNode edges in the story graph.

Note that CheckIsomorphism, CheckAttribute, CheckConstraint, and CheckNegativeNode edges in the story graph do not correlate to links in the story pattern. Figure 4.10 shows a cut-out of the story graph from the example from Figure 2.16. The figure shows that all references from the story pattern are mapped to BindNormal and CheckLink edges in the story graph. Edges in the opposite direction exist if the reference's corresponding association is bidirectional. As t0 and t1 are of the same type, CheckIsomorphism edges are between them.

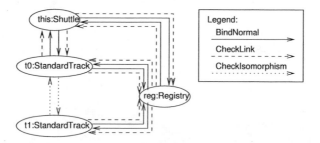

Figure 4.10: Cut-out of the story graph from the example from Figure 2.16

When searching a graph matching for the story pattern, i.e. to find an order for a matching sequence, the nodes and edges of the story graph are visited corresponding to the *selection rules* described in the following. We distinguish between *matching* an edge and *marking* an edge: *Matching* denotes that the edge is added to the solution and it implies marking of the edge. An edge that is just *marked* is not added to the solution and it will not be regarded any more. In contrast to the edges, all nodes need to be matched. An edge can only be matched if its source node is already matched. Initially, the this node is matched. Following the rules leads to a traversal through the graph. In the following, we describe when an edge can be matched and which edges are marked if the edge is matched:

- A BindNormal edge can be matched when its source node is bound and the target node is unbound. If it is matched, the target node is matched and also the BindNormal edge in the opposite direction is marked. Further, both CheckLink edges between the source and the target node are marked. Finally, all BindNormal edges that lead to the target state are marked. If the target node is the source of CheckIsomorphism edges and if the targets of these CheckIsomorphism edges are bound, the corresponding edges are matched. If the target is unbound, the edges are just marked. In this case, the check for isomorphism is performed when the target node is bound.

- A CheckLink edge can be matched only if the source and target nodes are matched. When matching such an edge, the CheckLink edge in the opposite direction is marked, too.

- A BindOptional edge can be matched when all BindNormal edges are matched. The story graph is modified as described for the BindNormal edges.

- Similar to CheckLink edges, a CheckNegativeLink edge requires matched source and target nodes. The CheckNegativeLink in the opposite direction is marked also when matching the edge.

- CheckIsomorphism edges can be matched when source and target states are matched. The matching leads to no further modifications on the story graph as the CheckIsomorphism edge in the opposite direction has been marked when binding its source node.

- CheckAttribute edges can be matched when their source node, which is always identical with the target node, is matched.

- CheckConstraint edges are similar to CheckAttribute edges. They can be marked when all nodes that are required to check the constraint are matched.

- A CheckNegativeNode edge can be marked when all nodes that are source of the CheckNegativeNode edges, which lead to the node marked to be negative, are matched, too. Matching such an edge leads to marking of all of these edges.

We explained how to derive a story graph from a story pattern and introduced rules how to visit the story graph. Even when following the rules, multiple different possibilities exist to explore the story graph. Each possibility will lead to another matching sequence. As each matching sequence leads to a different WCET (see above), we have to find one of the matching sequences with the optimal (minimal) WCET. How to derive the WCET from the matching sequence is described formally in Appendix D.

WCET Optimization In order to determine the optimal matching sequence, we use a brute force back tracking search method, as presented in Appendix D. As the costs for matching an edge depend on the previously matched edges, classical shortest path algorithms are not applicable. Our algorithm requires exponential run-time in relation to the number of references of a story pattern and the existing bidirectional cycles.

As a method with exponential time might lead to problems in practice, we improved the algorithm: We use a heuristic, we ensure a monotonically decreasing of the upper WCET bound, and we introduce a lower WCET bound. The heuristic [Sei05] is applied to obtain acceptable values for the WCET in the average case. It determines a solution so that its WCET can be used as first upper bound. This cuts the search space of possible solutions at the beginning of our algorithm. Our algorithm will recognize solutions as infeasible as soon as the execution time is greater or equal the heuristics WCET. If a solution is found with a shorter WCET, this value is used as new upper bound. This way of using a first upper bound and then decreasing the upper bound monotonically reduces the computation time significantly.

WCET of an Activity Diagram   When the WCETs of all activities are determined (and optimized), standard approaches will be applied to compute the WCET of the whole action, specified by the activity diagram. To determine this WCET, WCNIs are specified for the loops of the activity diagram. Currently, we determine the WCET just for activity diagrams consisting of one activity.

WCET of evalCont   To obtain the WCETs of the implementation of the continuous parts, also a WCET analysis is required. This can also be done by summing up the elementary operations.

Determination of Required Resources

The resources (like memory) required by a component at run-time can be determined in a similar way: As it is known how the component specification will be mapped to code, the resources required by the whole component can be determined by summing up the required resources of the single elementary code-fragments. Nevertheless, we follow another strategy to obtain the required memory:

As we use the factory pattern for an implementation of a component's associated data structure (see Section 4.2.1), dynamic memory allocation just takes place due to reconfiguration, when whole component instances are instantiated or deinstantiated. This occurs in a controlled and predictable manner.

The resource requirements of a basic component that does not embed further components are static and simply determined by testing. Due to the applied factory pattern, the resource requirements of structural hierarchical components are derivable straight forward by testing and respecting the different possible configurations and the resource requirements of the configuration's components.

4.2.4   Real-Time Scheduling

We described in Section 4.1 that an IPANEMA application consists of a periodic real-time thread that triggers the evalCont and evalDiscrete methods in each period. One task, when mapping the specification to a platform specific model, consisting of one periodic real-time thread, is to choose the thread's parameters appropriately. A period needs to be chosen so that on the one hand, the implementations of the continuous components are stable and on the other hand, all deadlines, specified in the hybrid reconfiguration charts, are met.

A first approach depicted in Figure 4.11 could be to choose a period T such that $w_c + w_d \leq T$ for w_c the WCET of the continuous part and w_d the WCET of the discrete part. Although this would ensure that both parts are evaluated within the period, such a period is not always feasible: As mentioned in Section 2.4.3, the period has to be below a specific upper bound to guarantee stability for continuous configurations. Thus, the upper bound of the duration of the period is prescribed by the continuous configurations. This upper bound T_{max} is the minimum of the periods required by all possible continuous configurations to guarantee a stable digital implementation. In realistic applications, the WCETs of side-effects are often a multiple of this upper bound. Obviously, the whole evalDiscrete method is in this case not executable in a periodic thread with a period less or equal T_{max}.

Figure 4.11: Periodic evaluation of the continuous and discrete system parts with a long period

As jitter or delay in the evaluation of the continuous part causes instability as well, we do not affect the continuous part, but we split up the discrete part so that each of the split up parts fits into the time between the end of the continuous evaluation and the end of the period. This split up is not trivial and leads to additional effort. This additional effort is avoided if an RTOS is applied that meets the POSIX PSE50 standard, as the priority scheduler, which is required for all such RTOS, can be used to perform the split up if we create threads and set the scheduling parameters appropriately. In the remainder of this section, we will determine a scheduling that ensures meeting all deadlines, specified in the model, for platforms that meet the POSIX PSE50 standard.

The upper part of Figure 4.12 shows the thread that periodically evaluates the continuous system part w_c, followed by the evaluation of the *atomic* part with WCET w_d^a of the discrete system part. The white-filled arrow denotes triggering of the transition. The black-filled arrow marks the transition's deadline. The atomic part contains the items when firing a transition that must definitely be evaluated between two evaluations of the continuous system part in order to achieve each component to be in a stable state:

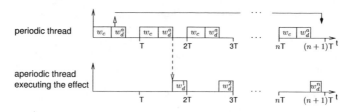

Figure 4.12: Periodic evaluation of the continuous and discrete system parts with rolled out execution of the side-effect

When adapting the current attribute (item 5 in Section 4.2.2), the components required by the target configuration need to be instantiated and initialized (item 7) in the same discrete part, as these components are required for the next evaluation of the continuous part. In order to utilize memory efficiently, the deinstantiation of the components, not required for the target configuration (item 6), has to take place before components are instantiated (item 7). Therefore, we require items 5, 6, and 7 to be executed within the atomic part to ensure that the components are always in a stable state.

As mentioned in Section 4.1, the evaluation of the discrete system part consists of the evaluation of the discrete parts of all active components of the system according to their hierarchy. Thus, items 5, 6, and 7 of all components are executed within the atomic part. As this requires that at least the events that are raised by the superordinated components have been raised, we also execute item 4 within the atomic part. Due to the temporal dependencies, we also execute items 1 - 3 within the atomic part. Note that even the sum of the WCETs of items 1 - 7 is usually much smaller than the WCET of a transition's side-effect (item 8). Therefore, item 8 (and due to the temporal dependency also item 9) is rolled out to an aperiodic thread. This aperiodic thread is started by the atomic part. As all discrete state changes and reconfigurations take place within the atomic part between two evaluations of the continuous part, all components are in a well-defined state when the continuous part is evaluated.

The advantage is, that the continuous system part is still evaluated without jitter or delay and that the side-effect obtains just the remaining processor resources. This design exploits the fact that the discrete side-effect has no impact on the evaluation of the continuous system part.

A special case occurs when the WCET w_d of items 8 and 9 is so small that these items can be executed within one period: If $w_d \leq T - w_c - w_d^a$ with $w_d := w_d^1 + \ldots + w_d^n$ (see Figure 4.12) the side-effect does not need to be rolled out into an aperiodic thread.

Period Determination

The main problem when performing the mapping to our platform specific model is to determine the period of the periodic thread: On the one hand, this period needs to be small enough to guarantee stability for the continuous controller configurations. On the other hand, we require the period to be as big as possible so that as less side-effects as possible need to be rolled out to aperiodic threads. As mentioned above, each continuous controller configuration provides an upper bound for the period. So, the minimum of these upper bounds is an upper bound for the period of our system. However, the greater the period the greater is the worst-case delay between triggering a transition and detecting this triggering (cf. Figure 4.12). How to determine the period for basic discrete components has been described in [BGS05]. In the remainder of this section, this is extended for the hybrid case.

Figure 4.12 points out an effect that we call *scheduling paradox*: As just mentioned, decreasing the period usually leads to a shorter delay and thus to an earlier termination of the aperiodic thread. When choosing a shorter period in our application, the side-effect needs to be split up into more parts. Thus, executing the whole side-effect spans more periods and thus, the continuous part is evaluated more times. Thus, decreasing the period can lead to a later termination of a side-effect, although the delay till recognizing the activated transition is shorter.

In the remainder of this section, we will present our algorithm to determine a period that guarantees stability and that guarantees to meet all deadlines. If multiple solutions exist, we will choose the greatest period in order to minimize the threads to be rolled out.

Figure 4.12 points out the worst-case delay between triggering a transition (indicated by the white-filled arrow) and starting the execution of the transition. In this case, the transition became triggered immediately after the check for activation has been performed. Thus, there is a delay of one period till the transition is recognized to be triggered and a delay of w_d^a till the execution of the side-effect starts. The delay is even greater if the evaluation of the continuous system part of the first period was shorter than its worst-case execution time. Then, w_d^a started earlier than indicated in the figure. The additional delay δ is the difference of the worst-case execution time and the actual execution time. The upper bound of this additional delay is obviously w_c which leads to Equation 4.1 for the delay Δ.

$$\Delta := T + w_d^a + \delta \qquad (4.1)$$

After this delay Δ, an aperiodic thread with the WCET w_d is started, executing the side-effect. This aperiodic thread is frequently interrupted by the periodic thread that executes for the time given by $w_c + w_d^a$. The number n of interrupts is equal to the number of periods that elapse till the aperiodic thread terminates. This leads to a response time R as shown in Equation 4.2.

$$R := \Delta + w_d + n(w_c + w_d^a) \text{ with } n = \left\lceil \frac{w_d}{T - w_d^a - w_c} \right\rceil$$
$$\Leftrightarrow \qquad (4.2)$$
$$R = T + w_d^a + \delta + w_d + (w_c + w_d^a) \left\lceil \frac{w_d}{T - w_d^a - w_c} \right\rceil$$

In order to meet the deadline d, a period has to be chosen such that $d \geq R$. If the side-effect is so short that $w_d \leq T - w_c - w_d^a$ holds (see above), the side-effect finishes at the latest after $T + w_c + w_d + w_d^a$. Thus, $d \geq T + w_c + w_d + w_d^a$ has to hold which leads to $w_c + w_d + w_d^a \leq T \leq d - (w_c + w_d + w_d^a)$.

If the discrete atomic part of the system starts two aperiodic threads, e.g. as a component's orthogonal AND state is active and it executes two side-effects or, because two components execute side-effects, the one with the shorter deadline will obtain the higher priority conform to the deadline monotonic priority assignment [But97]. For this thread, also $d \geq R$ has to hold. For the lower priority thread changes that w_d in Equation 4.2 is replaced by the sum of its own WCET and the WCET of the aperiodic thread with the higher priority as both side-effects have to be finished before its deadline. Thus, we obtain two inequalities and have to determine a period that fulfills both inequalities. If more aperiodic threads may be started, the number of inequalities increases accordingly.

Note that each transition leads to a set of inequalities and that we have to determine a value for T that fulfills the inequalities for all transitions. For the possible values of T, an upper and a lower bound exist: The upper bound T_{up} is given by the continuous configurations (see above) and the lower bound is given by $w_c + w_d^a$ (see Figure 4.12). If no T between the time bounds exists that solves the inequalities, the time restrictions of the model are too hard, so that no implementation is derivable for the specific target platform.

In case we execute multiple applications on the same target system, e.g. to benefit from resource optimization by flexible resource management, we may not derive implementations for the applications each demanding 100% processor load. Then each application would be executable on the target system alone, but both applications would not be schedulable at all. Therefore, we introduce a utilization factor ν indicating how much processor load the application may use. Then, we adopt the formula for the response time (Equation 4.2) to Equation 4.3.

$$R = T + \frac{1}{\nu}(w_d^a + \delta + w_d + (w_c + w_d^a)) \left\lceil \frac{w_d}{\nu T - w_d^a - w_c} \right\rceil \qquad (4.3)$$

As a processor utilization less than 100% does not guarantee schedulability (a processor load of $ln2 \approx 0.693$ guarantees schedulability) [But97], a schedulability analysis has to be performed before multiple applications are executed on the same target system.

4.2.5   Synthesizing Profiles for Flexible Resource Management Systems

When using the extended model, introduced in Section 3.2.5, to specify the system behavior, the specified information is used to derive an implementation consisting of multiple profiles (cf. Section 2.1.4). As described in [BGGO04a], the basic idea is to associate discrete states and transitions to each profile. When a profile switch is initiated, the hybrid reconfiguration chart has to switch to a state that belongs to the corresponding profile if necessary. Then, a hybrid reconfiguration chart is just allowed to switch between the states that belong to the current profile. If a transition that is not marked as blockable crosses two profiles, it could not be ensured to fire the transition whenever it is triggered as the current profile may not be left. Therefore, a profile must be closed with respect to the required transitions.

In [BGGO04a], an algorithm for the synthesis of profiles from extended hybrid reconfiguration chart models has been presented. This algorithm will be described informally in the remainder of this section. Its formalization is given in Appendix E.

As mentioned above, a profile is defined in this approach as a set of discrete states and a set of outgoing transitions. As the profiles need to be closed with respect to the required transitions, we call such profiles *permanent*. When deriving profiles, we are interested in profiles that we call *optimal*: A profile is optimal, iff no other permanent profile exists that consists of more states or transitions and requires the same amount of resources at the maximum. Thus, the profile that consists of the whole hybrid reconfiguration chart, i.e. all states and all transitions, is optimal.

To compute further profiles, we define a specific upper bound for the required resources. We use a previously synthesized profile that requires more resources than defined by the upper bound and remove all states requiring more resources than specified by the bound. If a transition requires more resources than specified by the bound, we remove it and its source state. Then, we remove all states whose outgoing required transitions point to a state that does not belong to the new synthesized profile and thus, we ensure that the resulting profile is permanent. The new synthesized profile is optimal due to its construction: As only the states and transitions are removed that require more resources or that invalidate permanence, no other permanent profile exists that consists of more states or transitions and requires the same amount of resources at the maximum. To synthesize multiple profiles, we start with the full hybrid reconfiguration chart, define upper bounds for the resources, and apply the outlined synthesis algorithm.

Applying the profile synthesis algorithm to the hybrid reconfiguration chart of the AccelerationControl component, as shown in Figure 3.15, leads to two different profiles: one profile Advanced consisting of the whole hybrid reconfiguration chart and one profile Standard consisting just of the states VelocityControl and PositionControl and their transitions. Note that profile Standard is fully contained in profile Advanced.

Profile Attributes   We define the quality of a profile by the maximum of the qualities of its states. The maximal (minimal resp.) requirement of a profile's resource is the maximum (minimum resp.) of the states' requirement of that resource, which depends on the states' configurations. The WCETs for entering and leaving a profile and the maximal allowed assignment delay when requesting resources are derived from the temporal annotations of the hybrid reconfiguration chart:

An implementation of a hybrid reconfiguration chart requests resources only when changing the current state. We realize the state change so that all resource requests occur during the atomic part of the discrete evaluation when executing a transition. For example, memory is requested when executing item 7 when firing a transition (see Section 4.2.2). Thus, the assignment delay w_δ increases the execution time of this atomic part. Therefore, we replace w_d^a from Equation 4.2 with $w_d^{a'} := w_d^a + w_\delta$ when determining the period for a platform that supports flexible resource management. We determine the period T so that all inequalities are fulfilled and w_δ is maximized.

When an application is forced by the operating system to leave a profile, this is done by triggering an enforceable transition. After a delay, the execution of the atomic part starts. This delay is up to one period plus the deadline of a transition that may currently be executing when the profile switch is initiated. After executing items 1 - 6, the old profile is left. Entering the new profile requires just the WCET of item 7.

Reachability

To derive the profile reachability graph for one or multiple applications, it is important which profiles can be reached from which profiles. Obviously, a profile ρ_1 is reachable from a profile ρ_2 if ρ_2 is fully contained in ρ_1. A profile ρ_2 is reachable from a profile ρ_1 if for all nodes of ρ_1 that do not belong to ρ_2 an enforceable transition exists that leads to a node of ρ_2. In our example, profile Standard is reachable from profile Advanced and vice versa.

Temporary Profiles   An optimal profile may not be reachable from another one due to the fact that not enough enforceable transitions exist. Then, we add *temporary* profiles to our profile graph to improve the connectivity using a series of steps and accept non optimal profiles temporarily. It is to be noted, that such a sequence of enforced transitions has to respect T^{MIET} to ensure that the component is still able to do its regular work.

To construct a path of (eventually non-optimal) profiles from a start profile to a target profile, we construct a path backwards starting at the target profile. Therefore, we first determine the set of states N' from which the target profile can be reached via enforceable transitions. As after each enforced transition the hybrid reconfiguration automaton runs without being interrupted by enforced transitions for the minimal inter enforceable time, we determine then the set of states $N \subseteq N'$ from which required transitions do not leave N'. We iteratively determine N' as the set of states from which N can be reached via enforceable transitions and so on. This algorithm terminates if the start profile is included in N' (and the corresponding transitions) or the expansion is terminated, i.e. the set N did not grow during an iteration. This algorithm is formalized in Appendix E, too.

We construct the connections in the profile graph as follows: We add a direct edge between two optimal profiles, if for all states of the source profile, the target profile is directly reachable via an enforceable transition (see above). Otherwise, the procedure outlined above is used to derive additional required temporary profiles.

4.2.6   Discussion

In the previous sections, we described how to map the architecture, the behavior, and the temporal requirements, specified by our PIM, to a PSM, which is based on the UML profile for Schedulability, Performance, and Time Specification and on the IPANEMA run-time framework. The architecture is mapped to a class structure. For the realization of behavior, we distinguish between the discrete part and the continuous part of the hybrid component's behavior. The implementation exploits the abstract representation of a hybrid component that is provided by the notion of interface state charts to obtain an efficient implementation of the specified reconfiguration.

Different temporal requirements have been specified in the PIM. As the WCETs of the implementation are obviously dependent on the target platform, the behavior must be implemented dependent on the target platform to meet the temporal requirements. Therefore, we described in Section 4.2.3 how to exploit the model-based specification to automatically derive and to optimize the WCETs and further resource requirements from the PIM, based on PM-specific values for elementary operations.

After determining the WCETs, the PIM is automatically mapped to active objects which are implemented as threads. The scheduling attributes like period, priorities, or deadlines are derived from the WCETs and from the temporal requirements. They guarantee that all specified real-time requirements are met. Finally, we showed how to exploit the extended models to implement a component by multiple profiles, enabling advanced resource management. The resulting PSM has been shown in Figure 4.3.

Possible extensions which could be subject to future work are for example to improve the determination of the WCET: On the one hand, the mapping from the elementary operations to assembler code instructions could be considered to determine an exacter WCET. To obtain a less pessimistic WCET estimation, an execution time analysis on the hardware level, which considers techniques like caching or pipelining, is required. Extensions to also support determination of WCETs of activity diagrams consisting of multiple activities are planned.

Further, the code generation could use different strategies to obtain different resource requirements for profiles. Thus, it is imaginable to obtain a WCET optimized implementation that requires more memory and to obtain a memory optimized implementation that leads to long WCETs. Another approach could use different boundaries for the to-many multiplicities in class diagrams: If the upper bound for a to-many association is set to a low value, the implementation will require less memory and will lead to short WCETs, but it will not be able to work in huge scenarios (e.g. in such a case a registry might handle just 5 shuttles). If the bound is set to a high value, it will require more memory and have longer WCETs, but it will allow more complex scenarios (e.g. the registry will allow 100 shuttles to enter its track section).

4.3   From the Platform Specific Model to Source Code

In Section 4.2, we described that our PSM consists of structures, described by class diagrams, methods, and tagged values that describe WCETs, threads inclusive scheduling parameters, and profiles. Further, we showed how to map the specified architecture, reconfiguration, hybrid behavior, and real-time requirements to this PSM with respect to a platform model. As the PSM contains all information, required for an implementation, the mapping to source code of a programming language is straight forward:

The architecture has been implemented by a structure that is described by classes and associations. Their implementation is straight forward as for example described in

[Zün02, KNNZ00]. The code generation is supported by the run-time framework IPANEMA: It encapsulates the specifics of different target platforms and provides a unique C++ interface. Thus, the code synthesized for the hybrid components does not have to be different for every different target platform. We just have to apply another implementation of the run-time framework. When another programming language is chosen as target, obviously another implementation of the framework is required.

The behavior is implemented by the methods of the classes. These methods realize either items 1 - 9 from Section 4.2.2 (similar to the implementation presented in [Bur02]) or they implement the activity diagrams, which specify the continuous behavior (see Section 4.2.2). Although item 8 requires starting an aperiodic thread if necessary, this is also straight forward. In order to realize the results of the real-time scheduling, just threads need to be initiated and initialized with the determined scheduling parameters.

Implementing the enforceable and blockable transitions and the synthesized profiles requires some more effort: An enforceable transition is implemented like two transitions: One transition that is triggered like an un-enforceable one and a second one with the same action and deadline constraints but that is triggered only if a specific internal event is available and a time guard that refers to an internal clock and the T^{MIET} time evaluates to true (see Appendix A). Such an internal event is never raised by the environment, but just by the FRM. Blockable transitions are implemented by extending their guards with specific boolean attributes which are set to false if the transition is blocked, to true otherwise.

This section points up that the MDA approach requires comparatively a lot of effort to derive the PSM. As mentioned in Section 2.1.1, this mapping to the PSM describes the *concepts* for the implementation. When the concepts are sophisticated and reasonable, this effort pays off as then mapping the PSM to code is straight forward. Even the mapping to other target languages is straight forward.

4.4   Conclusion

In this chapter, we synthesized an automatic implementation of the platform independent model, introduced in Chapter 3. In order to enable and to support this mapping, we first introduced the IPANEMA platform. Then, we followed the MDA process and worked out the concepts for the implementation in form of the mapping to the platform specific model. Our sophisticated platform specific model enables a straight forward mapping to code.

Thus, our modeling language is not just a theoretical concept which allows analysis as introduced in Section 3.2.6, it provides also an automatic implementation that is conform to its semantics and especially respects the specified real-time requirements.

In order to use the outlined modeling language, analysis, and automatic implementation, we obviously require tool support. We explicitly did not want to provide one new tool that provides modeling support for the basic continuous, basic discrete, and hybrid hierarchical components, as experience showed that such an overall tool would lack acceptance by both control engineers and software engineers. As both groups of engineers usually prefer to continue using their well-known and well-approved CAE tool or CASE tool respectively, we realized a tool integration instead of developing a new overall tool. How this integration has been realized is presented in the next chapter.

Chapter 5

Tool Support

This work does not only show how to develop mechatronic systems on the conceptual level. Even tool support has been created to integrate tools from different domains. First, this integration is presented, and then the tools and the outlined integration are used for an evaluation of the application example.

5.1 Tool Integration

As shown in the previous chapters, mechatronic systems consist of multiple components for different purposes. As the components are designed by different engineers from different domains and as the engineers usually prefer working with tools, they are used to and that are established in their domain, usually multiple different domain specific tools are applied. Therefore, it is preferable to integrate existing, well-approved, domain-specific tools instead of building one overall tool for the design of all components.

In our case, tool integration has to integrate architecture and behavior of hybrid components, specified by the different tools. This integration has been presented conceptually in Chapter 3. For this integration, just the externally relevant information of the embedded components is required. This is obtained from the components' interface description (note that the interface state chart of a continuous component consists of just one discrete state, the in- and outputs, and the signal flow information between the in- and outputs).

Thus, we provide a component description consisting of three parts which are combined into one exchange document per component [BGK04, BGM+06]:

- The externally relevant interface information, provided by the component's interface state chart,

- a behavioral description at the source code level, and

- a tool-specific description of all details of the component that allows modifications using the respective originating tool.

Figure 5.1 illustrates how to achieve the desired integration between different tools: The tools export hybrid components in form of XML exchange documents (see Appendix F for the DTD). Further, the tools can import such hybrid components to integrate them into their model. The integration itself is carried out using only the interface descriptions, considering the individual components as black boxes.

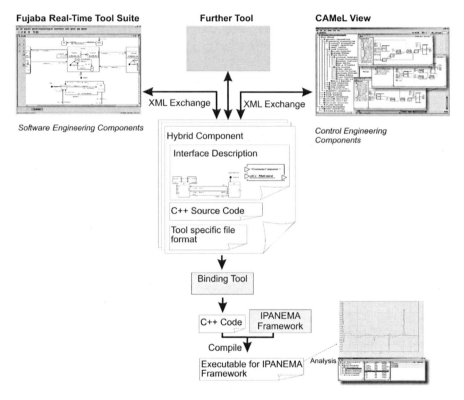

Figure 5.1: Tool integration

Due to the generality of this integration approach, the outlined integration is not limited to the tools which are used in the application example (namely the *Fujaba Real-Time Tool Suite*[1] and *CAMeL-View*[2]). All tools that provide import and export of hybrid components can be integrated.

---

[1] www.fujaba.de
[2] www.ixtronics.de

In order to obtain an executable application, the binding tool (see Figure 5.1) extracts the source code from the exchange document. As we intend to obtain executable applications for the run-time framework IPANEMA (see Section 4.1), the source code of each hybrid component has to adhere to IPANEMA's structure and to its API as presented in Figure 4.1. Thus, the code of the hybrid components, generated by different tools, is integrated without taking their internals into account.

5.1.1 CAMeL-View

In order to design feedback-controllers, we applied the CAE tool CAMeL-View. It is used for example to specify the dynamics of a physical system or the behavior of feedback-controllers by block diagrams (cf. Section 2.4.1).

In order to achieve the projected integration, controller block hierarchies are exported as hybrid components, consisting of the required interface description and generated C++ code implementing the block's behavior (see Section 2.4.3). The hybrid component export has been realized in [Boi05].

5.1.2 Fujaba Real-Time Tool Suite

The Fujaba Tool Suite currently offers a wide range of UML based diagrams. The core of the CASE tool supports among others class diagrams, activity and story diagrams, and state machines. For the design of mechatronic systems, the Fujaba Tool Suite has been extended to the Fujaba Real-Time Tool Suite [BGH+05c] which provides support for component diagrams, real-time statecharts, hybrid reconfiguration charts, interface state charts, and real-time coordination patterns. A C++ code generator has been implemented for the Fujaba Real-Time Tool Suite that maps such models to C++ code for the target platform IPANEMA as described in Chapter 4. Modelchecking and consistency analyses are supported as described in Sections 2.3 and 3.2.6.

5.2   Evaluation

In order to evaluate the concepts presented in the previous chapters, we generated and executed the convoy coordination application example. As the IPANEMA extensions, which have been required for the execution of hybrid components (see Section 4.1), are currently not available for a real-time platform, we executed the generated application on a Windows system without application of a flexible resource management system. Obviously, this allows just a proof of functional correctness by testing/simulating and we cannot proof temporal correctness. Due to our experience with purely discrete systems which have been implemented for Real-Time Java [BBF+00] and whose real-time requirements have been implemented in a similar manner [Bur02, BGS05], we are optimistic that the presented concepts to implement the specified real-time behavior are correct. Although we do not use a real-time platform for this evaluation, we will measure and present execution times.

The generated application is executable and can be executed on the target system to coordinate convoys and to control the velocity. Nevertheless, the design process for the development of safety-critical mechatronic systems requires intensive testing before the application is executed on the target system. One kind of testing is called *Hardware in the Loop* (*HIL*) simulation: In a HIL simulation, the generated application is tested without the real, physical plant. Instead of this, a model of the plant is used in a computer simulation. This computer simulation provides all required input signals and simulates how the real physical system would react to the output signals. Therefore, CAMeL-View synthesizes additional classes that compile with our generated application and which lead to an extended application that allows stimulating input signals and capturing output signals by CAMeL-View. Stimulation and capturing allow systematic testing. A screenshot of a CAMeL capture is shown in Figure 5.1 in the lower right corner.

Tables 5.1 and 5.2 list the classes, generated by Fujaba and by CAMeL-View. They list the LoC[3] and the memory each classes' instance requires after initialization (before reconfiguration took place). Note again, that the CAMeL-View code generation is not part of this work. For completeness, we include the CAMeL-View code also in this evaluation. In Table 5.1, it is important to know that a ReconfigurationChart instance is part of the corresponding Component instance, i.e. 4.78 kBytes of the 19.05 kBytes of an AccelerationControl instance are used for the AccelerationControlReconfigurationChart instance. The values for the reconfigurable components AccelerationControl, DriveTrain, and Shuttle are the values after initialization, when they are still in their initial state. Table 5.2 shows just one value per feedback-controller: The memory of a PilotControl instance and a PilotControlHierarchy instance is included in the value for the PilotControlComponent instance.

The application requires at start-up 7552 kBytes. 5412 kBytes of this memory is required for the classes which enable the coupling to CAMeL-View. This is not required when executing the application after testing with the real physical plant.

Applying the method from Section 4.2.3 to determine the WCET of the story diagram from Figure 2.16 with the values for the elementary WCETs from Appendix C leads to a WCET of 9.250 μsec. Testing the story diagram leads to a WCET of 4.817 μsec. Although this is an acceptable worst-case estimation, the discrepancy between measurement and calculation shows that more sophisticated methods need to be applied for determining the elementary operations' WCETs. Further evaluation about the WCET optimization and determination has been presented in [BGST05].

With $T_{max} = 1000\mu$sec for the minimal upper bound for the continuous configurations (see Section 4.2.4) and choosing 2000μsec for the deadlines in the models presented within this thesis leads to a period $T = T_{max} = 1000\mu$sec. We also evaluated our modelchecking approach. The results have been presented in [GST+03].

---

[3]*Lines of Code* without empty lines and without commentaries

Component	Files	LoC	Memory per Instance [kBytes]
AccelerationControl	AccelerationControl.h	23	19.05
	AccelerationControl.cpp	70	
	AccelerationControlReconfigurationChart.h	114	4.78
	AccelerationControlReconfigurationChart.cpp	1186	
		Σ 1393	
DriveTrain	DriveTrain.h	24	51.00
	DriveTrain.cpp	49	
	DriveTrainReconfigurationChart.h	110	4.66
	DriveTrainReconfigurationChart.cpp	786	
		Σ 969	
Shuttle	Shuttle.h	19	64.60
	Shuttle.cpp	46	
	ShuttleReconfigurationChart.h	111	4.76
	ShuttleReconfigurationChart.cpp	933	
		Σ 1109	
		Σ 3471	

Table 5.1: Synthesized Fujaba classes

5.3 Conclusion

This chapter presented our approach to integrate tools from different domains in order to support modeling *and* automatic implementation of systems consisting of hybrid components. In order to integrate source code generated by different tools, we require the generated code to adhere to the framework's API.

In the second part of this chapter, we evaluated the prototypic realization of the C++ code generator. The evaluation showed that the dynamic instantiation and deinstantiation of the components will show benefit especially when the system's configurations have huge differences in their resource requirements. The method to determine the WCET of a story pattern leads to good estimations. It has to be noted that the code, generated by the Fujaba Real-Time Tool Suite, is not optimized. Several optimizations will improve the resource requirements.

Component	Files	LoC	Memory per Instance [kBytes]
PilotControl	PilotControl.h	15	2.92
	PilotControl.cpp	55	
	PilotControlComponent.h	11	
	PilotControlComponent.cpp	26	
	PilotControlHierarchy.h	10	
	PilotControlHierarchy.cpp	36	
		Σ 153	
PositionControl	PositionControl.h	15	3.02
	PositionControl.cpp	60	
	PositionControlComponent.h	11	
	PositionControlComponent.cpp	26	
	PositionControlHierarchy.h	10	
	PositionControlHierarchy.cpp	36	
		Σ 158	
Sum	Sum.h	15	2.90
	Sum.cpp	55	
	SumComponent.h	11	
	SumComponent.cpp	27	
	SumHierarchy.h	10	
	SumHierarchy.cpp	37	
		Σ 155	
VelocityControl	VelocityControl.h	13	2.64
	VelocityControl.cpp	47	
	VelocityControlComponent.h	11	
	VelocityControlComponent.cpp	25	
	VelocityControlHierarchy.h	10	
	VelocityControlHierarchy.cpp	35	
		Σ 141	
		Σ 607	

Table 5.2: Synthesized CAMeL-View classes

Chapter 6

Related Work

In this work, we presented a new approach for the model-based design, analysis, and implementation of embedded, hybrid, mechatronic, reconfigurable real-time systems. Of course, multiple other approaches exist for the design of reconfigurable hybrid systems. In these approaches, reconfiguration is either restricted to the components' module boundaries or they lack of modeling or analyzing complex systems. In contrast to the existing approaches, our approach is integrated in a seamless design process, which guarantees real-time requirements even for complex distributed systems and which also provides an automatic and efficient mapping to code which even implements the specified and verified real-time requirements:

In our design process, we separate the design of real-time communication protocols, real-time behavior, and hybrid behavior. This separation is exploited in the compositional verification of huge, distributed systems. Together with the step-wise refinement, the compositional modelchecking ensures the correctness of the overall system, consisting of communicating, reconfigurable components with real-time requirements. The implementation of our models follows the MDA approach, it respects the specified real-time requirements, and it provides an efficient implementation of the reconfiguration supported by the abstraction, given by the notion of nodes (cf. Section 4.2.2). A first comparison of our approach with traditional approaches to model reconfiguration (see Section 3.2.7) showed that our approach reduces visual complexity and simplifies analyses and thus enables ruling the system's complexity.

In this chapter, we examine the existing approaches with respect to the categories *modeling support*, *MDA support*, and *support for formal analyses* [BGH05a]. These categories are described in detail below:

Modeling Support

For the modeling support of the approaches, we judge how the existing approaches support describing the *structure/composition* as it is a crucial prerequisite to model complex systems. In complex systems, *modularity* is a major concern a suitable approach has to fulfill. For the support of modularity, an appropriate notion of *interfaces* is required and we consider whether these *interface notions are sufficient to ensure correct embedding*, and whether the interfaces are *static* or if they change during run-time (*dynamic interfaces*).

As models have to integrate concepts from software, electrical, mechanical, and control engineering, the approaches should support both *continuous* and discrete behavior. For the discrete system part, we require a *state machine* like notation with possibly *hierarchical states*, *orthogonal states*, and *history*.

In order to support self-optimizing systems which require adapting their behavior and structure to their current context at run-time, we consider whether *reconfiguration* can be described at all and whether the combination of discrete and continuous behavior is supported by *blinding out* active configurations or by *exchanging* moduls as in the case of hybrid automata. In addition, we look if reconfiguration can cross module boundaries and whether the different configurations are exploited to enable an improved *resource management*.

MDA Support

Here, the question is which of the levels platform independent model (PIM), platform specific model (PSM), and code are populated in the approach. Depending on the supported levels, we judge whether the approach can be employed in the earlier or later phases only or whether it supports all development phases.

An important follow up criterion is then which kind of transformations/synthesis steps are supported and what degree of automation is offered, as this determines to a great extent how well the model-driven philosophy is really supported. We have *PIM* $\rightarrow$ *PSM*, *PSM* $\rightarrow$ *Code*, and the direct synthesis *PIM* $\rightarrow$ *Code*. For each of these transformation steps the correct *timing of the activation* and the correct schedulability has to be guaranteed.

Support for Formal Analyses

Due to the safety-critical character of mechatronic systems, formal analyses are required to ensure correctness of the models. As stressed in [CBP+04], a *formal semantics* is a crucial prerequisite for any reasonable modeling approach as otherwise no reasonable analysis of the properties of the model is possible. In addition, such a semantics is required to be *implementable* (and the models should be implemented accordingly) as otherwise the analysis result does not necessarily hold for the final system. If the model is mapped to multiple tasks, the approaches should support schedulability analysis.

To ensure relevant system properties for all possible system traces, we require techniques for the complete formal verification which should be supported in an automatic fashion. Relevant criteria are *real-time behavior* and *hybrid behavior*. An important requirement in practice is also that a *scalable* tool support exists which supports *modular* or *compositional* reasoning. Therefore, the definition of *refinement* is essential.

Outline

Instead of first describing all regarded related approaches and then discussing them, we grouped multiple related and similar approaches into single sections and discussed them in a block to improve readability. We begin with approaches for the design of non-hybrid real-time systems and then present approaches for the design of hybrid, reconfigurable systems.

Note that we judge the related approaches on the basis of the information provided by the cited references and that they did not have been validated by proper experiments with the tools.

6.1 Real-Time Systems

Many different approaches exist for the design of real-time systems. Although they do not support reconfiguration, we discuss them with respect to their support for real-time systems. Some of them are based on models enriched with sufficient information to derive an appropriate implementation of the specified real-time behavior automatically. These approaches lack high-level constructs to specify complex systems and their notion is partly not related to the UML standard. Further, the used models partly contain source code, so that they cannot benefit from the advantages of the MDE approach (see Section 2.1).

In contrast, other approaches which are UML-based provide a modular, component-based architecture and provide high-level constructs to reduce complexity. Most of these approaches are based on semantics which are not realizable, because of the *zero execution time* assumption (cf. Section 2.1.5). Other approaches provide adequate means to specify the necessary real-time requirements by syntactically enriched models in order to synthesize code automatically, but the proposed code generation algorithms do not respect these details properly.

6.1.1 Low-level Approaches

For example in [HSG+01], the application framework VERTAF (Verifiable Embedded Real-Time Application Framework) is sketched, where a low-level object model is specified. Active objects are annotated with periods, deadlines and WCETs. The resulting model is checked for schedulability and implemented automatically.

[SKW00] describes the implementation of a low level automata model. The implementation algorithm maps the specification to a *multi-tasking model* which describes how the actions of the model are placed into physical threads. The annotation of WCETs and deadlines in the model enables this mapping.

[GKWS03] uses the CASE tool Rational Rose[1] to model UML components, ports, their interaction and actions which describe how a component's port reacts to incoming events and triggers output ports. These models are partly imported into an ESML (Embedded

---

[1]http://www.rational.com

Systems Modeling Language) - model, where they are extended by information needed for scheduling and partitioning (i.e. every port is associated with a period that determines how often the port checks for incoming events and a WCET is assigned for each action). This information is used to distribute the components automatically to multiple processors and to guarantee schedulability.

Discussion

Modeling Support   [GKWS03] is the only approach that supports specifying the system's structure. It supports the notion of components and ports which specify static interfaces. Support for dynamic interfaces to ensure consistent models does not exist.

Due to the lack of high-level constructs, like hierarchical and orthogonal states, guards, or time guards, these approaches are not applicable for complex mechatronic components. Further, they do not allow integrating continuous behavior.

MDA Support   The model applied in [HSG⁺01] is just on the PSM level as it contains platform specific information like WCETs. The models of [SKW00, GKWS03] can be seen as low level PIMs. The multi-tasking model and the ESML model are on the PSM level and they are enriched with platform specific timing annotations. The timing annotations, specified in all three approaches lead to an automatic implementation of the specified real-time behavior. The approaches do not provide support to derive them automatically (like WCETs or periods in our case). Further, they lack of a seamless model-based approach to benefit from the advantages of MDA and MDE.

Support for Formal Analyses   Verification is not possible, as the three approaches lack of a formal semantics. The mapping to tasks enables scheduling analysis.

6.1.2   High-level Approaches

As UML became the standard in software engineering and due to the advantages of model-driven engineering, a lot of UML-related approaches emerged which use model-based, object-oriented modeling paradigms for the design of embedded, mechtronic, real-time systems. Attemps like [AKZ96, Dou, Gom00], ROOM [SGW94], UML/RT [SR98], Embedded UML [MLLG01], or UML2.0 [Obj05b] show the need to use UML for the specification of real-time systems.

State Machine Extensions   Plenty of extensions of UML state machines have been proposed which introduce different high-level constructs to model more complex temporal dependencies than provided by the standard when and after constructs [LQV01, BlLM02, Har98, KP92, PAS94]. With these extensions, triggering transitions or executing side-effects is delayed and transition activations or available events are valid for a specified amount of time.

Timed Automata   The statechart extensions mentioned above focus on the verification of system properties, but do not consider code generation. This is also true for hierarchical timed automata [DM01, DMY02], timed automata (e.g. [HNSY92, LPY97]), and the approach described in [KMR02]. In [KMR02], a UML state machine is mapped to two timed automata – one to describe transitions, the other to model the event queue. Timed automata introduce clocks which can be reset to zero when firing a transition. Locations are associated with boolean expressions called time invariants and transitions are enriched by time guards. Their semantics is similar to the one of our real-time statechart model.

In [ADF$^+$01, AFP$^+$02], locations of the flat timed automaton UPPAAL [LPY97] are associated with tasks inclusive WCETs and deadlines. These extensions enriche the model with the information required for code generation and a prototype synthesizing C-Code has been implemented.

Masse   In [MKH03], Rational Rose RT is used to specify an application's structure and behavior. An analyzer-tool parses the generated code and presents all possible scenarios. The developer is required to add scheduling information for each scenario which is used to convert the singlethreaded code, generated by Rose RT, to a multithreaded application.

Modecharts & MacBeth   Modecharts [JM94] are another high-level form of state transition systems for the specification of real-time systems. They offer the concepts of hierarchy, parallelism and even inter-level transitions. Their semantics is defined by a mapping to Real Time Logic (RTL) which enables modelchecking as described in [YMS95]. Actions are executed only while residing in states and not when firing transitions. The model respects that actions require time and thus they are associated with deadlines or –if needed– with periods. [PMS95] describes code generation for the target language ESTEREL. MacBeth [PI01] is related to Modecharts and introduces several new modeling concepts.

Discussion

Modeling Support   The presented approaches do not focus on structure, modularity, and interfaces. They provide high-level constructs for different automata models like hierarchy, orthogonal states, or history. Some approaches even provide constructs to specify complex temporal trigger conditions. Modecharts models are restricted, as deadlines and trigger conditions are specified just relative to the current state's (mode's) point of entry and there is no possibility of specifying them relative to preceding states. None of the approaches supports the specification of hybrid behavior or reconfiguration.

MDA Support   The presented statechart extensions [LQV01, BlLM02, Har98, KP92, PAS94] and timed automata models are PIMs, but when the locations of timed automata are associated with platform specific information like WCETs in [ADF$^+$01, AFP$^+$02], we obtain a PSM. The latter approach has the advantage that it enables code generation, but it is restricted to flat automata. Thus, it does not take the additional syntactical constructs of hierarchical timed automata into account. Further, it is not really sufficient for hard real-time systems, as it does not take into account the delays that occur when transitions are fired, arguing that these delays are small compared to the WCETs.

Although some of the presented approaches provide useful high-level constructs to specify temporal behavior for systems without any hard real-time constraints, they are not sufficient to specify hard real-time systems. The models just deliver points in time when transitions are triggered, but the approaches do not provide support for mapping the model to a PSM or to code.

[MKH03] has the drawback that an embedded application usually consists of plenty of scenarios. Thus, there is the need to manually add a lot information before the model is transformed into a multithreaded application.

Modechart's and MacBeth's mappings to code are restricted, as the code generator regards only the timing intervals which trigger the transitions and not the deadlines or periods.

Support for Formal Analyses   As most of the approaches focus on formal verification, they provide a formally defined semantics, but most of them are not implementable due to the zero execution time assuption (cf. Section 2.1.5). Implemented on a real physical machine, the points of time, when a transition is triggered, will usually not be recognized precisely, so that the transitions will fire with a delay. Even if this delay is short, it is not appropriate for hard real-time systems. The models providing an implementable semantics [ADF$^+$01, AFP$^+$02, MKH03, PMS95, PI01] do not provide appropriate code generators which respect the specified temporal requirements. Support for schedulability analysis is not provided either. They also do not provide notion for refinement.

6.2   Hybrid, Reconfigurable Systems

The approaches presented in the previous section all have in common that they have been created for the design of non-hybrid, real-time systems. Thus, they do not integrate continuous behavior with the discrete behavior and they do not support reconfiguration. Such approaches are discussed in this section.

6.2.1   Classical Approaches

Block Diagrams and MATLAB/Simulink/Stateflow   As described in Section 2.4, block diagrams are used to specify feedback-controllers. The standard approach to model an exchange of feedback-controllers is to include discrete blocks. When integrating such discrete control elements into block diagrams, the alternative controller outputs are fed into a discrete block whose behavior is described by a statechart. Dependent on the statechart's current discrete state, the corresponding continuous signals are blind out or directed to the block's output. This enables switching between the output signals of different controllers. Conditionally blocks which are only evaluated if explicitly triggered are another option to model reconfiguration. Thus, a statechart can be used to only trigger the required elements of the currently active configuration instead of blinding out the results of the not required ones.

The de facto industry standard employing this concept is MATLAB/Simulink and Stateflow.[2] Formal verification of MATLAB/Simulink and Stateflow models of moderate size can be accomplished by an automatic transformation to hybrid automata (see Section 6.2.2) via the Hybrid System Interchange Format (HSIF) (cf. [ASK04]).

Hybrid Bond Graphs *Bond graphs* are used to model physical behavior. Different bond graph elements and active bonds between them model the exchange of power. The bond graph elements are simple, non domain-specific structures like resistances, capacities etc. Thus, bond graphs are applicable in different domains. Further block diagram elements are used to specify the dynamics of a system. Therefore, bond graphs combine the power exchange and the dynamics within one diagram. In *hybrid bond graphs* [MB95, MB98] *controlled junctions* are introduced into the bond graph. A finite state machine (FSM) is associated with each controlled junction. Each state of the FSM is of type on or off, indicating if the controlled junction acts like a normal junction or as a 0 value source. The controlled junctions, used to blind out single elements, are similar to discrete or conditionally blocks in block diagrams.

SCADE Drive The SCADE Drive Tool Suite [Hoh04] (esterel-technologies) is a tool chain for design, simulation, modelchecking, and C-code generation. Its code generator is certified. Modeling reconfiguration is similar to MATLAB/Simulink.

Discussion

Modeling Support Modularity is provided by all three approaches, but the interfaces are static in all approaches. When specifying complex mechatronic systems, the models become huge and lead to a high visual complexity which is difficult to manage by the engineer. The only possibility, provided by the discussed approaches, to reduce the visual complexity is to combine multiple blocks from a block diagram into *hierarchical blocks* [Oga02].

The approaches integrate discrete and continuous behavior and thus they enable the specification of hybrid systems. Reconfiguration is specified by kinds of workarounds: Every single controller configuration is always active – independent of the system's current discrete state (state of the statechart or states of the controlled junctions). As they just blind out some configurations instead of replacing them, such designs do not really specify reconfiguration. These approaches lead to a waste of resources when implementing such models, as all blocks are permanently evaluated – even the ones of the inactive configurations.

---

[2]http://www.mathworks.com

MDA Support   The models are on the PIM level and support direct mapping to code. The existing code generators do not respect WCETs of side-effects and thus lack of the implementation of real-time behavior.

Support for Formal Analyses   The semantics of MATLAB/Simulink models is formally defined by [ASK04] which enables hybrid modelchecking of models of adequate size. Concepts how to handle complexity problems in verification –e.g. compositinal modelchecking– do not exist.

From the model-based engineering's point of view, such models have further drawbacks in the analyzability. Especially when a diagram consists of multiple discrete blocks or controlled junctions, it is not obvious which configurations exist. Each possible combination of the discrete states (each global discrete state) may lead to another configuration. Then, a complex exploration of the state space has to be performed to provide the set of reachable global discrete states which leads to the set of possible configurations. In particular, such an analysis is required to check the consistency of each configuration, e.g. to determine if all required input signals are available and not blinded out by one of the discrete blocks.

6.2.2   Hybrid Behavioral Models

The hybrid behavioral models, described in this section, overcome some of the drawbacks of the previously discussed approaches. They provide adequate state machine like notations:

Hybrid Automata and Hybrid I/O Automata   The discussion of block diagrams and hybrid bond graphs showed that there is a strong relation between the system's current global discrete state and the current configuration. In the mentioned approaches, there is no direct mapping from the discrete states to the configurations. Hybrid automata [HHWT95, ACH+95] overcome this drawback by simply assigning a specific continuous controller to each discrete state of a finite automata model. [ASK04] presents an algorithm for the automatic transformation of MATLAB/Simulink and Stateflow models to hybrid automata. Hybrid I/O automata [LSV01] further support communicating hybrid automata.

Correctness of hybrid automata is verified by hybrid modelcheckers (e.g. HyTech,[3] d/dt,[4] RED,[5] CheckMate[6]) in a non-compositional manner. [Lam93] introduces how to specify hybrid systems in TLA$^+$ (Temporal Logic of Actions) which has been extended in [HGK98] to compositional TLA (cTLA). Using cTLA, hybrid systems are specified in a compositional, modular manner, by introducing *processes*. Each process is specified by a state-transition system. When verifying a property that is related to just a subset of all processes, only this subset has to be verified.

---

[3]http://www-cad.eecs.berkeley.edu/~tah/HyTech/
[4]http://www-verimag.imag.fr/~tdang/ddt.html
[5]http://cc.ee.ntu.edu.tw/~val/
[6]http://www.ece.cmu.edu/~webk/checkmate

Giotto   Within the Fresco project,[7] the high-level programming language Giotto [HKSP02, HHK01] has been created. Similar to automata models, a Giotto program consists of modes and mode switches. The behavior of a mode is described by C code. Each mode is associated with a period, specifying how often its behavior is executed, and a WCET for the corresponding C code. Switch-frequencies specify how often a switch is evaluated. The Giotto program is automatically implemented for a *virtual embedded machine* that realizes the timing specifications for the target platform.

In [HKSP02], it is described how MATLAB/Simulink has been extended for the specification of Giotto programs: Reconfiguration is specified within such Giotto Simulink models by *Giotto case blocks*, switching between different parts of the Simulink model. Each combination of these case-dependent parts of the Simulink model build one of the modes.

Hybrid Statecharts   Hybrid statecharts as defined in [KP92] introduce hierarchical and orthogonal discrete states. This allows modeling more complex systems as these constructs reduce the visual complexity of the models. Their semantics is formally defined which allows formal verification.

High-level Pr/T Nets   In [Bri97], it is demonstrated how to use high-level predicate/transition-nets (Pr/T nets) for the modeling of hybrid systems. [Tac01] describes analyses and implementation of these models. In [RR03, RR04], the modeling approach has been extended to support even reconfigurating systems. In these Pr/T nets, a (quasi-continuous) feedback-controller is modeled by a Pr/T net. Associating hierarchical places with such nets in a high-level Pr/T net enables modeling the exchange of feedback-controllers by dismarking a place and marking another one. Refinement or replacement rules (which are similar to graph transformation systems [KNNZ00]) are used for modeling dynamic modifying nets.

As it is possible to specify duration and delay times in these nets, these works respect that firing transitions consumes time. The formal semantics of Pr/T Nets enables formal verification in principle. Using the SEA approach [RSAT00] leads to automatic implementation of the model.

Discussion

Modeling Support   All approaches [HHWT95, ACH+95, LSV01, Lam93, HGK98, HKSP02, HHK01, KP92, Bri97, Tac01, RR03, RR04] have in common, that they have been designed for the specification of behavior, but there is no integration with an architectural description (similar to UML component diagrams or UML class diagrams).[8] Therefore, these models are used for the specification of the behavior of single components (in terms of UML), but a distributed system or a system with a modular, hierarchical architecture requires an extension of the model or the integration with other approaches.

---

[7]http://www.eecs.berkeley.edu/~tah/Talks/the_fresco_project.html
[8]Note that most of these approaches are older than the UML.

Hybrid statecharts, as defined in [KP92], introduce hierarchy in the behavior, which reduces visual complexity and thus overcomes one of the drawbacks of hybrid automata. Nevertheless, the presented approaches do not support the structured, separated design of architecture, communication, and reconfiguration and their later integration like the approach presented in this work.

The interface of a hybrid automaton, a Giotto program, a hybrid statechart, or a high-level Pr/T net (its in- and outputs) has to be the union of the interfaces of its continuous controllers. Thus, each continuous controller has to respect all inputs and has to blind out the unused signals in its internal representation. This shows that the model lacks of the information which input signals are required in which discrete states. In order to check consistency, i.e. to check if all available signals are sufficient for a safe application of the controller, it has to be extracted from the model of the continuous controller which signals are required and which ones are not used to produce the output. Especially when reconfiguration leads to configurations with different interfaces –which is usual in the domain of mechatronic systems– a description of the dynamic of the interface is required to ensure consistent configurations, i.e. to ensure that all required input signals and further used output signals are available. Although Hybrid I/O Automata [LSV01] distinguish between input and output variables and input and output actions, these inputs and outputs are static and thus independent of the automaton's current discrete state.

When using MATLAB/Simulink to specify reconfigurating Giotto programs, all configurations are combined in one Giotto Simulink model. The single possible configurations just become obvious when mapping the Giotto Simulink model to the Giotto program. Thus, the Giotto Simulink model has the same drawbacks as the classical approaches, described in Section 6.2.1.

MDA Support   Except Giotto and the high-level Pr/T nets, all models define a PIM that lacks of automatic implementation due to the *zero execution time* assumption (see Section 2.1.5). Giotto programs and high-level Pr/T nets are platform specific and contain temporal annotations which are respected appropriately in the implementation.

Support for Formal Analyses   The semantics of the presented approaches is formally defined. Hybrid automata and statechart models and high-level Pr/T nets lack of verification of complex systems due to the state explosion problem and due to the lack of compositional approaches. The compositional approach, presented in [HGK98], is just useful, if a property has to be verified which is related to a subset of all processes. For the verification of the whole system, there is no benefit in this approach.

The focus of Giotto is implementation. Giotto supports schedulability analysis, but verification is not addressed. Correctness could be ensured if the Giotto program is synthesized from a verified model – e.g. a Masaccio model [Hen00] (see Section 6.2.3).

6.2.3   Modular, Component-Based Approaches

An essential drawback of the approaches, presented in the previous section, is the lack of support for distributed, modular, component-based architectures. In this section, we present approaches that overcome this drawback.

SAE AADL and MetaH   One approach towards a modular architecture is SAE AADL [FGHL04], the successor of MetaH.[9] A SAE AADL specification consists of multiple processes, threads, and subprograms that are distributed on different processors. Communication between the threads is described by ports and connections, similar to UML 2.0.

CHARON   CHARON [ADE+01] provides a hierarchical automata model for the specification of behavior. Additionally, it provides a hierarchical architectural model, similar to ROOM actor diagrams [SGW94] whose concepts influenced the design of UML component diagrams. CHARON's transitions are non-urgent and thus, they do not have to be fired instantaneous [AIK+03] which leads to delays when firing transitions. Sensing, computation, and actuation are assumed to be performed within one period. This disengagement from the zero execution time assumption enables a more realistic implementation (cf. Section 2.1.5). A *dynamic dependency graph* ensures that algebraic constraints which are evaluated dependent on the system's current discrete state are evaluated in the dependency order, i.e. an assignment is not processed before its right-hand variables are updated. [AGLS01] defines *refinement* for hybrid CHARON models.

HyROOM   HyROOM [SPP01, BBP+02] distinguishes between a hierarchical architectural model and a hierarchical behavioural model, similar to CHARON. The discrete states of the behavioral model are associated with MATLAB/Simulink blocks to specify hybrid behavior.

HyCharts   As described in [SPP01], a HyROOM model can be mapped to a HyChart [GSB98, Sta01] model. This consists of an architectural model and a behavioral model as well, but the continuous parts are not specified by MATLAB/Simulink blocks, but by ordinary differential equations. By adding *relaxations* to the state machine, the behavior becomes implementable, but additional behavior is added as well. The semantics of the models is defined formally, which enables verification.

Masaccio   Masaccio [Hen00] which is like Giotto (see Section 6.2.2) part of the Fresco project is also based on components. It builds complex components by the parallel and serial composition of atomic discrete and atomic continuous components. It defines the interface of a component which contains (among others) dependency relations, describing which continuous output signals depend on which continous input signals.

---

[9]http://www.htc.honeywell.com/metah

HybridUML and HL³   HybridUML [BBHP04] defines a profile for UML 2.0 which allows the specification of architecture and hybrid behavior, as well. Its formal semantics is defined by a transformation to the HL^3 language. HL^3 models are implemented by a mapping to a multi-CPU computer system.

UML^h   In UML^h [FNW98], the architecture is specified by extended UML class diagrams that distinguish between discrete, continuous and hybrid classes. Hybrid behavior is specified by a textuell description of mathematic correlations between discrete and continuous variables, similar to the object-oriented extension of Z [FJW97].

Ptolemy II   Similar to Charon, HybridUML, or HyROOM, Ptolemy II [HLL$^+$03] distinguishes between architectural and behavioral design. In contrast to the aforementioned approaches, Ptolemy II provides different semantic domains (*models of computation*). Among others, it supports semantics for continuous time, discrete time, (distributed) discrete events, finite state machines, synchronous dataflow, and timed multitasking. Ptolemy II even supports combination and integration of these models of computation.

SysML   A request for proposals for *UML for System Engineering (UML for SE)* [Obj03b] by the OMG currently addresses UML in the context of technical systems. The idea of UML for SE is to provide a language that supports the system engineer in modeling and analyzing software, hardware, logical and physical subsystems, data, personnel, procedures, and facilities.

One distinguishing proposal for UML for SE which is already adopted by the OMG is the *Systems Modeling Language (SysML)* [Obj05a][10] extending a subset of the UML 2.0 specification. SysML introduces the notion of blocks which are based on UML classes and components. This naming may cause confusion as *blocks* and *block diagrams* are used in the engineering domain for the specification of feedback-controllers (see Section 2.4.1). Further, SysML introduces flow ports which are similar to our continuous ports. A syntactic construct like our hybrid ports, which groups multiple continuous or discrete ports, does not exist.

Parametric Constraints allow specifying parametric (arithmetic) relations between numerical attributes of block instances. Continuous components could be modeled by defining the corresponding differential equations by parametric constraints for a class, but to the best of our knowledge, concrete examples for this issue do not exist. The nodes of activity diagrams are extended with continuous functions, in- and outputs, and flow information for the exchange of continuous data.

Latest activity in the SysML community reveals discrepancy, so that the SysML partners split up. After publishing a unique SysML version 0.9, and publishing a version 1.0 [Obj05a], it appears highly probable that a second SysML dialect will appear.

---

[10]http://www.sysml.org

Time Weaver   In [dR03], a framework for the component-based development of real-time systems is presented. The framework allows the specification of temporal annotations, like deadlines and periods, which enables schedulability analyses. Reconfiguration is specified by mode switches similar to discrete blocks in MATLAB/Simulink.

Discussion

Modeling Support   All presented tools and techniques support the specification of a system's architecture or structure by a notion of classes or component diagrams. All approaches support modular architecture and interface descriptions of the modules. Nevertheless, they do not respect that a module can change its interface due to reconfiguration which can lead to incorrect configurations. Masaccio is the only approach respecting dependency relations in the interface description. Further, none of the approaches supports intelligent resource management like our approach by using the benefits that stem from the flexible resource management system (see Sections 2.1.4 and 3.2.5).

Except SysML, all approaches allow the specification of continuous behavior by block diagrams, differential equations, or similar textual descriptions. Discrete behavior is specified by state machines, mostly with support for orthogonal states and history. They integrate continuous and discrete behavior, and thus they enable the specification of hybrid behavior. Except Time Weaver, the approaches embed the continuous models in the discrete state machines.

SysML's parametric constraints and the activity extensions are a first step towards the integration of continuous behavior with UML, but it is doubtful if control engineers will use parametric constraints for the specification of feedback-controllers instead of the well-approved block diagrams as presented in Section 2.4.1. Reconfiguration is not adressed at all in SysML.

In the other approaches, reconfiguration is restricted as each component is just able to switch between continuous feedback-controllers that are one level below the reconfigurating component in the architectural view. A reconfiguration of non-continuous components (e.g. components that show hybrid behavior themselves) or the reconfiguration via multiple layers in the architectural view requires additional modeling effort (see Section 3.2.7).

MDA Support   Although SAE AADL provides a modular, distributed model, the notion of threads and processes is not platform independent, so that the design is influenced by the process-view of a target platform. The other models are located on the PIM level.

CHARON, HyCharts, and HybridUML are the only approaches allowing an automatic implementation, whereby HybridUML implementations always require a multi-CPU system and still assume side-effects to consume no time. HyCharts change the model by adding additional behavior to provide an implementation. CHARON is restricted to simple, short side-effects as sensing, computation, and actuation are assumed to be performed within one period. The dynamic dependency graph respects just algebraic constraints, but as described in Section 2.4.3, the dependency relations between the variables used for the implementation of the differential constraints need to be respected, too.

As Masaccio models, which are on the PIM level, might be used to derive Giotto models, which are on the PSM level, these are the only approaches supporting the MDA process.

Support for Formal Analyses CHARON, Masaccio, HybridUML, HL^3, UML^h, HyROOM, and HyCharts have a formally defined semantics, but due to the assumption of zero-execution times or zero-reaction times, most of them are not implementable. CHARON is the only approach providing an implementable semantics. HyCharts are implementable after defining *relaxations* to the temporal specifications. They respect that idealized continuous behavior is not implementable on discrete computer systems. Further, CHARON provides a semantic definition of refinement. Ptolemy II even provides multiple semantics and supports their integration.

Automatic verification of the real-time behavior including the reconfiguration is supported by CHARON. It even supports hybrid modelchecking. Compositional modelchecking of real-time properties as presented in Section 2.3 is possible for CHARON and HyCharts in principle due to their definition of refinement. Schedulability analysis is supported by CHARON, Ptolemy II, and Time Weaver.

Although the approaches separate the architectural description from the behavioral description, they do not support the separated specification and verification of communication, real-time behavior and hybrid behavior and their later step-wise integration.

6.3   Conclusion

The discussions in this chapter point out that current approaches have drawbacks in modeling support, MDA support, support for formal analysis, or in multiple of these categories. Although many approaches enable ruling the complexity by a modular, component-based architecture and by behavioral models that support history and hierarchical and orthogonal states, our approach is the only one that supports reconfiguration via multiple hierarchical levels. This is supported by the additional high-level modeling construct of the implied state change for modeling reconfiguration. Further, our approach enables reconfiguration by adapting the structure instead of just exchanging whole models or blinding out unused parts of the system. This is enabled by associating whole configurations instead of single components to the system's discrete states.

None of the presented approach supports dynamic interfaces like our notion of interface state charts. Such an interface description is required to ensure consistent configurations and reconfiguration.

For the specification and implementation of real-time behavior, our approach supports all three layers of the MDA approach. The transformations between the MDA layers respect the specified real-time requirements appropriately.

The presented approaches either do not support formal analysis or this is restricted to simple models as it does not scale for complex systems. Our approach is the only one that integrates high-level models, specifying hybrid behavior and reconfiguration, in a well-structured approach for the verification of the real-time behavior of complex, distributed systems. We do not support hybrid modelchecking, but we ensure that embedding hybrid or continuous components does not invalidate the results of the real-time modelchecking.

Chapter 7

Conclusion and Future Work

In this work, we presented a UML-based language for modeling reconfigurable mechatronic systems. This language allows the specification of reconfiguration by integrating structure and behavior. One key issue is the description of a component's dynamic interface. It provides an abstraction of the detailed component's realization and thus, it simplifies analyses and enables the verification of complex systems. The latter one is supported by the integration of our approach with compositional real-time modelchecking.

The presented modeling language is not just a theoretical construct that provides a semantics that simplifies formal analyses – the detailed description how to implement the models shows that the semantics is implementable. When implementing these models, we follow the MDA approach. First, we worked out the concepts for the implementation and used them to generate the intermediate platform specific model. Thereby, we determine the scheduling parameters which ensure that all specified real-time requirements are met. The abstraction, provided by the description of the dynamic interfaces, helps to obtain implementations which are of manageable size despite of reconfiguration. After working out the concepts, the final mapping to source code of a target language is straight forward.

The tool integration of the CAE Toool *CAMeL-View* and the CASE Tool *Fujaba Real-Time Tool Suite* enables the application of our approach by continuing using well-approved tools. It does not only integrate models, but also the synthesized source code.

Although, we presented a seamless approach for modeling and implementing reconfigurable mechatronic systems and although we integrated this approach with compositional real-time modelchecking, new trends in software engineering become obvious which require extension of the presented work:

When changing behavior and structure of a system, reconfiguration is just the first step. A new trend deals with *compositional adaptation*, i.e. the behavior and the structure is changed, but the possible configurations are not all known at design time or their number is infinite. A first attempt to model compositional adaptation is given in [BG05]. There, *reconfiguration rules* which are based on graph transformation systems are introduced to specify compositional adaptation. Obviously, such a model also needs to be implemented, the reconfiguration rules need to be respected appropriately in the verification, and the model requires a formally defined semantics. This may be subject to future work.

Independent of the use of such reconfiguration rules, the verification should be extended to also respect the hybrid capabilities in the verification. In order to be scalable for complex systems, a compositional approach is required. Therefore, there is the need to apply hybrid modelchecking for the verification of a component and to extend the real-time coordination patterns to *hybrid coordination patterns*. In such a pattern, there are not just discrete signals transmitted between the communication partners, continuous values are also exchanged. An abstraction that may be useful for hybrid modelchecking could be to provide lower and upper bounds of the derivates of the continuous system parts.

Another open issue is how to instantiate the coordination patterns: It is neither required nor feasible to have active coordination patterns between all components of a system. In our application example, the coordination patterns just need to be instantiated if two shuttles are closed to each other. This issue is discussed in [Sch06].

One trend in software engineering is to specify possible scenarios and to synthesize the components' behaviors from these scenarios. In future work, this could be supported for real-time systems as we described in [GKB05] or for hybrid systems. Such a synthesis could be supported by the concepts of [UKM03] to identify unspecified behavior in the set of scenarios.

In order to improve modeling of controller-exchange, further fading should be supported. Instead of just allowing output cross-fading, support for input cross-fading could be useful. This leads to another topic which should be considered in future work: Our hybrid models should be analyzed for stability like for example in [SKK04].

Further improvements should respect dynamic qualities for profiles: In our example, the PositionControlWithPilotControl state has the highest quality. Thus, the profile that includes this state has also the highest quality, but as long as state VelocityControl is active, the switch to the profile that includes state PositionControlWithPilotControl does not lead to any benefit. It is just useful to switch to this profile, when the system is under position control. Thus, the profile should obtain a low quality as long as state VelocityControl is active and the quality should be increased if the system resides in state PositionControl.

When implementing a single component, we implement it for just one processor. An interesting extension would be to implement a component on a distributed, networked system. The determination of WCETs could be improved by respecting processor architectures and taking into account worst-case assumptions about pipelining, caching etc.

List of Figures

Bibliography

[ACH+95]   R. Alur, C. Courcoubetis, N. Halbwachs, T.A. Henzinger, P.-H. Ho, X. Nicollin, A. Olivero, J. Sifakis, and S. Yovine. The Algorithmic Analysis of Hybrid Systems. *Theoretical Computer Science*, 138(3-34), 1995.

[ADE+01]   R. Alur, T. Dang, J. Esposito, R. Fierro, Y. Hur, F. Ivancic, V. Kumar, I. Lee, P. Mishra, G. Pappas, and O. Sokolsky. Hierarchical Hybrid Modeling of Embedded Systems. In *First Workshop on Embedded Software*, 2001.

[ADF+01]   Tobias Amnell, Alexandre David, Elena Fersman, M. Oliver Möller Paul Pettersson, and Wany Yi. Tools for Real-Time UML: Formal Verification and Code Synthesis. In *Workshop on Specification, Implementation and Validation of Object-oriented Embedded Systems (SIVOES'2001)*, June 2001.

[AFP+02]   Tobias Amnell, Elena Fersman, Paul Pettersson, Hongyan Sun, and Wang Yi. Code Synthesis for Timed Automata. *Nordic Journal of Computing (NJC)*, 9(4), 2002.

[AGLS01]   Rajeev Alur, Radu Grosu, Insup Lee, and Oleg Sokolsky. Compositional Refinement of Hierarchical Hybrid Systems. In *Proceedings of the Fourth International Conference on Hybrid Systems: Computation and Control (HSCC'01)*, volume 2034 of *Lecture Notes in Computer Science*, pages 33–48. Springer-Verlag, 2001.

[AIK+03]   Rajeev Alur, Franjo Ivancic, Jesung Kim, Insup Lee, and Oleg Sokolsky. Generating Embedded Software from Hierarchical Hybrid Models. In *Proceedings of the 2003 ACM SIGPLAN conference on Language, compiler, and tool for embedded systems*, pages 171–182. ACM Press, 2003.

[AKZ96]   Maher Awad, Juha Kuusela, and Jurgen Ziegler. *Object-Oriented Technology for Real-Time Systems: A Practical Approach Using OMT and Fusion.* Prentice Hall, 1996.

[ASK04]   Aditya Agrawal, Gyula Simon, and Gabor Karsai. Semantic Translation of Simulink/Stateflow models to Hybrid Automata using Graph Transformations. In *International Workshop on Graph Transformation and Visual Modeling Techniques, Barcelona, Spain*, 2004.

[BBF+00] Greg Bollella, Ben Brosgol, Steve Furr, Savid Hardin, Peter Dibble, James Gosling, and Mark Turnbull. *The Real-Time Specification for Java^{TM}*. Addison-Wesley, 2000.

[BBHP04] Kirsten Berkenkötter, Stefan Bisanz, Ulrich Hannemann, and Jan Peleska. Executable HybridUML and its Application to Train Control Systems. In Hartmut Ehrig, Werner Damm, Jörg Desel, Martin Große-Rhode, Wolfgang Reif, Eckehard Schnieder, and Engelbert Westkämper, editors, *Integration of Software Specification Techniques for Applications in Engineering*, volume 3147 of *Lecture Notes in Computer Science*, pages 145–173. Springer-Verlag, 2004.

[BBP+02] K. Bender, M. Broy, I. Peter, A. Pretschner, and T. Stauner. Model based development of hybrid systems. In *Modelling, Analysis, and Design of Hybrid Systems*, volume 279 of *Lecture Notes on Control and Information Sciences*, pages 37–52. Springer-Verlag, July 2002.

[BBW00] Guillem Bernat, Alan Burns, and Andy Wellings. Portable Worst-Case Execution Time Analysis Using Java Byte Code. In *Proceedings of the 12th Euromicro Conference on Real-Time Systems (Euromicro-RTS 2000)*, 2000.

[BG03] Sven Burmester and Holger Giese. The Fujaba Real-Time Statechart PlugIn. In *Proc. of the Fujaba Days 2003, Kassel, Germany*, pages 1–8, October 2003.

[BG05] Sven Burmester and Holger Giese. Visual Integration of UML 2.0 and Block Diagrams for Flexible Reconfiguration in Mechatronic UML. In *Proc. of the IEEE Symposium on Visual Languages and Human-Centric Computing (VL/HCC'05), Dallas, Texas, USA*, pages 109–116. IEEE Computer Society Press, September 2005.

[BGGO04a] Sven Burmester, Matthias Gehrke, Holger Giese, and Simon Oberthür. Making Mechatronic Agents Resource-aware in order to Enable Safe Dynamic Resource Allocation. In B. Georgio, editor, *Proc. of Fourth ACM International Conference on Embedded Software 2004 (EMSOFT 2004), Pisa, Italy*, pages 175–183. ACM Press, September 2004.

[BGGO04b] Sven Burmester, Holger Giese, Alfonso Gambuzza, and Oliver Oberschelp. Partitioning and Modular Code Synthesis for Reconfigurable Mechatronic Software Components. In *Proc. of European Simulation and Modelling Conference (ESMc'2004), Paris, France*, pages 66–73, October 2004.

[BGH05a] Sven Burmester, Holger Giese, and Stefan Henkler. Visual model-driven development of software intensive systems: A survey of available techniques and tools. In *Proc. of the Workshop on Visual Modeling for Software Intensive Systems (VMSIS) at the the IEEE Symposium on Visual Languages and*

Human-Centric Computing (VL/HCC'05), Dallas, Texas, USA, pages 11–18, September 2005.

[BGH05b]   Sven Burmester, Holger Giese, and Martin Hirsch. Syntax and Semantics of Hybrid Components. Technical Report tr-ri-05-264, University of Paderborn, Paderborn, Germany, October 2005.

[BGH+05c]   Sven Burmester, Holger Giese, Martin Hirsch, Daniela Schilling, and Matthias Tichy. The Fujaba Real-Time Tool Suite: Model-Driven Development of Safety-Critical, Real-Time Systems. In *Proc. of the 27th International Conference on Software Engineering (ICSE), St. Louis, Missouri, USA*, pages 670–671, May 2005.

[BGHS04]   Sven Burmester, Holger Giese, Martin Hirsch, and Daniela Schilling. Incremental Design and Formal Verification with UML/RT in the FUJABA Real-Time Tool Suite. In *Proceedings of the International Workshop on Specification and vaildation of UML models for Real Time and embedded Systems, SVERTS2004, Satellite Event of the 7th International Conference on the Unified Modeling Language, UML2004*, pages 1–20, October 2004.

[BGK04]   Sven Burmester, Holger Giese, and Florian Klein. Design and Simulation of Self-Optimizing Mechatronic Systems with Fujaba and CAMeL. In *Proc. of the Fujaba Days 2004, Darmstadt, Germany*, pages 19–22, September 2004.

[BGM+06]   Sven Burmester, Holger Giese, Eckehard Münch, Oliver Oberschelp, Florian Klein, and Peter Scheideler. Tool Support for the Design of Self-Optimizing Mechatronic Multi-Agent Systems. *International Journal on Software Tools for Technology Transfer (STTT)*, 2006. (accepted).

[BGO04a]   Sven Burmester, Holger Giese, and Oliver Oberschelp. Hybrid UML Components for the Correct Design of Self-optimizing Mechatronic Systems. Technical Report tr-ri-03-246, University of Paderborn, Paderborn, Germany, January 2004.

[BGO04b]   Sven Burmester, Holger Giese, and Oliver Oberschelp. Hybrid UML Components for the Design of Complex Self-optimizing Mechatronic Systems. In *Proc. of 1st International Conference on Informatics in Control, Automation and Robotics (ICINCO 2004), Setubal, Portugal*, pages 222–229. IEEE, August 2004.

[BGO06]   Sven Burmester, Holger Giese, and Oliver Oberschelp. Hybrid UML Components for the Design of Complex Self-optimizing Mechatronic Systems. In José Braz, Helder Araújo, Alves Vieira, and Bruno Encarnaçao, editors, *Informatics in Control, Automation and Robotics I*, pages 281–288. Springer, 2006.

[BGS05]   Sven Burmester, Holger Giese, and Wilhelm Schäfer. Model-Driven Archi-
            tecture for Hard Real-Time Systems: From Platform Independent Models to
            Code. In *Proc. of the European Conference on Model Driven Architecture -
            Foundations and Applications (ECMDA-FA'05), Nürnberg, Germany*, pages
            25–40, November 2005.

[BGST05]   Sven Burmester, Holger Giese, Andreas Seibel, and Matthias Tichy. Worst-
            Case Execution Time Optimization of Story Patterns for Hard Real-Time
            Systems. In *Proc. of the 3rd International Fujaba Days 2005, Paderborn,
            Germany*, pages 71–78, September 2005.

[BGT05]   Sven Burmester, Holger Giese, and Matthias Tichy. Model-Driven Development
            of Reconfigurable Mechatronic Systems with Mechatronic UML. In *Model
            Driven Architecture: Foundations and Applications*, volume 3599 of *Lecture
            Notes in Computer Science (LNCS)*, pages 47–61. Springer-Verlag, August
            2005.

[BlLM02]   V. Del Bianco, l. Lavazza, and M. Mauri. Formalization of UML Statecharts
            for Real-Time Software Modeling. In *Proceedings of the 6th International
            Conference on Integrated Design and Process Technology, IDPT2002*, 2002.

[BO04]   Carsten Böke and Simon Oberthür. Flexible Resource Management - A
            framework for self-optimizing real-time systems. In *IFIP Working Conference
            on Distributed and Parallel Embedded Systems (DIPES2004), Toulouse, France*,
            August 2004.

[Boi05]   Vadim Boiko. Erweiterung des CAE-werkzeugs CAMeL-View um eine modulare
            Codegenerierung zur Unterstützung hybrider UML Komponenten, 2005.

[BR99]   Loic P. Briand and Daniel M. Roy. *Meeting Deadlines in Hard Real-Time
            Systems: The Rate Monotonic Approach*. IEEE Computer Press, 1999.

[Bri97]   Maria Elisabeth Brielmann. *Modellierung und Entwurf heterogener Systeme*.
            PhD thesis, University of Paderborn, Paderborn, Germany, 1997.

[Bur02]   Sven Burmester. Generierung von Java Real-Time Code für zeitbehaftete UML
            Modelle. Master's thesis, University of Paderborn, Department of Computer
            Science, Paderborn, Germany, September 2002.

[But97]   Giorgio C. Buttazzo. *Hard Real Time Computing Systems: Predictable Schedul-
            ing Algorithms and Applications*. Kluwer international series in engineering
            and computer science: Real-time systems. Kluwer Academic Publishers, 1997.

[BW01]   Alan Burns and Andy Wellings. *Real-Time Systems and Programming Lan-
            guages: Ada 95, Real-Time Java and Real-Time POSIX*. Addison-Wesley, 3rd
            edition, 2001.

[CBP+04]   Luca Carloni, Maria D. Di Benedetto, Roberto Passerone, Alessandro Pinto, and Alberto Sangiovanni-Vincentelli. *Modeling Techniques, Programming Languages and Design Toolsets for Hybrid Systems.* Project IST-2001-38314 COLUMBUS - Design of Embedded Controllers for Safety Critical Systems, WPHS: Hybrid System Modeling, July 2004. Version: 0.2, Deliverable number: DHS4-5-6.

[CUT02]   The OMG's Model Driven Architecture, January 2002.

[dAH01]   Luca de Alfaro and Thomas A. Heizinger. Interface Automata. In Volker Gruhn, editor, *Proceedings of the Joint 8th European Software Engineering Conference (ESEC) and 9th ACM SIGSOFT Symposium on the Foundation of Software Engineering (FSE-9), Vienna, Austria, September 10-14*, pages 109–120. ACM Press, 2001.

[Dit99]   Carsten Ditze. *Towards Operating System Synthesis.* PhD thesis, Department of Computer Science, University of Paderborn, Paderborn, Germany, 1999.

[DM01]   Alexandre David and M. Oliver Möller. From HUPPAAL to UPPAAL: A Translation from Hierarchical Timed Automata to Flat Timed Automata. Unpublished BRICS RS-01-11, Department of Computer Science, University of Aarhus, March 2001.

[DMY02]   Alexandre David, Oliver Möller, and Wang Yi. Formal Verification of UML Statecharts with Real-Time Extensions. In Ralf-Detler Kutsche and Herbert Weber, editors, *Proceedings of 5th International Conference on Fundamental Approaches to Software Engineering (FASE 2002)*, number 2306 in Lecture Notes in Computer Science, pages 218–232, Grenoble, France, 2002. Springer-Verlag.

[Dou]   Bruce Powel Douglass. Real-Time Design Patterns. Unpublished. (http://www.ilogix.com/whitepaper_PDFs/RTPatterns.pdf).

[dR03]   Dionisio de Niz and Raj Rajkumar. Time Weaver: A Software-Through-Models Framework for Embedded Real-Time Systems. In *Proceedings of the 2003 ACM SIGPLAN conference on Language, compiler, and tool for embedded systems*, pages 133–143. ACM Press, 2003.

[EKRNS00] Thilo Ernst, Clemens Klein-Robbenhaar, André Nordwig, and Tobias Schrag. Modellierung und Simulation hybrider Systeme mit Smile. *Informatik Forschung und Entwicklung*, 15(1):33–50, 2000.

[Erp00]   Edwin Erpenbach. *Compilation, Worst-Case Execution Times and Schedulability Analysis of Statechart Models.* PhD thesis, University of Paderborn, Department of Mathematics and Computer Science, February 2000.

[FdO99]   J.A. Ferreira and P. Estima de Oliveira. Modelling Hybrid Systems using Statecharts and Modelica. In *Proc. 7th IEEE International Conference on Emerging Technologies and Factory Automation, Barcelona (Spain)*, 1999.

[FGHL04]   Peter H. Feiler, David P. Gluch, John J. Hudak, and Bruce A. Lewis. Embedded Systems Architecture Analysis Using SAE AADL. Technical Report CMU/SEI-2004-TN-005, Carnegie Mellon University, June 2004.

[FGK+04]   Ursula Frank, Holger Giese, Florian Klein, Oliver Oberschelp, Andreas Schmidt, Bernd Schulz, Henner Vöcking, and Katrin Witting. *Selbstoptimierende Systeme des Maschinenbaus: Definitionen und Konzepte*. HNI-Verlagsschriftenreihe, Band 155, Paderborn, Germany, 2004.

[FJW97]   Viktor Friesen, Stefan Jähnichen, and Matthias Weber. Specification of Software Controlling a Discrete-Continuous Environment. In *Proceedings of the 1997 international conference on Software engineering, Boston, Massachusetts, United States*, 1997.

[FNW98]   Viktor Friesen, Andre Nordwig, and Matthias Weber. Object-Oriented Specification of Hybrid Systems Using UMLh and ZimOO. In *Proceedings of the 11th International Conference of Z Users on The Z Formal Specification Notation, Berlin, Germany*, volume 1493 of *Lecture Notes in Computer Science (LNCS)*, pages 328–346. Springer-Verlag, 1998.

[GB03]   Holger Giese and Sven Burmester. Real-Time Statechart Semantics. Technical Report tr-ri-03-239, University of Paderborn, Paderborn, Germany, June 2003.

[GBSO04]   Holger Giese, Sven Burmester, Wilhelm Schäfer, and Oliver Oberschelp. Modular Design and Verification of Component-Based Mechatronic Systems with Online-Reconfiguration. In *Proc. of 12th ACM SIGSOFT Foundations of Software Engineering 2004 (FSE 2004), Newport Beach, USA*, pages 179–188. ACM, November 2004.

[GH06]   Holger Giese and Martin Hirsch. Checking and Automatic Abstraction for Timed and Hybrid Refinement in Mechatronic UML. Technical Report tr-ri-05-266, University of Paderborn, Paderborn, Germany, 2006. (to appear).

[GHJV95]   E. Gamma, R. Helm, R. Johnson, and J. Vlissides. *Design Patterns: Elements of Reusable Object Oriented Software*. Addison-Wesley, Reading, MA, 1995.

[Gie03]   Holger Giese. A Formal Calculus for the Compositional Pattern-Based Design of Correct Real-Time Systems. Technical Report tr-ri-03-240, Computer Science Department, University of Paderborn, July 2003.

[GKB05]   Holger Giese, Florian Klein, and Sven Burmester. Pattern Synthesis from Multiple Scenarios for Parameterized Real-Timed UML models. In Stefan

Leue and Tarja Systä, editors, *Scenarios: Models, Algorithms and Tools*, volume 3466 of *Lecture Notes in Computer Science (LNCS)*, pages 193–211. Springer-Verlag, April 2005.

[GKWS03]   Zonghua Gu, Sharath Kodase, Shige Wang, and Kang G. Shin. A Model-Based Approach to System-Level Dependency and Real-Time Analysis of Embedded Software. In *The 9th IEEE Real-Time and Embedded Technology and Applications Symposium, Toronto, Canada*, May 2003.

[GMK02]   Ioannis Georgiadis, Jeff Magee, and Jeff Kramer. Self-organising Software Architectures for Distributed Systems. In *Proceedings of the first workshop on Self-healing systems, Charleston, South Carolina, USA*, pages 33–38. ACM Press, October 2002.

[Gom00]   Hassan Gomaa. *Designing Concurrent Distributed and Real Time Applications with UML*. Addison-Wesley, August 2000.

[GS04]   Holger Giese and Daniela Schilling. Towards the Automatic Verification of Inductive Invariants for Invinite State UML Models. Technical Report tr-ri-04-252, University of Paderborn, Paderborn, Germany, December 2004.

[GSB98]   Radu Grosu, Thomas Stauner, and Manfred Broy. A Modular Visual Model for Hybrid Systems. In *Formal Techniques in Real Time and Fault Tolerant Systems (FTRTFT'98)*. Springer-Verlag, 1998.

[GST⁺03]   Holger Giese, Daniela Schilling, Matthias Tichy, Sven Burmester, Wilhelm Schäfer, and Stephan Flake. Towards the Compositional Verification of Real-Time UML Designs. Technical Report tr-ri-03-241, University of Paderborn, Paderborn, Germany, July 2003.

[GTB⁺03]   Holger Giese, Matthias Tichy, Sven Burmester, Wilhelm Schäfer, and Stephan Flake. Towards the Compositional Verification of Real-Time UML Designs. In *Proc. of the European Software Engineering Conference (ESEC), Helsinki, Finland*, pages 38–47. ACM press, September 2003.

[Hah99]   Martin Hahn. *OMD - Ein Objektmodell für den Mechatronikentwurf*. PhD thesis, University of Paderborn, Paderborn, Germany, 1999.

[Har98]   D. Harel. *Modeling reactive systems with statecharts*. McGraw-Hill, 1998.

[Hen00]   Thomas A. Henzinger. Masaccio: A formal model for embedded components. In *Proceedings of the First IFIP International Conference on Theoretical Computer Science (TCS), Lecture Notes in Computer Science 1872, Springer-Verlag, 2000, pp. 549-563.*, 2000.

[HGK98]   P. Herrmann, G. Graw, and H. Krumm. Compositional Specification and
            Structured Verification of Hybrid Systems in cTLA. In *The First IEEE In-
            ternational Symposium on Object-Oriented Real-Time Distributed Computing,
            April 20 - 22, 1998*, page 335ff, Kyoto, Japan, 1998. IEEE Computer Press.

[HHK01]   Thomas A. Henzinger, Benjamin Horowitz, and Christoph M. Kirsch. Giotto:
            A Time-triggered Language for Embedded Programming. In *Proceedings of
            the IEEE 91:84-99, 2003. A preliminary version appeared in the Proceedings of
            the First International Workshop on Embedded Software (EMSOFT), Lecture
            Notes in Computer Science 2211, Springer-Verlag*, pages 166–184, 2001.

[HHWT95]   Thomas A. Henzinger, P.-H. Ho, and H. Wong-Toi. HyTech: The Next
            Generation. In *Proc. of the 16th IEEE Real-Time Symposium*. IEEE Computer
            Press, December 1995.

[HKSP02]   Thomas A. Henzinger, Christoph M. Kirsch, Marco A.A. Sanvido, and Wolf-
            gang Pree. From Control Models to Real-Time Code Using Giotto. In *IEEE
            Control Systems Magazine 23(1):50-64, 2003. A preliminary report on this
            work appeared in C.M. Kirsch, M.A.A. Sanvido, T.A. Henzinger, and W.
            Pree, A Giotto-based helicopter control system, Proceedings of the Second
            International Workshop on Embedded Software (EMSOFT), Lecture Notes in
            Computer Science 2491, Springer-Verlag, 2002, pp. 46-60.*, 2002.

[HKW04]   Guillaume Hutzler, Hanna Klaudel, and D. Y. Wang. Towards Timed Au-
            tomata and Multi-agent Systems. In *Formal Approaches to Agent-Based
            Systems: Third International Workshop, FAABS 2004, Greenbelt, MD*, vol-
            ume 3228 of *Lecture Notes in Computer Science (LNCS)*, pages 161–172.
            Springer-Verlag, April 2004.

[HLL+03]   Christopher Hylands, Edward Lee, Jie Liu, Xiaojun Liu, Stephen Neuendorffer,
            Yuhong Xiong, Yang Zhao, and Haiyang Zheng. Overview of the Ptolemy
            Project. TechReport UCB/ERL M03/25, Department of Electrical Engineering
            and Computer Science, University of California, Berkeley, July 2003.

[HNSY92]   Thomas A. Henzinger, Xavier Nicollin, Joseph Sifakis, and Sergio Yovine.
            Symbolic Model Checking for Real-Time Systems. In *Proc. of IEEE Symposium
            on Logic in Computer Science*. IEEE Computer Press, 1992.

[Hoh04]   Wolfram Hohmann. Supporting Model-Based Development with Unambiguous
            Specifications, Formal Verification and Correct-by-Construction Embedded
            Software. In *Proc. of SAE World Congress 2004*, 2004.

[Hon98]   U. Honekamp. *IPANEMA - Verteilte Echtzeit-Informationsverarbeitung in
            mechatronischen Systemen*. PhD thesis, University of Paderborn, 1998.

[HP98]   David Harel and Michael Politi. *Modeling Reactive Systems with Statecharts: The STATEMATE Approach.* McGraw-Hill, 1998.

[HPSS87]   David Harel, Amir Pnueli, Jeanette P. Schmidt, and R. Sherman. On the Formal Semantics of Statecharts. In *Proceedings of the 2nd IEEE Symposium on Logic in Computer Science (LICS), Ithaca, NY, USA*, pages 54–64, 1987.

[HSG+01]   Pao-Ann Hsiung, Feng-Shi Su, Chuen-Hau Gao, Shu-Yu Cheng, and Yu-Ming Chang. Verifiable Embedded Real-Time Application Framework. In *Seventh Real-Time Technology and Applications Symposium (RTAS '01), Taipei, Taiwan*, 2001.

[HVB+05]   Christian Henke, Henner Vöcking, Joachim Böcker, Norbert Fröhleke, and Ansgar Trächtler. Convoy Operation of Linear Motor Driven Railway Vehicles. In *Proc. of the Fifth International Symposium on Linear Drives for Industry Applications, Hyogo, Japan*, September 2005.

[ILM92]   R. Isermann, K.-H. Lachmann, and D. Matko. *Adaptive Control Systems.* Prentice Hall, Herfordshire, 1992.

[JM94]   F. Jahanian and A.K. Mok. Modechart: A Specification Language for Real-Time Systems. In *IEEE Transactions on Software Engineering, Vol. 20*, December 1994.

[Ken02]   Stuart Kent. Model Driven Engineering. In M. Butler, L. Petre, and K. Sere, editors, *Proceedings of the Third International Conference on Integrated Formal Methods (IFM 2002), Turku, Finland*, volume 2335 of *Lecture Notes in Computer Science*, pages 286 – 298. Springer-Verlag, May 2002.

[KMR02]   A. Knapp, S. Merz, and C. Rauh. *Model Checking timed UML State Machines and Collaborations.* 7th International Symposium on Formal Techniques in Real-Time and Fault Tolerant Systems (FTRTFT 2002), Oldenburg, September 2002, Lecture Notes in Computer Science volume 2469 pages 395-414. Springer-Verlag, 2002.

[KNNZ00]   H.J. Köhler, U. Nickel, J. Niere, and A. Zündorf. Integrating UML Diagrams for Production Control Systems. In *Proc. of the 22nd International Conference on Software Engineering (ICSE), Limerick, Ireland*, pages 241–251. ACM Press, 2000.

[KP92]   Y. Kesten and A. Pnueli. Timed and Hybrid Statecharts and their Textual Representation. In J. Vytopil, editor, *Formal Techniques in Real-Time and Fault-Tolerant Systems*, volume 571 of *Lecture Notes in Computer Science*. Springer-Verlag, 1992.

[KPSB04]   Ingolf Krüger, Wolfgang Prenninger, Robert Sandner, and Manfred Broy. De-
           velopment of Hierarchical Broadcasting Software Architectures Using UML 2.0.
           In Hartmut Ehrig, Werner Damm, Jörg Desel, Martin Große-Rhode, Wolfgang
           Reif, Eckehard Schnieder, and Engelbert Westkämper, editors, *Integration of
           Software Specification Techniques for Applications in Engineering*, volume 3147
           of *Lecture Notes in Computer Science (LNCS)*, pages 29–47. Springer-Verlag,
           2004.

[Kud05]   Margarete Kudak. Modulare Echtzeitverifikation hybrider UML-Komponenten.
           Master's thesis, University of Paderborn, Department of Computer Science,
           Paderborn, Germany, 2005.

[Lam93]   Leslie Lamport. Hybrid Systems in TLA+. In *Hybrid Systems*, volume 736 of
           Lecture Notes in Computer Science (LNCS), pages 77–102. Springer-Verlag,
           1993.

[Leu98]   Hing Leung. On finite automata with limited nondeterminism. *Acta Infor-
           matica*, 35(7):595–624, 1998.

[LPY97]   K. Larsen, P. Pettersson, and W. Yi. UPPAAL in a Nutshell. *Springer
           International Journal of Software Tools for Technology*, 1(1), 1997.

[LQV01]   Luigi Lavazza, Garbiele Quaroni, and Matteo Venturelli. Combining UML
           and formal notations for modelling real-time systems. In Volker Gruhn, editor,
           *Proceedings of the Joint 8th European Software Engineering Conference (ESEC)
           and 9th ACM SIGSOFT Symposium on the Foundation of Software Engineering
           (FSE-9), Vienna, Austria, September 10-14*, pages 196–206. ACM Press, 2001.

[LSV01]   Nancy Lynch, Roberto Segala, and Frits Vaandrager. Hybrid I/O Automata
           Revisited. In *Proceedings of the 4th International Workshop on Hybrid Systems:
           Computation and Control (HSCC 2001), Rome, Italy, March 28-30, 2001*,
           volume 2034 of *Lecture Notes in Computer Science*, pages 403–417. Springer-
           Verlag, 2001.

[MB95]   Pieter J. Mosterman and Gautam Biswas. Modeling Discontinuous Behavior
           with Hybrid Bond Graphs. In *Proc. of the Intl. Conference on Qualitative
           Reasoning, Amsterdam, the Netherlands*, pages 139–147, May 1995.

[MB98]   Pieter J. Mosterman and Gautam Biswas. A Theory of Discontinuities in
           Physical System Models. *Journal of the Franklin Institute*, 334B(6):401–439,
           January 1998.

[MKH03]   Jamison Masse, Saehwa Kim, and Seongsoo Hong. Tool Set Implementation for
           Scenario-based Multithreading of UML-RT Models and Experimental Valida-
           tion. In *The 9th IEEE Real-Time and Embedded Technology and Applications
           Symposium, Toronto, Canada*, May 2003.

[MLLG01] Grant Martin, Luciano Lavagno, and Jean Louis-Guerin. Embedded UML: a merger of real-time UML and co-design. In *Proceedings of the ninth international symposium on Hardware/software codesign, Copenhagen, Denmark*, pages 23–28, 2001.

[NSZ03] Ulrich A. Nickel, Wilhelm Schäfer, and Albert Zündorf. Integrative Specification of Distributed Production Control Systems for Flexible Automated Manufacturing. In M. Nagl and B. Westfechtel, editors, *DFG Workshop: Modelle, Werkzeuge und Infrastrukturen zur Unterstützung von Entwicklungsprozessen*, pages 179–195. Wiley-VCH Verlag GmbH and Co. KGaA, 2003.

[Obj03a] Object Management Group. *MDA Guide Version 1.0*, May 2003. Document omg/2003-05-01.

[Obj03b] Object Management Group. *UML for System Engineering, Request for Proposal*, March 2003. Document ad/03-03-41.

[Obj05a] Object Management Group. *Systems Modeling Language (SysML) Specification, Version 1.0 alpha*, November 2005. Document ad/05-11-05.

[Obj05b] Object Management Group. *UML 2.0 Superstructure Specification*, August 2005. Document ptc/05-07-04.

[Obj05c] Object Management Group. *UML Profile for Scheduling, Performance, and Time Specification, Version 1.1*, January 2005. Document formal/05-01-02.

[Oga87] Katsuhiko Ogata. *Discrete-Time Control Systems*. Prentice Hall, 1987.

[Oga02] Katsuhiko Ogata. *Modern Control Engineering*. Prentice Hall, 2002.

[OGBG04] Oliver Oberschelp, Alfonso Gambuzza, Sven Burmester, and Holger Giese. Modular Generation and Simulation of Mechatronic Systems. In *Proc. of the 8th World Multi-Conference on Systemics, Cybernetics and Informatics (SCI), Orlando, USA*, pages 1–6, July 2004.

[PAS94] A. Peron and A.Maggiolo-Schettini. Transitions as Interrupts: A New Semantics for Timed Statecharts. In *In Proceedings of TACS '94, volume 789 of Lecture Notes in Computer Science, Springer-Verlag*, 1994.

[PB00] Peter P. Puschner and Alan Burns. Guest Editorial: A Review of Worst-Case Execution-Time Analysis. *Real-Time Systems*, 18(2/3):115–128, May 2000.

[PI01] Carlos Puchol and Subramanian K. Iyer. The MacBeth Specification, Modeling and Programming Language. In *Seventh Real-Time Technology and Applications Symposium (RTAS '01), Taipei, Taiwan*, May 2001.

[PMS95]   C. Puchol, A.K. Mok, and D.A. Stuart. Compiling Modechart Specifications. In
           16th IEEE Real-Time Systems Symposium (RTSS '95), Pisa, Italy, December
           1995.

[RR03]   Franz Josef Rammig and Carsten Rust. Modeling of Dynamically Modifiable
           Embedded Real-Time Systems. In *9th IEEE International Workshop on
           Object-oriented Real-time Dependable Systems (WORDS 2003F),* October
           2003.

[RR04]   Carsten Rust and Franz Josef Rammig. A Petri Net Based Approach for the
           Design of Dynamically Modifiable Embedded Systems. In Bernd Kleinjohann,
           editor, *Design Methods and Applications for Distributed Embedded Systems,*
           Proc. IFIP TC 10 Conference DIPES 2004. IFIP WG 10.5, Kluwer Academic
           Publishers, 23 - 26 August 2004.

[RSAT00]   C. Rust, F. Stappert, P. Altenbernd, and J. Tacken. From High-Level Specifi-
           cations down to Software Implementations of Parallel Embedded Real-Time
           Systems. In *Proceedings of the conference on Design, automation and test in
           Europe, Paris, France,* pages 686–691. ACM Press, 2000.

[Sch05a]   Bernhard Schätz. Interface Descriptions for Embedded Components. In
           *3rd Workshop on Object-oriented Modeling of Embedded Real-Time Systems,
           Paderborn, Germany,* October 2005.

[Sch05b]   Matthias Schwarz. Mechatronic UML Components for Flexible Resource
           Management Systems. Master's thesis, University of Paderborn, Department
           of Computer Science, Paderborn, Germany, November 2005.

[Sch06]   Daniela Schilling. *Software-Verifikation Mechatronischer Systeme.* PhD thesis,
           University of Paderborn, 2006. (to appear).

[Sei05]   Andreas Seibel. Story Diagramme für Eingebettete Echtzeitsysteme, February
           2005.

[SGW94]   Bran Selic, Garth Gullekson, and Paul Ward. *Real-Time Object-Oriented
           Modeling.* John Wiley & Sons, Inc., 1994.

[SKK04]   A. Stathaki, F. N. Koumboulis, and R. E. King. An Application of Logic-Based
           Switching for a Class of Hybrid Industrial Controllers. In *12th Mediterranean
           Conference on Control and Automation, Kusadasi, Aydin, Turkey,* June 2004.

[SKW00]   M. Saksena, P. Karvelas, and Y. Wang. Automatic Synthesis of Multi-Tasking
           Implementations from Real-Time Object-Oriented Models. In *Proceedings
           of the Third IEEE International Symposium on Object-Oriented Real-Time
           Distributed Computing,* Newport Beach, California, 2000. IEEE Computer
           Press.

[SPP01]   T. Stauner, A. Pretschner, and I. Péter. Approaching a Discrete-Continuous
            UML: Tool Support and Formalization. In *Proc. UML'2001 workshop on Prac-
            tical UML-Based Rigorous Development Methods – Countering or Integrating
            the eXtremists*, pages 242–257, Toronto, Canada, October 2001.

[SR98]   Bran Selic and Jim Rumbaugh. Using UML for Modeling Complex Real-Time
            Systems. Techreport, ObjectTime Limited, 1998.

[Sta01]   Thomas Stauner. *Systematic Development of Hybrid Systems*. PhD thesis,
            Technische Universität München, 2001.

[Tac01]   Jürgen Tacken. *Durchgängiger Entwurf eingebetteter Realzeitsysteme*. PhD
            thesis, University of Paderborn, Paderborn, Germany, 2001.

[TBA04]   Bedir Tekinerdogan, Sevcan Bilir, and Cem Abatlevi. Integrating Platform
            Selection Rules in the Model Driven Architecture Approach. In *Proc. of Model
            Driven Architecture: Foundations and Applications (MDAFA 2004), Linköping,
            Sweden*, June 2004.

[UKM03]   Sebastian Uchitel, Jeff Kramer, and Jeff Magee. Behaviour Model Elaboration
            using Partial Labelled Transition Systems. In *Proc. of the European Software
            Engineering Conference (ESEC), Helsinki, Finland*, pages 19–27. ACM press,
            September 2003.

[Vöc03]   Henner Vöcking. Multirate-Verfahren und Umschaltstrategien für verteilte
            Reglersysteme. Master's thesis, University of Paderborn, 2003.

[YMS95]   Jin Yang, A.K. Mok, and D. Stuart. A new generation modechart verifier. In
            Real-Time Technology and Applications Symposium, Chicago, Illinois, May
            1995.

[Zün02]   Albert Zündorf. *Rigorous Object Oriented Software Development*. Habilitation-
            Thesis Version 0.3, University of Paderborn, 2002.

Index

Appendix A

Formalization

In Chapter 3, we presented our modeling approach to specify structure and behavior of reconfigurable mechatronic systems. In order to enable automatic code generation as presented in Chapter 4 and to enable automatic analysis techniques as outlined in section 3.2.6, a formally defined semantics is required. Sections A.1 – A.4 define the syntax and formal semantics of hybrid components and hybrid reconfiguration charts. Basically, this is taken from [BGH05b] which extends the formalization from [GBS004] and integrates it with formalization from [BGO04a]. Section A.5 integrates syntax and semantics with our compositional modelchecking approach first presented in [GTB$^+$03].

A.1 Prerequisites: Formal Definitions

This section defines the employed basic mathematical notations:

We use $\mathbb{R}$ to denote the set of the real numbers, $\mathbb{N}_0$ to denote the natural numbers including 0, $[a, b]$ with $a, b \in A$ and $a \leq b$ to denote the interval of all elements $c \in A$ with $a \leq c \leq b$, $\wp(A)$ to denote the power set of A, and $[A \rightarrow B]$ and $[A \rightharpoonup B]$ to denote the set of total resp. partial functions from A to B. $EQ(V_l, V_r)$ denotes the set of all equations of the form $v_l = f^i(v_r^1, ..., v_r^n)$ with operations f^i of arity n and left- and right-hand side variables of the equation $v_l \in V_l$, $v_r^1, ..., v_r^n \in V_r$. $COND(V)$ denotes the set of all conditions over variables of V. The set of possible constants and operations is named OP. The set of possible constants is named OP_{const}.

As a special case we assume a set of operations $\{\perp_i\}$ which do not explicitly define for an equation $v_l = \perp_i(v_r^1, ..., v_r^n)$ any specific restrictions on the relation between the input and output trajectories. The set of all these operations is denoted by $OP_\perp$.

Other than the vector equations usually employed by control engineers, we employ a set of variables V to denote each single value and describe the mapping by a function $[V \rightarrow \mathbb{R}]$. All values of a vector of the length n can be represented in a similar fashion as $[[0, n] \rightarrow \mathbb{R}]$.

$f \otimes g$ further denotes the composition of the two functions $f : A_1 \rightarrow B_1$ and $g : A_2 \rightarrow B_2$ with disjoint definition sets $A_1 \cap A_2 = \emptyset$ defined by $(f \otimes g)(x)$ equals $f(x)$ for $x \in A_1$ and $g(x)$ for $x \in A_2$. The combination of two updates $a_1 \oplus a_2$ further denotes the composition of the two functionals $a_1 : [A_1 \rightarrow B_1] \rightarrow [A'_1 \rightarrow B'_1]$ and $a_2 : [A_2 \rightarrow B_2] \rightarrow [A'_2 \rightarrow B'_2]$ with disjoint sets $A_1 \cap A_2 = \emptyset$ and $A'_1 \cap A'_2 = \emptyset$ defined by $(a_1 \oplus a_2)(x \otimes y) := a_1(x) \otimes a_2(y)$.

A.2   Flat behavioral models

In this section, the syntax and semantics of hybrid reconfiguration automata are specified. They are the basis for hybrid reconfiguration charts. Therefore, we first define the syntax and semantics of a continuous model in Section A.2.1. This is used to define hybrid automata (Section A.2.2), which will be the base for the definition of hybrid reconfiguration automata (Section A.2.3). The definitions are extensions of the ones from [GBSO04]. The applied formal mathematical definitions are defined in Section A.1.

A.2.1   Continuous Behavior

In our example, the continuous feedback-controller components VelocityControl, PositionControl, PilotControl, and Sum are used. Their behavior is usually specified by means of differential equations in form of block diagrams as described in Section 2.4. Such block diagrams are formalized using the following concept of a continuous block.

Syntax

A continuous block provides a sufficient syntactical structure for the employed concept of differential equations. Its sytax is defined by Definition 1.

Definition 1 *A continuous block M is described by a 7-tuple $(V^x, V^u, V^y, F, G, C, X^0)$ with V^x the state variables, V^u the input variables, and V^y the output variables. For the implicitly defined state flow variables $V^{\dot{x}}$ and auxiliary variables $V^a = V^y \cap V^u$, the set of equations $F \subseteq EQ(V^{\dot{x}} \cup V^a, V^x \cup V^u \cup V^a)$ describes the flow of the state variables, the set of equations $G \subseteq EQ(V^y \cup V^a, V^x \cup V^u \cup V^a)$ determines the output variables, and $X^0 \subseteq [V^x \rightarrow \mathbb{R}]$ the set of initial states. The invariant C with $C \in COND(V^x)$ is further used to determine the set of valid states.*

A block M is only *well-formed* when for the system of differential equations $F \cup G$ holds that there are no cyclic dependencies, no double assignments, all undefined referenced variables are contained in $V^u - V^y$, and a value is assigned to all state variables ($V^{\dot{x}}$) and output variables (V^y).

To define a proper notion of refinement later in Definition 13 in Section A.2.3, we denote dependencies between input and output variables using $D(M) \subseteq V^u \times V^y$. The external visible dependencies $D^e(M)$ are accordingly defined as $D^e(M) := D(M) \cap ((V^u - V^y) \times (V^y - V^u))$.

Definition 2 *The interface $I(M)$ of a continuous block M is defined as the external visible input and output variables $(V^u - V^y, V^y - V^u)$.*

We can compose two continuous models if their variable sets are not overlapping and the resulting sets of equations are well formed as follows:

Definition 3 *The* composition *of two continuous models* $M_1 = (V_1^x, V_1^u, V_1^y, F_1, G_1, C_1, X_1^0)$ *and* $M_2 = (V_2^x, V_2^u, V_2^y, F_2, G_2, C_2, X_2^0)$ *denoted by* $M_1 \| M_2$ *is again a continuous model* $M = (V^x, V^u, V^y, F, G, C, X^0)$ *with* $V^x := V_1^x \cup V_2^x$, $V^u := V_1^u \cup V_2^u$, $V^y := V_1^y \cup V_2^y$, $F := F_1 \cup F_2$, $G := G_1 \cup G_2$, C *is derived from* C_1 *and* C_2 *as* $C = \{(x_1 \otimes x_2) | x_1 \in C_1 \wedge x_2 \in C_2\}$, *and the set of initial states is* $X^0 = \{((l_1, l_2), (x_1 \otimes x_2)) | (l_1, x_1) \in X_1^0 \wedge (l_2, x_2) \in X_2^0\}$.

$M_1 \| M_2$ is well-formed iff $V_1^x \cap V_2^x = \emptyset$, $V_1^u \cap V_2^u = \emptyset$, $V_1^y \cap V_2^y = \emptyset$, and $F \cup G$ are well-formed. A composition is *consistent* if the resulting continuous model is well-formed.

Semantics

The state space of a continuous behavior is $X = [V^x \rightarrow \mathbb{R}]$ which describes all possible assignments for the state variables. A trajectory $\rho_u : [0, \infty] \rightarrow [V^x \rightarrow \mathbb{R}]$ for the set of differential equations F and input $u : [0, \infty] \rightarrow [V^u \rightarrow \mathbb{R}]$ with $\rho_u(0) = x$ for the current continuous state $x \in X$ and $\rho_u(t) \in C$ for all $t \in [0, \infty]$ describes a valid behavior of the continuous system. The output variables V^y are determined by $\theta_u : [0, \infty] \rightarrow [V^y \rightarrow \mathbb{R}]$ using G analogously. The semantics for a continuous model M is given by all possible triples of environment and system trajectories (u, ρ_u, θ_u) denoted by $[\![M]\!]$.

A.2.2   Hybrid Automata

Before defining the syntax and semantics of a hybrid reconfiguration automaton, like for example the one depicted in Figure 3.5, we define the syntax and semantics of a standard hybrid automaton with static interfaces similar to hybrid I/O automata [LSV01].

Syntax

The syntax of a hybrid automaton is defined by Definition 4, its interface by Definition 5:

Definition 4 *A* hybrid automaton *is described by a 6-tuple* (L, D, I, O, T, S^0) *with* L *a finite set of locations,* D *a function over* L *which assigns to each* $l \in L$ *a continuous model* $D(l) = (V^x, V^u, V^y, F(l), G(l), C(l), X^0(l))$ *(cf. Definition 1) with identical variable sets,* I *a finite set of input signals,* O *a finite set of output signals,* T *a finite set of transitions, and a set of initial states* $S^0 \subseteq \{(l, x) | l \in L \wedge x \in X^0(l)\}$. *For any transition* $(l, g, g', a, l') \in T$ *holds that* $l \in L$ *is the source-location,* $g \in COND(V^x \cup V^u)$ *the continuous guard,* $g' \in \wp(I \cup O)$ *the I/O-guard,* $a \in [[V^x \rightarrow \mathbb{R}] \rightarrow [V^x \rightarrow \mathbb{R}]]$ *the continuous update, and* $l' \in L$ *the target-location. For every* $l \in L$ *we require that* $D(l)$ *is well-formed.*

Definition 5 *The* interface $I(M)$ *of a hybrid automaton* M *is defined as the external visible event sets and input and output variables* $(I - O, O - I, V^u - V^y, V^y - V^u)$.

Note that the presented definition of a hybrid automaton easily permits to still employ the concepts of real-time statecharts such as clocks. We simply have to define clock variables v_i whose values are determined by equations $\dot{v}_i = 1$ in F to encode this feature into a hybrid automaton.

The parallel composition of two hybrid automata is defined as follows:

Definition 6 *For two hybrid automata M_1 and M_2 the parallel composition $(M_1\|M_2)$ results in a hybrid automaton $M = (L, D, I, O, T, S^0)$ with $L = L_1 \times L_2$, $D(l, l') = D_1(l)\|D_2(l')$, $I = I_1 \cup I_2$, $O = O_1 \cup O_2$. The resulting transition relation is $T = \{((l_1, l_2), g_1 \wedge g_2, g_1^i \cup g_2^i, (a_1 \oplus a_2), (l_1', l_2'))|(l_1, g_1, g_1^i, u_1, l_1') \in T_1 \wedge (l_2, g_2, g_2^i, u_2, l_2') \in T_2 \wedge g_1^i \cap (I_2 \cup O_2) = g_2^i \cap (I_1 \cup O_1)\} \cup \{((l_1, l_2), g_1, g_1^i, u_1, (l_1', l_2))|(l_1, g_1, g_1^i, u_1, l_1') \in T_1 \wedge g_1^i \cap (I_2 \cup O_2) = \emptyset\} \cup \{((l_1, l_2), g_2, g_2^i, u_2, (l_1, l_2'))| (l_2, g_2, u_2, l_2') \in T_2 \wedge g_2^i \cap (I_1 \cup O_1) = \emptyset\}. S^0 \text{ is defined as } S_1^0 \times S_2^0.$*

The automaton M is only well-defined when for all reachable $(l, l') \in L$ holds that $D((l, l'))$ is well-formed and the internal signal sets are disjoint $((O_1 \cap I_1) \cap (O_2 \cap I_2) = \emptyset)$. The composition of hybrid automata is only *consistent* when the resulting automaton is well-defined.

In order to abstract from signals –e.g. signals that are exchanged between automata– we define the *hiding of signals* as in Definition 7 which is taken from [BGO04a].

Definition 7 *For a hybrid automaton $M = (L, D, I, O, T, S^0)$ the* hiding *of some signals $A \subseteq I \cup O$ denoted by $M\backslash_A$ is defined as the hybrid automaton $M' = (L, D, I', O', T', S^0)$ with $I' = I - A$, $O' = O - A$, and $T' = \{(l, g, g^i - A, u, l)|(l, g, g^i, u, l) \in T\}$.*

Semantics

For $X = [V^x \to \mathbb{R}]$, the set of possible continuous state variable bindings, the inner state of a hybrid automaton can be described by a pair $(l, x) \in L \times X$. There are two possible ways of state modifications: Either by firing an instantaneous transition $t \in T$ changing the location as well as the state variables or by residing in the current location which consumes time and alters just the control variables.

When staying in state (l, x), firing an instantaneous transition $t = (l', g, g^i, a, l'')$ is done iff

- the transitions source location equals the current location: $l = l'$,

- the continuous guard is fulfilled: $g(x \otimes u) = \text{true}$ for $u \in [V^u \to \mathbb{R}]$ the current input variable binding,

- the I/O-guard is true for the chosen input and output signal sets $i \subseteq I$ and $o \subseteq O$: $i \cup o = g^i$, and

- the continuous update still fulfills the invariant of the target location $a(x) \in C(l'')$.

The resulting state will be $(l'', a(x))$ and we note this firing by $(l, x) \rightarrow_{(i \cup o)} (l'', a(x))$. Iff no instantaneous transition can fire, the hybrid automaton resides in the current location l for a non-negative and non-zero time delay $\delta > 0$. Let $\rho_u : [0, \delta] \rightarrow [V^x \rightarrow \mathbb{R}]$ be a trajectory for the differential equations $F(l)$ and the external input $u : [0, \delta] \rightarrow [V^u - V^y \rightarrow \mathbb{R}]$ with $\rho_u(0) = x$. The state for all $t \in [0, \delta]$ will be $(l, \rho_u(t))$. The output variables $V^y - V^u$ and internal variables $V^y \cap V^u$ are determined by $\theta_u : [0, \delta] \rightarrow [V^y \rightarrow \mathbb{R}]$ using $G(l)$ analogously. We additionally require that for all $t \in [0, \delta]$ holds that $\rho_u(t) \in C(l)$.

The trace semantics is thus given by all possible infinite execution sequences $(u_0, l_0, \rho_{u_0}^0, \theta_{u_0}^0, \delta_0) \rightarrow_{e_0} (u_1, l_1, \rho_{u_1}^1, \theta_{u_1}^1, \delta_1) \ldots$ denoted by $[\![M]\!]_t$ where all $(l_i, \rho_{u_i}^i(\delta_i)) \rightarrow_{e_i} (l_{i+1}, \rho_{u_{i+1}}^{i+1}(0))$ are valid instantaneous transition executions.

Other aspects of hybrid behavior, such as zeno behavior and the distinction between *urgent* and *non-urgent* transitions, are omitted here. A suitable formalization can be found, e.g., in [HHWT95].

A.2.3 Hybrid Reconfiguration Automata

In this section, syntax and semantics of hybrid reconfiguration automata, like the one from Figure 3.5, are defined formally.

Syntax

We define the syntax of hybrid reconfiguration charts as in Definition 8.

Definition 8 *A hybrid reconfiguration automaton is described by a 6-tuple (L, D, I, O, T, S^0) with L a finite set of locations, D a function over L which assigns to each $l \in L$ a continuous model, $D(l) = (V^x(l), V^u(l), V^y(l), F(l), G(l), C(l), X^0(l))$ conf. to Definition 1, I a finite set of input signals, O a finite set of output signals, T a finite set of transitions, and $S^0 \subseteq \{(l, x) | l \in L \wedge x \in X(l)\}$ the set of initial states. For any transition $(l, g, g^i, a, l') \in T$ holds that $l \in L$ is the source-location, $g \in COND(V^x(l) \cup V^u(l))$ the continuous guard, $g^i \in \wp(I \cup O)$ the I/O-guard, $a \in [[V^x(l) \rightarrow \mathbb{R}] \rightarrow [V^x(l') \rightarrow \mathbb{R}]]$ the continuous update, and $l' \in L$ the target-location. For every $l \in L$ we require that $D(l)$ is well-formed.*

The automaton additionally allows that each location has its own variable sets. We use V^x to denote the union of all $V^x(l)$. V^u and V^y are derived analogously. We further use $V^x(F(l))$ to denote the *state variable set*. All assigned output variables are analogously named *provided output variable set* $(V^y(F(l) \cup G(l)))$ and all input variables employed are named *required input variable set* $(V^u(F(l) \cup G(l)))$.

Definition 9 *The (static) interface $I(M)$ of a hybrid reconfiguration automaton M is defined as the external visible event sets and input and output variables $(I - O, O - I, V^u - V^y, V^y - V^u)$.*

The parallel composition follows directly from the non reconfigurable case. In the case of hybrid reconfiguration automata, a correct parallel composition has to ensure that for all reachable $(l, l') \in L$ holds that $D((l, l'))$ does not contain cyclic dependencies.

Additional Terms Further, we define the terms *fading location* and *regular location* in Definition 10 and *passive location* in Definition 11 similar to the ones presented in [BGO04a]. The fading locations are inspired by the idea of [LSV01] and represent fading transitions as time consuming intermediate states.

Definition 10 *For a hybrid reconfiguration automaton $M = (L, D, I, O, T, S^0)$, a location $l_f \in L$ with $D(l_f) = (V^x(l_f), V^u(l_f), V^y(l_f), F(l_f), G(l_f), C(l_f), X^0(l_f))$ is a* fading location *iff*

- *the invariant consists of just one inequality with respect to the variable v and an upper bound d_{max}: $C(l_f) \equiv (v \leq d_{max})$,*

- *v is a clock: $\exists v \in V^x(l_f)$ with $(\dot{v} = 1) \in F(l_f)$,*

- *v is reset to zero when entering l_f: for all $(l, g, g', a, l_f) \in T$ holds that $(v = 0) \in a$,*

- *exactly one transition exists leaving l_f: $|\{(l_f, g, g', a, l')|(l_f, g, g', a, l') \in T\}| = 1$, and*

- *for this transition holds $g \equiv d_{min} \leq v \leq d_{max}$, $g' = true$, and $a = Id$.*

All non fading locations are regular locations.

Definition 11 *For a hybrid reconfiguration automaton $M = (L, D, I, O, T, S^0)$ a regular location $l_p \in L$ is a* passive location *iff the location and all transitions leaving it have no continuous constraints.*

Semantics

The semantics can be derived from the hybrid automata semantics (see Section A.2.2) by always taking into account the location dependent notion $V^x(l)$ etc. instead of the location independent V^x.

Interface Automata

While the previously outlined concept of the hybrid automaton (see Section A.2.2) permits to model and formalize static structures with static interfaces that describe hybrid behavior, advanced mechatronic systems in contrast integrate complex reconfiguration scenarios which cannot be modeled in an appropriate manner with static interfaces (cf. [GBSO04]). If we thus consider *dynamic interfaces*, we also have to address the resulting problems that receiving and sending of signals as well as reading or writing the continuous variables has to be done in a coordinated fashion as otherwise a consistent behavior cannot be guaranteed. As reading from a currently undefined continuous out variable results in unpredictable and therefore unsafe control behavior, this kind of inconsistency must be excluded for mechatronic systems.

As described in Section 3.2.3, we face the problem by the introduction of interface automata. The externally relevant behavior, covered by the interface automaton, only includes the real-time behavior as well as the state-dependent continuous interface. Therefore, the notion of an interface automaton is restricted as follows:

Definition 12 *A hybrid automaton* $M = (L, D, I, O, T, S^0)$ *is an* interface automaton *iff*

- *for its continuous part D holds that the set of auxiliary variables is empty: $V^y \cap V^u = \emptyset$,*

- *all $v \in V^x$ are clocks: $\dot{v} = 1$,*

- *the update a for any transition (l, g, g^i, a, l') is restricted to OP_{const}, and*

- *the continuous input/output behavior for V^y is not determined (G is restricted to $OP_\perp$).*

Note that the concrete operations used in G do not restrict the possible trajectories and that they are only used to abstract from the evaluation dependencies.

Such an interface automaton can then be employed to enable a safe, strict hierarchical aggregation of sub-components by a super-component (see Figures 3.6, 3.11, or 3.14) by providing a more suitable notion of interface than the *static interface* of a component as defined in Definition 14.

Refinement and Abstraction

To study what a correct relation between the realization of a component and its interface automaton is, we write for a possible execution sequence of states and transitions of a hybrid automaton $M = (L, D, I, O, T, S^0)$ with $(u_0, l_0, \rho^0_{u_0}, \theta^0_{u_0}, \delta_0) \rightarrow_{e_0} (u_1, l_1, \rho^1_{u_1}, \theta^1_{u_1}, \delta_1) \in [\![M]\!]_t$ simply $(l_0, \rho^0_{u_0}(0)) \rightarrow_{(u_0, \rho^0_{u_0}, \theta^0_{u_0}, \delta_0)} (l_0, \rho^0_{u_0}(\delta_0)) \rightarrow_{e_0} (l_1, \rho^1_{u_1}(0)) \rightarrow_{(u_1, l_1, \rho^1_{u_1}, \theta^1_{u_1}, \delta_1)} (l_1, \rho^1_{u_1}(\delta_1))$ to represent the state changes in a more uniform manner. We thus have the concept of a hybrid path $\pi = (u_0, \theta^0_{u_0}, \delta_0); e_0; \dots; (u_n, l_n, \theta^1_{u_n}, \delta_n); e_n$ such that we write $(l_0, \rho^0_{u_0}(0)) \rightarrow_\pi (l_n, \rho^n_{u_n}(\delta_n))$ iff it holds that $(l_0, \rho^0_{u_0}(0)) \rightarrow_{(u_0, \rho^0_{u_0}, \theta^0_{u_0}, \delta_0)} (l_0, \rho^0_{u_0}(\delta_0)) \rightarrow_{e_0} \dots (l_n, \rho^n_{u_n}(0)) \rightarrow_{(u_n, l_n, \rho^n_{u_n}, \theta^n_{u_n}, \delta_n)} (l_n, \rho^n_{u_n}(\delta_n))$.

For $e'_i = e_i - (O \cap I)$ the externally relevant events and $\theta^i_{u_i} = \theta^i_{u_i}|_{V^y(l_i) - V^u(l_i)}$ the output minus the internal variables, we have an abstract path $\pi' = (u_0, \theta^0_{u_0}, \delta_0); e'_0; \dots; (u_n, \theta^1_{u_n}, \delta_n); e_n; \dots$ and we write $(l_0, \rho^0_{u_0}(0)) \Rightarrow_{\pi'} (l_n, \rho^n_{u_n}(\delta_n))$. Note that $w; e; w'$ with $e = \emptyset$ is collapsed to $w; w'$ as no externally relevant events are received or emitted. The offered discrete as well as continuous interactions for a state (l, x) are further denoted by the set offer$(M, (l, x))$ which is defined as $\{e | \exists (l, x) \Rightarrow_e (l', x)\} \cup \{(du/dt)(0) | \exists (l, x) \Rightarrow_{(u, \theta_u, \delta)} (l, x')\}$.

An appropriate notion of hybrid refinement for the interface is then defined as follows:

Definition 13 *For two hybrid reconfiguration automata M_I and M_R holds that M_R is a* refinement *of M_I denoted by $M_R \sqsubseteq M_I$ iff a relation $\Omega \subseteq (L_R \times X_R) \times (L_I \times X_I)$ exists, so that for every $c \in (L_R \times X_R)$ a $c'' \in (L_I \times X_I)$ exists such that $(c, c'') \in \Omega$ and for all $(c, c'') \in \Omega$ holds*

$$\forall c \Rightarrow_\pi c' \quad \exists c'' \Rightarrow_\pi c''' \quad : (c', c''') \in \Omega \qquad and \qquad (A.1)$$

$$\textit{offer}(M_R, c) \supseteq \textit{offer}(M_I, c'') \qquad \textit{and} \qquad (A.2)$$

$$\forall((l_R, x_R), (l_I, x_I)) \in \Omega : D^e(D_R(l_R)) \subseteq D^e(D_L(l_I)). \qquad (A.3)$$

Refinement is transitive which is expressed by Theorem 1.

Theorem 1 *For three hybrid reconfiguration automata M_A, M_B and M_C holds*

$$M_C \sqsubseteq M_B \wedge M_B \sqsubseteq M_A \Rightarrow M_C \sqsubseteq M_A. \qquad (A.4)$$

Proof 1 *As $M_C \sqsubseteq M_B$ and $M_B \sqsubseteq M_A$, there exist $\Omega_{CB} \subseteq (L_C \times X_C) \times (L_B \times X_B)$ and $\Omega_{BA} \subseteq (L_B \times X_B) \times (L_A \times X_A)$ cf. Definition 13. We chose $\Omega_{CA} = \{(c, c'') | \exists (c, \bar{c}) \in \Omega_{CB} \wedge \exists (\bar{c}, c'') \in \Omega_{BA}\}$. The requirement that for every c an entry c'' exists in Ω_{CA} is fulfilled, as an entry $\bar{c}$ exists for every c in Ω_{CB} and an according entry c'' exists for every $\bar{c}$ in Ω_{BA}.*

- *Equation A.1 follows directly from the construction of Ω_{CA}.*

- *Due to Equation A.2 from Definition 13, it holds for all c, $\bar{c}$, and c'' with $(c, \bar{c}) \in \Omega_{CB}$ and $(\bar{c}, c'') \in \Omega_{BA}$: $\textit{offer}(M_C, c) \supseteq \textit{offer}(M_B, \bar{c})$ and $\textit{offer}(M_B, \bar{c}) \supseteq \textit{offer}(M_A, c'')$. Thus, $\textit{offer}(M_C, c) \supseteq \textit{offer}(M_A, c'')$ is fulfilled.*

- *Due to Equation A.3 from Definition 13, it holds for all (l_C, x_C), (l_B, x_B), and (l_A, x_A) with $((l_C, x_C), (l_B, x_B)) \in \Omega_{CB}$ and $((l_B, x_B), (l_A, x_A)) \in \Omega_{BA}$: $D^e(D_C(l_C)) \subseteq D^e(D_B(l_B))$ and $D^e(D_B(l_B)) \subseteq D^e(D_A(l_A))$. Thus, $D^e(D_C(l_C)) \subseteq D^e(D_A(l_A))$ is fulfilled.*

A.3   The Component Model

The structure of a complex system, as explained in Section 2.1.2, is described by UML components. Components are a specialization of UML encapsulated classifiers, which correspond to UML/RT capsules [SR98] and the ROOM concept of actors [SGW94]. Components interact with their environment only via one or more signal-based boundary objects called *ports*. Each port plays a particular role in a collaboration that the component has within its context. Additionally, UML connectors, which correspond to UML/RT connectors and ROOM bindings, are signal-based communication channels that interconnect multiple ports. In our approach, we refined the UML approach and introduced hybrid components. Their behavior, i.e. how they realize such interactions, is described by behavioral models, as described in Section A.2. In this section, we first formalize static component structures. By extending this formalization, we obtain then the formal model for variable reconfigurating structures. In the third part of this section, we formalize the syntactic refinement, described by Figure 3.17 in Section 3.2.6.

A.3.1   Static Component Structures

To model mechatronic systems, we have to extend the UML component model to also support the description of quasi-continuous control behavior. Our straight forward approach to this is to add besides signals also quasi-continuous variables to ports of our hybrid components. While a signal is sent and received at a discrete point in time (cf. SignalEvent in UML), we assume that a quasi-continuous variable has a well-defined value for each point in time.[1] As an example take Figure 3.2 where the component structure of the shuttle system is depicted.

Syntax

To formalize such a structural description of a component diagram, we omit that a UML port can have multiple attached UML interfaces denoting the syntactical interface and instead employ only an unstructured set of signals.

Ports   A *discrete port type* P_d is therefore defined by a pair (I, O) with possible incoming signals I and outgoing signals O. For a *continuous port type* P_c, we use instead a pair (V^u, V^y) with V^u the input variables and V^y the output variables. Combining both definitions, a *hybrid port type* P_h is a 4-tuple (I, O, V^u, V^y) which includes both signals as well as variables. For sake of simplicity, we simply use empty signal or variable sets for continuous resp. discrete port types in the following.

In addition, for each port type $P = (I, O, V^u, V^y)$, the inverse port type $\overline{P} := (O, I, V^y, V^u)$ is defined by simply exchanging the in and out signal sets as well as the in and out variable sets. A *port declaration* is then a pair (N_i, P_i) with N_i a unique port name of the port name set $\mathcal{N}_{po}$ and P_i a discrete, continuous, or hybrid port type. We further refer to a port type P_i of N_i simply using $type(N_i)$ and refer to the sets I_i, O_i, V_i^u and V_i^y resp. using $I(N_i)$ etc.

Components   The interface of a component is defined by the boundary ports, which interact with the environment. In the example of Figure 3.2, the position of the discrete ports identifies it as a boundary port of component Shuttle which is thus part of the component interface. We thus define the *static interface* of a component simply as a set of port declarations as follows:

Definition 14 *The* static interface *I of a component is a set of port declarations* $\{(N_1, P_1), \ldots, (N_n, P_n)\}$ *with for all* $1 \leq i \leq n$ *and* $1 \leq j \leq n$ *with* $i \neq j$ *holds* $N_i \neq N_j$.

Besides the external connections via ports, a component may also embed other components for which an external interface must be known. Thus, a component includes besides its external port sets also a set E of occurrences of embedded components which is each represented by a pair (N_j, I_j) with N_j the unique occurrence name of the occurrence name

---

[1]Usually, quasi-continuous variables also may have a quasi-continuous value domain, however, this might not always be the case (e.g. quasi-continuous variables may also be employed to encode boolean flags etc.).

set $\mathcal{N}_o$ and I_j the interface of that component. To denote a port with port name N_i within the interface of an occurrence with unique name N_j, we further use $type(N_j.N_i)$ and refer to the sets I_i, O_i, V_i^u and V_i^y resp. using $I(N_j.N_i)$ etc. The dt:DriveTrain component with occurrence name dt and component interface DriveTrain, which is embedded into the Shuttle component as depicted in Figure 3.2, is an example for such an embedding.

Finally, also the *internal behavior* of the component may send or receive a given set of signals as well as read or write continuous variables. These signals and variables are defined by the special internal interface B. To describe the mapping between external ports, the ports of embedded components, and ports of the internal behavior as depicted in Figure 3.5 by means of connector links, a set of links $map \subseteq (\mathcal{N}_{po} \cup (\mathcal{N}_o.\mathcal{N}_{po})) \times (\mathcal{N}_{po} \cup (\mathcal{N}_o.\mathcal{N}_{po}))$ is used.

Using the above introduced concepts, a static internal component structure can be defined as follows:

Definition 15 *The static internal structure or* configuration *of a component is a tuple* (I, B, E, map) *with I the component's static interface, B the interface of the internal behavior, $E = \{(N_1, I_1), \ldots, (N_n, I_n)\}$ the set of embedded occurrences consisting of a unique occurrence name N_i from the occurrence name set $\mathcal{N}_o$ and the occurrence's interface I_i, and map a mapping to describe the connectors between ports of these different interfaces. For all $1 \leq i \leq n$ and $1 \leq j \leq n$ with $i \neq j$ must hold $N_i \neq N_j$.*

In some cases, I is equal to B, but when the realizations of the embedded occurrences consume signals from B, these signals do not appear in I. We define consistency for static internal structures as follows:

Definition 16 *A static internal structure as introduced in Definition 15 is* consistent *iff*

1. *map is symmetric $((a, b) \in map \Rightarrow (b, a) \in map)$,*

2. *The mapping map is unique $((a, b) \in map \Rightarrow \nexists (a, c) \in map : c \neq b)$,*

3. *for all $(p, q) \in map$ holds that p and q refer either to ports of the external port set I, ports of the internal behavior B, or ports of embedded occurrences,*

4. *for all $(p, q) \in map$ holds that $type(p) = \overline{type(q)}$, and*

5. *any ports of the external port set I, the internal behavior B, or an embedded occurrence is mapped by map to exactly one counterpart.*

Note, that item 5 seems to be contradictory to Figure 3.4, but recall that the AccelerationControl component from this figure is not described by a static component structure. Variable component structures are described in Section A.3.2.

Behavior Of course, this description of the structure does not define any behavior formally and precisely. Therefore, we have to integrate the structural description, defined by Definition 15, with the behavioral models from Section A.2. Thus, we define the relation between the interface of a behavioral model and a static internal structure:

Definition 17 *A continuous block M with interface $I(M) = (V^u - V^y, V^y - V^u)$ realizes a given port set $L = \{(N_0, (V_0^u, V_0^y)), \ldots, (N_n, (V_n^u, V_n^y))\}$ of continuous ports iff*

- $V^u - V^y = \bigcup_{i=1}^{n} \{N_i.v | v \in V_i^u\}$ *and*
- $V^y - V^u = \bigcup_{i=1}^{n} \{N_i.v | v \in V_i^y\}$.

We write $M \vdash L$.

Definition 18 *A hybrid automaton M with interface $I(M) = (I - O, O - I, V^u - V^y, V^y - V^u)$ realizes a given port set of hybrid ports $L = \{(N_0, (I_0, O_0, V_0^u, V_0^y)), \ldots, (N_i, (I_n, O_n, V_n^u, V_n^y))\}$ iff*

- $I - O = \bigcup_{i=1}^{n} \{N_i.a | a \in I_i\}$,
- $O - I = \bigcup_{i=1}^{n} \{N_i.a | a \in O_i\}$,
- $V^u - V^y = \bigcup_{i=1}^{n} \{N_i.v | v \in V_i^u\}$, *and*
- $V^y - V^u = \bigcup_{i=1}^{n} \{N_i.v | v \in V_i^y\}$.

We write $M \vdash L$.

Using the introduced concepts for the component interface, internal component structure, and behavior, we can now define what a (hybrid) component looks like.

Definition 19 *The component realization $C = (S, M, P, prop)$ consists of a component structure $S = (I, B, E, map)$, an internal behavior $M = (m_1, \ldots, m_n)$, a set of properties P, and a function $prop : \{M\} \cup (\bigcup_{i=1..n} \wp(m_i)) \to P$ that assigns a property to the behavior or to some of the behavior's syntactical elements. It must hold that $M \vdash B$.*

Semantics

The semantics of a component realization C embedding occurrences $E = \{(N_1, I_1), \ldots, (N_n, I_n)\}$ as defined in Definition 19 is not just defined by the parallel composition of M with the automata or blocks which realize the embedded occurrences, i.e. the semantics is not just defined as $M || (M_1 || \ldots || M_n)$ with $M_i \vdash I_i$ for $i \in \{1, n\}$. Additionally, the structural connections encoded with the relation map have to be reflected in the behavioral model. Therefore, a hybrid automaton $behavior((S, M, P, prop))$ realizing the forwarding behavior implicitly specified within the relation map has to be constructed as follows: Let $S = (I, B, E, map)$ and $M = (L, D, I, O, T, S^0)$, with $D(l) = (V^x, V^u, V^y, F(l), G(l), C(l), X^0(l))$. $behavior((S, M, P, prop)) = M' = (L, D', I', O', T', S^0)$ with $D'(l) = (V^x, V^{u'}, V^{y'}, F(l), G'(l), C(l), X^0(l))$ is defined as follows:

- The set L of locations and the set of initial states S^0 is in M like in M',

- the set V^x of continuous state variables, their flow $F(l)$, the locations' conditions $C(l)$ and the initial continuous states $X^0(l)$ is in D like in D',

- the source signals of the connectors become input signals: $I' = I \cup \bigcup_{(N,N') \in map} I(N)$,

- the target signals of the connectors become output signals: $O' = O \cup \bigcup_{(N,N') \in map} O(N)$,

- additional transitions, each with the same source and target locations, map in every location the source signals of the connectors to its target signals: $T' = T \cup \{(l, true, \{N.a, N'.a\}, id, l) | l \in L \ \wedge (N, N') \in map \wedge a \in I(N)\}$,[2]

- the source variables of the connectors become input variables: $V^{u'} = V^u \cup \bigcup_{(N,N') \in map} V^u(N)$,

- the target variables of the connectors become output variables: $V^{y'} = V^y \cup \bigcup_{(N,N') \in map} V^y(N)$, and

- the connectors are implemented by equations, mapping the source variables to target variables: $G'(l) = G(l) \cup \{N.v := N'.v | (N, N') \in map, v \in V^u(N)\}$.[3]

The behavior of a component realization $C = (S, M, P, prop)$ with component structure $S = (I, B, E, map)$ is then given by $behavior((S, M, P, prop))$. The behavior of a component instance with instance name $N \in \mathcal{N}_o$ and component behavior M is further given by $M|_{+N}$ where $x|_{+N}$ denotes that all signal and variables of x are accordingly extended by the prefix N.

A.3.2   Variable Component Structures & Reconfiguration

The described notion of a component realization with a static internal structure and the definition of its semantics must be extended when the internal structure is variable as in the case of hybrid reconfiguration automata or hybrid reconfiguration charts. Recall that for example the AccelerationControl component changes its structure dependent on its current location (cf. Figure 3.4).

Syntax

To ensure that a hybrid component such as the DriveTrain component depicted in Figure 3.3 is consistent (cf. Definition 16), the AccelerationControl component would have to ensure that in all internal modes (see Figure 3.10) the same set of continuous variables is required and offered. However, as depicted in Figure 3.10, the required inputs are different.

---

[2]Note that due to item 4 of Definition 16, it holds that $I(N) = O(N')$.
[3]Note that due to item 4 of Definition 16, it holds that $V^u(N) = V^y(N')$.

To support the correct design of complex mechatronic systems despite the fact that continuous variables may only be available in a state-dependent manner, we further extend the introduced notion of an *interface* of a component by means of state information to support a safe, modular reconfiguration for the hierarchical embedding of reconfigurable hybrid behavior:

Definition 20 *A* dynamic interface *of a component C is a tuple $(M, I, P, prop)$ with $M = (L, D, I, O, T, S^0)$ an interface automaton, I the static interface of the component C, P a set of properties, and $prop : L \to P$ a function that assigns properties to the interface automaton's locations. Any $l \in L$ is a valid* mode.

Using the notion of dynamic interfaces, we specify a variable structure within a component, as shown for example in Figure 3.5, formally as follows:

Definition 21 *A* dynamic internal structure *of a component C with mode set L can be described using a function S which assigns to each mode $l \in L$ an internal structure $S(l) = (I(l), B(l), E(l), map(l))$, where each $(N, (M, I, P, prop), l') \in E(l)$ in contrast to the static case contains a dynamic interface (cf. Definition 20) and a required valid mode of that dynamic interface.*

Informally, C shows in each of its locations a different (external) interface $I(l)$. C's internal behavior shows also different interfaces, denoted by $B(l)$. Further, multiple component occurences are embedded into each location. Each of these component realizations is a refinement of its dynamic interface $(M, I, P, prop)$. The valid mode l' of the dynamic interface specifies that the according embedded component is required to be in a location that delivers the interface that is described by l'. All input and output signals and all in and out variables of the embedded components and of C's interface $I(l)$ are interconnected by the connectors specified by $map(l)$. Such a *dynamic internal structure S* is *structurally consistent* iff for all modes $l \in L$ holds that $S(l)$ interpreted as a static structure is consistent.

To describe that continuous ports are only available dependent on the current state of a component, we distinguish between *permanent ports* and *optional ports*. For $I^\cup = \bigcup_{l \in L} I_l$ and $I^\cap = \bigcap_{l \in L} I_l$ holds that any $(N, P) \in I^\cap$ is a permanent port, while any $(N, P) \in I^\cup \setminus I^\cap$ is an optional port.

Before defining a *reconfigurable component realization*, we integrate again the structural definition with the behavioral model. In the reconfigurable case, we integrate the structural description, defined by Definition 21, with the behavioral model of the hybrid reconfiguration chart from Section A.2.3:

Definition 22 *A hybrid reconfiguration automaton M realizes a given interface in form of a set of hybrid port declarations like in the case of a hybrid automaton. If M in mode $l \in L$ realizes a static interface $I(l)$, we write $M, l \vdash I(l)$. If M in addition refines an interface automaton M^I ($M \sqsubseteq M^I$; see Definition 13), it also realizes the dynamic interface (M^I, I) and we write $M \vdash (M^I, I)$.*

Using the introduced concepts, we define what a (hybrid) component in the case of reconfiguration looks like:

Definition 23 *The* reconfigurable (hybrid) component $C = (S, M, P, prop)$ *consists of an internal behavior* $M = (L, D, I, O, T, S^0)$, *a dynamic component structure S for L, a set P of properties, and a function* $prop : L \to P$ *that assigns properties to the internal behavior's locations. It must hold that for all $l \in L$ and $S(l) = (I(l), B(l), E(l), map(l))$ we have* $M, l \vdash B(l)$.

Semantics

An internal behavior M and a *dynamic internal structure* S are *behavioral consistent* iff for all $(l, g, g', a, l') \in T$ and all embedded dynamic interfaces in $(N, (M, I, P, prop), l'') \in E(l)$ and $(N, (M, I, P, prop), l''') \in E(l')$ hold that a corresponding transition between the required modes l'' and l''' exists. A function $t : L \times L \to I \cup O$ is assumed which denotes all signals that must be emitted to enforce the mode changes of the embedded interface automata.

We define the semantics of a reconfigurable component by extending its internal behavior, described by a behavioral consistent hybrid reconfiguration automaton $M = (L, D, I, O, T, S^0)$, with the behavior of the associated component reconfiguration and with the *dynamic internal structure* $S : L \to \S$. The former extension is realized similar to the approach from Section A.3.1 for the static case, the latter one by referring to the above introduced trigger function t:

Let $S(l) = (I(l), B(l), E(l), map(l))$ and $M = (L, D, I, O, T, S^0)$ with the continuous model $D(l) = (V^x(l), V^u(l), V^y(l), F(l), G(l), C(l), X^0(l))$. $behavior(S, M, P, prop) = M' = (L, D', I', O', T', S^0\})$ with the continuous model $D'(l) = (V^x(l), V^{u'}(l), V^{y'}(l), F(l), G'(l), C(l), X^0(l))$ is defined as follows:

- The set L of locations and the set of initial states S^0 is in M like in M',

- the set V^x of continuous state variables, their flow $F(l)$, the locations' conditions $C(l)$ and the initial continuous states $X^0(l)$ is in D like in D',

- the source signals of the connectors become input signals: $I' = I \cup \bigcup_{l \in L, (N, N') \in map(l)} I(N)$,

- the target signals of the connectors become output signals: $O' = O \cup \bigcup_{l \in L, (N, N') \in map(l)} O(N)$,

- transitions emit additional signals to enforce state changes as denoted by t. Additional transitions, each with the same source and target locations, map in every location the source signals of the connectors to its target signals: $T = \{(l, g, g' \cup t(l, l'), a, l') | (l, g, g', a, l') \in T\} \cup \{(l, true, \{N.a, N'.a\}, id, l) | l \in L \wedge (N, N') \in map \wedge a \in I(N)\}$,[4]

---

[4]Note that due to item 4 of Definition 16, it holds that $I(N) = O(N')$.

- the source variables of the connectors become input variables: $V^{u'}(l) = \bigcup_{(N,N')\in map(l)} V^u(N)$,

- the target variables of the connectors become output variables: $V^{y'}(l) = \bigcup_{(N,N')\in map(l)} V^y(N)$, and

- the connectors $map(l)$ of each location l are implemented by equations, mapping the source variables to target variables: $G'(l) = G(l) \cup \{N.v := N'.v | (N,N') \in map(l), v \in V^u(N)\}$.

The behavior of a *reconfigurable component realization* $C = (S, M, P, prop)$ with component structure S is then given by $behavior((S, M, P, prop))$. The *component behavior* of a component instance with instance name $N \in \mathcal{N}_o$ and behavior M of the *component realization* is then given by $M|_{+N}$.

A.3.3 Syntactical Refinement

Due to the fact that hierarchical composition in contrast to the general parallel composition restricts a potential overlapping of locations, the compatibility can be checked in many cases on the syntactical level without consideration of the full state-space of the model (cf. Figure 3.17). In these checks fading transitions and their durations play an important role. Formalizing their semantics leads to *simple interface automata* [BGO04a].

Definition 24 *An interface automaton* $M = (L, D, I, O, T, S^0)$ *is* simple *if it contains only passive and fading locations and two fading locations are never directly connected.*

In order to apply Theorem 2 from [BGO04a] (see Theorem 2 below), we define the set H of possibly reachable state combinations of a reconfigurable hybrid component and its embedded occurrences as follows:

Definition 25 *Let* $C = (S, M, P, prop)$ *be a reconfigurable hybrid component with* $M = (L, D, I, O, T, S^0)$, $S(l) = (I(l), B(l), E(l), map(l))$, *and* $E(l) = \{(N_1, (M_1, I_1, P_1, prop_1), l_1), \ldots, (N_n, (M_n, I_n, P_n, prop_n), l_n)\}$. *The set of* possibly reachable states *is* $H = \{(l, (l_1, \ldots, l_n)) | l \in L\}$. *We call* $M\|_H(M_1\| \ldots \|M_n) := behavior(C)\|(M_1\| \ldots \|M_n)$ *the* hierarchical parallel composition *of* M *and* $M_1\| \ldots \|M_n$.

The following theorem (taken from [BGO04a]) describes a simple syntactical rule which is sufficient to proof that a hierarchical parallel product does not have any timing errors. The basic idea is that the timing interval of a hybrid reconfiguration chart's fading transitions has to be conform with the one of its embedded simple interface state charts, as described in Section 3.2.6.

Theorem 2 *For the hierarchical parallel composition* $M_1\|_H M_2$ *of two hybrid automata* M_1 *and* M_2 *holds* $M_1\|_H M_2 \sqsubseteq M_1\backslash_{I_2\cup O_2}$ *if*

1. $I(M_1\|_H M_2) = I(M_1\backslash_{I_2 \cup O_2})$,

2. *all initial states are also contained in H:* $(\{(l_1, l_2) | (l_1, x) \in S_1^0 \wedge (l_2, y) \in S_2^0\} \subseteq H)$,

3. M_2 *is a simple interface state chart (cf. Definition 24), and*

4. *for all* $(l_1, l_2) \in H$ *and transition* $t_1 = (l_1, g_1, g_1^i, a_1, l_1') \in T_1$ *holds:*

   (a) *if* l_1' *is not a fading location, then for all* $t_2 = (l_2, g_2, g_2^i, u_2, l_2') \in T_2$ *with* $g_1^i \cap (I_2 \cup O_2) = g_2^i$ *must hold:*

      i. $g_2 = \text{true}$,

      ii. l_2' *is a passive location (cf. Definition 11), and*

      iii. $(l_1', l_2') \in H$.

   In addition at least one such transition in M_2 *must exist.*

   (b) *if* l_1' *is a fading location we can conclude that exactly one transition* $t_1' = (l_1', g_1', g_1^{i'}, a_1', l_1'') \in T_1$ *with* $g_1' \equiv d_{min}^1 \le v \le d_{max}^1$ *and* $g_1^{i'} = \emptyset$ *exists (see Definition 10). For any* $t_2 = (l_2, g_2, g_2^i, a_2, l_2') \in T_2$ *with* $g_1^i \cap (I_2 \cup O_2) = g_2^i$ *must hold:*

      i. $g_2 = \text{true}$,

      ii. l_2' *is a fading location, and*

      iii. $(l_1', l_2') \in H$.

   For the uniquely determined successor transition $t_2' = (l_2', g_2', g_2^{i'}, a_2', l_2'') \in T_2$ *with* $g_2' \equiv d_{min}^2 \le v \le d_{max}^2$ *must hold:*

      iv. l_2'' *is a passive location (cf. Definition 11),*

      v. $(l_1'', l_2'') \in H$, *and*

      vi. $[d_{min}^2, d_{max}^2] \subseteq [d_{min}^1, d_{max}^1]$ *must be satisfied.*

   Again, at least one such pair of transitions in M_2 *must exist.*

Proof 2 *Theorem 2 has been proved in [BGO04a]. There, we first chose an appropriate* Ω *conform to Definition 13, so that every state* (l, x) *of* M_1 *is related to an corresponding state of* $M_1\|_H M_2$. *Then, we will show that for every transition* t_I *of* M_1 *an according transition* t_R *of* $M_1\|_H M_2$ *exists and that* t_R *fires when* t_I *fires. Then, we can conclude that every path in* $[\![M_1\|_H M_2]\!]_t$ *corresponds to one of* $[\![M_1]\!]_t$, *which is used to show that equations (1) and (2) from Definition 13 hold. Due to the distinction between continuous steps and discrete steps and due to the distinction between fading and non-fading transitions, the proof consists of 3 different cases: Let* $X_R := [V_1^x \cup V_2^x \to \mathbb{R}]$, *choose* $\Omega = \{((l_1, l_2), x_R), (l_1, \tilde{x}_R)) | (l_1, l_2) \in H, x_R \in X_R\}$.

Case 1: Discrete non-fading transitions   *For all transitions $t_1 = (l_1, g_1, g_1^i, a_1, l_1') \in T_1$, with l_1' is not a fading location, exists one path in the automaton's semantics: $(l_1, x_1) \to_{g_1^i} (l_1', a_1(x_1)) \in [\![M_1]\!]_t$. Due to the requirement (4a) of this theorem, at least one transition $t_2 = (l_2, g_2, g_2^i, a_1, l_2') \in T_2$ exists with $g_2 =$ true, $g_2^i = g_1^i \cap (I_2 \cup O_2)$, $C_2(l_2) =$ true and $(l_1', l_2') \in H$. Due to Definition 6 $M_1 \|_H M_2$ contains a transition*

$$t = ((l_1, l_2), g_1 \wedge g_2, g_1^i \cup g_2^i, (a_1 \oplus a_2), (l_1', l_2')) \tag{A.5}$$

with $g_1^i \cap (I_2 \cup O_2) = g_2^i$. As $g_1 \wedge g_2 \overset{(4ai)}{=} g_1 \wedge \text{true} = g_1$ and as $g_1^i \cup g_2^i \overset{(4a)}{=} g_1^i \cup (g_1^i \cap (I_2 \cup O_2)) = g_1^i$, t is equal to

$$t = ((l_1, l_2), g_1, g_1^i, (a_1 \oplus a_2), (l_1', l_2')) \tag{A.6}$$

Note that firing of t just depends on the triggers g_1 and g_1^i and not on g_2 or g_2^i. Thus, for all $(l_1, l_2) \in H$ holds that an according path from (l_1, l_2) to (l_1', l_2') is in the semantics of $M_1 \|_H M_2$: $((l_1, l_2), x_R) \to_{g_1^i} ((l_1', l_2'), (a_1 \oplus a_2)(x_R)) \in [\![M_1 \|_H M_2]\!]_t$ and $(l_1', l_2') \in H$.

Therefore, for each $c := ((l_1, l_2), x_R) \in (L_1 \times L_2) \times X_R$ there exists a $c'' := (l_1, \tilde{x}_R)$ so that for $c' := ((l_1', l_2'), x_R') \in (L_1 \times L_2) \times X_R$, and $c''' := (l_1', \tilde{x}_R')$, holds: There exists the execution sequences $c \to_{g_1^i} c'$ and $c'' \to_{g_1^i} c'''$ with $(c, c'') \in \Omega$ and $(c', c''') \in \Omega$, which is a requirement for refinement, cf. Definition 13.

Case 2: Discrete fading transitions   *For all transitions $t_1 = (l_1, g_1, g_1^i, a_1, l_1') \in T_1$, with l_1' is a fading location, holds that a path is in the semantics of M_1 that represents firing of t_1, residing in l_1' for a specific time δ_0, and leaving l_1' after δ_0:*

$$(l_1, x_1) \to_{g_1^i} (l_1', \rho_0(0)) \to_{(u_0, \rho_{u_0}^0, \theta_{u_0}^0, \delta_0)} (l_1', \rho_0(\delta_0)) \to_\emptyset (l_1'', a_1'(\rho_0(\delta_0))) \in [\![M_1]\!]_t \tag{A.7}$$

with $\delta_0 \in [d_{min}^1, d_{max}^2]$. Due to requirement (4b) of this theorem there exists at least one transition

$$t_2 = (l_2, g_2, g_2^i, a_2, l_2') \in T_2 \tag{A.8}$$

with $g_2 =$ true, $g_2^i = g_1^i \cap (I_2 \cup O_2)$, and $(l_1', l_2') \in H$. As l_2' is a fading location, there exists a successor transition of t_2 (cf. Definition 10):

$$t_2' = (l_2', g_2', g_2^{i'}, a_2', l_2'') \in T_2 \tag{A.9}$$

with $g_2' \equiv d_{min}^2 \leq v \leq d_{max}^2$, $g_2^{i'} = \emptyset$, and $(l_1'', l_2'') \in H$. Due to Definition 6 $M_1 \|_H M_2$ contains a

$$t = ((l_1, l_2), g_1 \wedge g_2, g_1^i \cup g_2^i, (a_1 \oplus a_2), (l_1', l_2')) \tag{A.10}$$

with $g_1^i \cap (I_2 \cup O_2) = g_2^i$ and a transition

$$t' = ((l_1', l_2'), g_1' \wedge g_2', g_1^{i'} \cup g_2^{i'}, (a_1' \oplus a_2'), (l_1'', l_2'')) \tag{A.11}$$

with $g_1^{i'} \cap (I_2 \cup O_2) = g_2^{i'}$. As $g_1 \wedge g_2 \overset{(4bi)}{=} g_1 \wedge \text{true} = g_1$ and as $g_1^i \cup g_2^i \overset{(4b)}{=} g_1^i \cup (g_1^i \cap (I_2 \cup O_2)) = g_1^i$, t is equal to

$$t = ((l_1, l_2), g_1, g_1^i, (a_1 \oplus a_2), (l_1', l_2')) \tag{A.12}$$

Note that firing again just depends on the triggers g_1 and g_1^i and not on g_2 or g_2^i. Due to requirement (4b) holds: $g_1' \wedge g_2' \equiv (d_{min}^1 \leq d_{max}^1) \wedge (d_{min}^2 \leq d_{max}^2)$. As $[d_{min}^2, d_{max}^2] \subseteq [d_{min}^1, d_{max}^1]$ (cf. requirement (4b vi)), it follows that

$$g_1' \wedge g_2' \equiv d_{min}^2 \leq v \leq d_{max}^2. \tag{A.13}$$

As further $g_1^{i'} \cup g_2^{i'} \stackrel{(4b),(4biv)}{=} \emptyset \cup \emptyset = \emptyset$, t' is equal to

$$t' = ((l_1', l_2'), d_{min}^2 \leq v \leq d_{max}^2, \emptyset, (a_1' \oplus a_2'), (l_1'', l_2'')). \tag{A.14}$$

Note, that firing of t' just depends on $d_{min}^2 \leq v \leq d_{max}^2$. t' fires after the time $\delta_0 \in [d_{min}^2; d_{max}^2]$.

    Thus, for all $(l_1, l_2) \in H$ holds that every path in $[\![M_1 \|_H M_2]\!]_t$ corresponds to one of $[\![M_1]\!]_t$, like the one from equation (A.7): $((l_1, l_2), x_R) \rightarrow_{g_1^i} ((l_1', l_2'), (a_1 \oplus a_2)(x_R)) \rightarrow_{(u_0, \rho_{u_0}^0, \theta_{u_0}^0, \delta_0)} ((l_1', l_2'), (\rho^0(a_1 \oplus a_2)(x_R))) \rightarrow_\emptyset ((l_1'', l_2''), (\rho^0(a_1 \oplus a_2)(x_R))) \in [\![M_1 \|_H M_2]\!]_t$. Further it holds: $(l_1', l_2') \in H$ and $(l_1'', l_2'') \in H$.

    Therefore, for each $c := ((l_1, l_2), x_R) \in (L_1 \times L_2) \times X_R$ there exists a $c'' := (l_1, \tilde{x}_R)$ so that for $c' := ((l_1'', l_2''), x_R') \in (L_1 \times L_2) \times X_R$, and $c''' := (l_1'', \tilde{x}_R')$, holds: There exists the execution sequences $c \Rightarrow_\pi c'$ with $\pi = g_1^i; (u_0, \theta_{u_0}^0, \delta_0); \emptyset$ and $c'' \Rightarrow_\pi c'''$ with $(c, c'') \in \Omega$ and $(c', c''') \in \Omega$, which is again the above mentioned requirement for refinement, cf. Definition 13.

Case 3: Continuous transitions

Let $(l_1, \tilde{\rho}_{u_0}^0(0)) \rightarrow_{(\tilde{u}_0, \tilde{\rho}_{u_0}^0, \theta_{u_0}^0, \delta_0)} (l_1, \tilde{\rho}_{u_0}^0(\delta_0))$ be a path from the semantics $[\![M_1]\!]$. For all $(l_1, l_2) \in H$ exists an according path in the semantics $[\![M_1 \|_H M_2]\!]_t$: $((l_1, l_2), \rho_{u_0}^0(0)) \rightarrow_{(u_0, \rho_{u_0}^0, \theta_{u_0}^0, \delta_0)} ((l_1, l_2), \rho_{u_0}^0(\delta_0))$.

    Therefore, for each $c := ((l_1, l_2), \rho_{u_0}^0(0)) \in (L_1 \times L_2) \times X_R$ there exists a $c'' := (l_1, \tilde{\rho}_{u_0}^0(0))$ so that for $c' := ((l_1, l_2), \rho_{u_0}^0(\delta_0)) \in (L_1 \times L_2) \times X_R$, and $c''' := (l_1', \tilde{\rho}_{u_0}^0(\delta_0))$, holds: There exists the execution sequences $c \rightarrow_{(u_0, \rho_{u_0}^0, \theta_{u_0}^0, \delta_0)} c'$ and $c'' \rightarrow_{(u_0, \rho_{u_0}^0, \theta_{u_0}^0, \delta_0)} c'''$ with $(c, c'') \in \Omega$ and $(c', c''') \in \Omega$, which is again the above mentioned requirement for refinement, cf. Definition 13.

Hybrid paths

Induction is used to show that the above results are valid for any path of discrete or continuous transitions. Therefore $\forall c = ((l_1, l_2), x_R) \exists c'' = (l_1, \tilde{x}_R)$ so that $\forall (c, c'') \in \Omega$ holds condition A.1:

$$\forall c \Rightarrow_\pi c' \quad \exists c'' \Rightarrow_\pi c''' \quad : (c', c''') \in \Omega \tag{A.15}$$

Environment interference

Since we showed that each part of a possible path corresponds to a discrete fading or non-fading or to the flow of a location, we conclude $offer(M_1, (l_1, x)) = \{g_1^i | \exists (l_1, g_1, g_1^i, a_1, l_1') \in T_1\} \cup \{(du/dt)(0) | \exists (l_1, x) \Rightarrow_{(u, \theta_u, \delta)} (l_1, x')\}$.

    Further, we conclude $offer(M_1 \|_H M_2, ((l_1, l_2), x)) = \{g_1^i | \exists ((l_1, l_2), g_1, g_1^i, a_1 \oplus a_2, (l_1', l_2')) \in T_{1\|H2}\} \cup \{(du/dt)(0) | \exists ((l_1, l_2), x) \Rightarrow_{(u, \theta, \delta)} (l, x')\}$. This is equivalent to $\{g_1^i | \exists (l_1, g_1, g_1^i, a_1, l_1') \in T_1\} \cup \{(du/dt)(0) | \exists l_1 \in L_1$ with $D(l_1) =$

$(V^x(l_1), V^u(l_1), V^y(l_1), F(l_1), G(l_1), C(l_1), X^0(l_1))\}$ *and for which exists trajectories* ρ_u *and* θ_u.

Therefore it holds: offer$(M_R, c) \supseteq$ *offer*(M_I, c''). *Due to Definition 13 and together with (A.15) follows that* $M_1\|_H M_2 \sqsubseteq M_1 \backslash_{I_2 \cup O_2}$.

Theorem 2 can be extended to the general case of $M_S\|_H(M_1\|\dots\|M_n)$ by induction. Due to the syntactical check of Theorem 2, the hierarchical composition by means of the underlying hybrid control software cannot invalidate the timing properties ensured by the embedding hybrid reconfiguration chart.

A.4 Advanced High-Level Modeling

In Chapter 3, we specified the behavior of the hybrid components by our high-level automata model, called *hybrid reconfiguration chart*. In contrast to the hybrid reconfiguration automata model, a hybrid reconfiguration chart allows the use of the high-level constructs

- committed locations,
- asynchronous comunication,
- history,
- hierarchy,
- exit(), entry(), and do() methods,
- transition priorities,
- stop states,
- fading transitions,
- implied state changes, and
- blockable and enforceable transitions.

In this section, we define the semantics of these high-level constructs by mapping them to the formally defined hybrid reconfiguration automata model.

A.4.1 Committed Locations

To model atomic sequences of actions, e.g. atomic broadcast or multicast, we provide a notion of *committed locations* in the hybrid reconfiguration chart model. A committed location is a location where no delay is allowed. If a committed location is entered, the next step must be the firing of a transition leaving this location. Thus, processes (automata) in committed locations may be interleaved only with processes in a committed location.

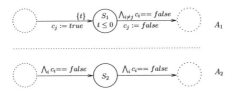

Figure A.1: Committed location

In Figure A.1, two orthogonal automata A_1 and A_2 are depicted. Location S_1 is modeled as *committed*. When S_1 is entered, an internal clock t is initialized and a variable c_j is set to *true*. To ensure that no time is consumed while S_1 is active, S_1 is associated with the invariant $t \leq 0$. To ensure that no other transition fires at that time all other transitions are labeled with the guard $\bigwedge_i c_i ==$ false.

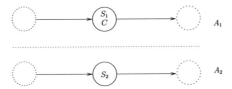

Figure A.2: Notation of committed location

For simplification, we will use the notion of Figure A.2 in both hybrid reconfiguration charts and hybrid automata to describe atomic steps.

A.4.2   Asynchronous Communication

Hybrid reconfiguration automata interact via synchronous events. To support asynchronous events in the hybrid reconfiguration chart model, we extend the synchronous communication by adding a queue for each event to the system.

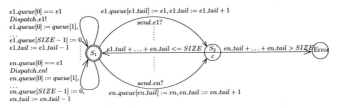

Figure A.3: Scheme for queuing asynchronous events

Figure A.3 shows the scheme for an automaton which is used to queue a given set of asynchronous events e1, ..., en. The automaton consists of the three states, S_1, S_2 and

Error. When the event send_e1 is sent by an automaton, the event is added to the queue. This is realized by the transition $S_1 \rightarrow S_2$, which adds the event to the array e1_queue. If the entire event queue is not full, the automaton will turn back to the initial state (here marked by the double line as location border). Otherwise, the automaton will switch to the *Error* state. If the automaton is in state S_1 consumed events are dispatched by the self-transitions $S_1 \rightarrow S_1$.

A.4.3 History

Within hierarchical states of hybrid reconfiguration charts, it is possible to define a history flag. Thus, we also introduce a mapping for history.

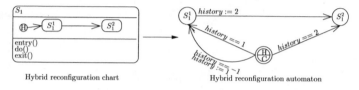

| Hybrid reconfiguration chart | Hybrid reconfiguration automaton |

Figure A.4: History

In Figure A.4 (left side), the hierarchical state S_1 of a hybrid reconfiguration chart contains the substates S_1^1, S_1^2 and the history flag (H). The effect of the latter one is that the state which last was active will be occupied again when S_1 is entered again. To realize this behavior in the hybrid reconfiguration automata model, a history location H and a variable history are added for each history flag. On each transition, the variable history is set to a unique value, representing a location, e.g. history:=1. When the state S_1 is entered for the first time, history is set to -1. From the history location H, a transition to every other location is added. Each individual outgoing transition from H is marked with a guard history==i, where i is the unique id of the target location. In Figure A.4 (right side), the transformed automaton is depicted. For flat history, as in the example, the construction is only done for the highest level of the hybrid reconfiguration chart. In case of deep history, the construction also has to be done for all other levels.

A.4.4 Hierarchy

In Figure A.5, the mapping of hierarchy is depicted by means of an orthogonal AND-state. The AND-state S_1 of the hybrid reconfiguration chart consists of the two parallel statecharts A_1, A_2. Each of them has two states S_1^1, S_2^1 resp. S_3^1, S_4^1. To map the behavior of the AND-state, three automata are necessary in the hybrid reconfiguration automata model. For each concurrent automaton, an equivalent separate automaton is created. Furthermore, a coordination automaton C which triggers the automata, implementing A_1 and A_2 respectively, is created.

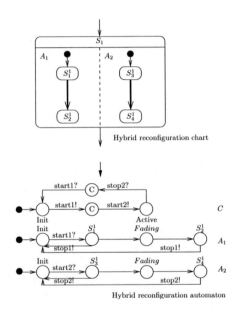

Figure A.5: Mapping of hierarchy

The mode of operation is as follows: If the AND-state in the hybrid reconfiguration chart is entered, the coordination automaton in the hybrid reconfiguration chart is activated first. Implemented by a committed location, the sub-automata are directly triggered. Whenever a sub-automaton decides to leave the AND-state (modeled by the transition back to the initial location), the coordination automaton ensures that all other sub-automata will leave the AND-state, too.

A.4.5   exit()- and entry()-methods

To handle the time consuming transitions, the exit()-operation of the source state, the data assignment (action()) and the target state's entry()-method have to be addressed first. They are mapped to the hybrid reconfiguration automata model by executing them sequentially in the entry action of an additional intermediate state. This leads to two different kinds of locations: *state locations*, representing states, and *action locations*, in which operations are executed.

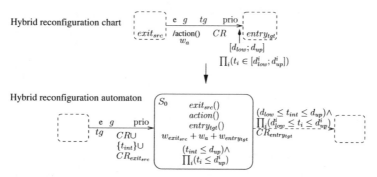

Figure A.6: Mapping of time consuming transitions

Figure A.6 shows how a transition is mapped to an additional action location and two transitions of a hybrid reconfiguration automaton. Solid arrows denote urgent, dashed arrows denote non-urgent transitions. If a transition is activated for a specific time interval, an urgent one fires immediately, a non-urgent one fires at any point of time of the interval. The two transitions connect the action location with the source and the target state. The event, guard, time guard and priority of the hybrid reconfiguration chart's transition are recovered in the urgent transition as these attributes shall trigger the actions.

The deadline is reused in the mapping multiple times. On the one hand, it is used to extend the invariant of the action location. On the other hand, it is used to prevent premature leaving of the action location before the point of time, specified by the lower bound of the deadline. As the last point of time when the action location may be left is specified by the upper bound of the deadline, it is used as the upper bound of the time guard of the non-urgent transition.

A.4.6 Transition Priorities

If a state has more than one outgoing transition and more than one of them is enabled at the same point in time, the transition with the highest priority fires. As priorities are not supported in the hybrid reconfiguration automata model, we have to provide a mapping for this concept. We have to distinguish between two cases: (1) a transition is only triggered by a guard and (2) a transition is triggered by a guard and an event. In the first case, we use the fact that boolean guards can be inverted. In the second case, the problem we have to deal with is that events cannot be inverted like boolean guards and that two participants running in parallel are synchronized when a transition fires.

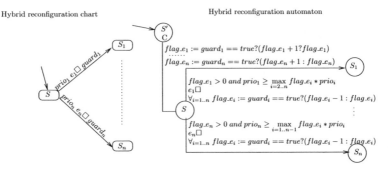

Figure A.7: Transformation of priority

In Figure A.7, the mapping scheme is depicted. A state S of a hybrid reconfiguration chart and its outgoing transitions $S \rightarrow S_1$ $(t_1), \ldots, S \rightarrow S_n$ (t_n) which are synchronized via events $e_i \square$ with $\square \in \{?, !\}$ and which are additionally marked with a guard $guard_i$ and a priority value $prio_i$ are mapped to a hybrid reconfiguration automaton. An additional state S' associated with a committed flag is added to the hybrid reconfiguration automaton. Due to the fact that S' is marked as committed, the state must be left immediately again after it was entered. In addition, for every event $e_i \square$, a variable $flag\_e_i$ is added. The flag characterizes whether the related event is enabled on both the sender and receiver side ($flag\_e_i == 1$), whether it is enabled only for one of the participants ($flag\_e_i == 0$), or wether it is not enabled for any of the participants ($flag\_e_i == -1$). The flag $flag\_e_i$ is tested and updated as follows:[5]

$$flag\_e_i := guard_i?(flag\_e_i + 1 : flag\_e_i)$$

If the guard $guard_i$ evaluates to true, $flag\_e_i$ is incremented. Otherwise, $flag\_e_i$ remains the same. From all outgoing transitions of the state S the guards are formed as follows:

$$flag\_e_i > 0 \; and \; prio_i \geq \max_{j=1..n, j \neq i} flag_j * prio_j$$

---

[5]$a?b : c$ is an abbreviation for if a then b else c.

flag_$e_i > 0$ is added to ensure that the original guard $guard_i$ is true and both participants are ready to synchronize. To ensure that only the transition with the highest priority fires, we additionally check that there is no other enabled transition with a higher priority than the current one.

$$\forall_{i=1...n}\text{flag\_}e_i := guard_i?(\text{flag\_}e_i - 1 : \text{flag\_}e_i)$$

When a transition fires, the value of all flags $flag_i$ has to be refreshed. If a $flag_i$ has been incremented before, it is thus accordingly decremented.

A.4.7 do()-method

Figure A.8 shows how a state S_1 and its do-method are mapped to two locations S_1 and S_1' in the hybrid reconfiguration automata model: The invariant is not modified. To model the periodic execution of the do()-operation, the new state S_1' is introduced. The non-urgent transitions $S_1 \rightarrow S_1'$ and $S_1' \rightarrow S_1$ are created. The do()-operation is assigned to the first one. The latter one resets the new introduced clock t and it is only triggered at $t \geq p_{low}$. To ensure that the do-operation is executed not later than p_{up}, the invariant $t \leq p_{up}$ is assigned to S_1', too. All transitions leading to S_1 in the hybrid reconfiguration chart are kept in the hybrid reconfiguration automaton. The leaving transitions are doubled so that one of them has its origin in S_1 and one in S_1'.

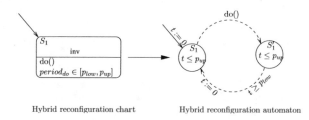

Hybrid reconfiguration chart   Hybrid reconfiguration automaton

Figure A.8: Ordinary states with do()-methods

A.4.8 Stop State

The hybrid reconfiguration chart model contains the stop state which denotes the termination of a statechart. In the hybrid reconfiguration automata model, there is no special stop state. This behavior is mapped in a correct manner as depicted in Figure A.9. A triggerless self-transition is added to the state so that the automaton stays in this location without causing a deadlock.

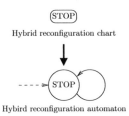

Figure A.9: Stop state

A.4.9   Fading Transitions

As introduced in Section 3.2.1, the fading transitions are a syntactical abbreviation. The mapping that defines the semantics of a fading transition becomes obvious by comparing Figures 3.5 and 3.6. The fading transition is mapped to an intermediate location, which we call *fading location*.

The configuration, associated with this location consists of the source locations configuration, the target locations configuration and one fading component for each output that is available in both, the source and the target configuration. If a component is part of the source and of the target configuration, two different instances of this component occur in the fading location. The fading component obtains the outputs of the source and the target configuration as input. The set G of the fading component consists of the equation f_{fade} from the fading transition specification. The set F contains one entry $\dot{t}_c = 1$ for a clock t_c.

The uniquely defined transition, leading from the source location to the fading location is associated with the event trigger, guard, time guard, and update from the fading transition specification. Further, a reset for a clock t_c is defined for this transition. Let $d = [d_{low}, d_{up}]$ be the duration interval of the fading transition. The fading location obtains an invariant $t_c \leq d_{up}$ and the uniquely defined transition from the fading location to the target location obtains a continuous guard $d_{low} \leq t_c \leq d_{up}$.

If the transition is not associated with a fading function, the intermediate fading location is just associated with the configuration of the source location. This can be seen as application of the default fading function $f_{fade} = 1$

A.4.10   Implied State Changes

The mapping, explained in Section A.4.9, is extended when the superordinated component specifies an implied state change. In order to ensure synchronous state changes in the superordinated and in the subordinated component, additional signals are added as shown in Figure A.10. The signal i1 ensures a synchronous switch to the intermediate state, the signal i2 ensures a synchronous switch to the target state. Note that we abstracted from the other details like guards etc. in Figure A.10.

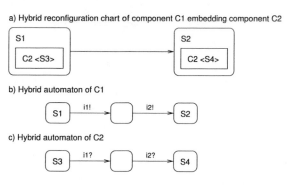

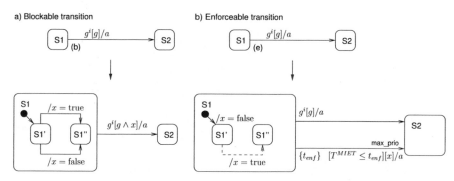

Figure A.10: Mapping of implied state changes

A.4.11   Blockable & Enforceable Transitions

As presented in Section 3.2.5 and in [BGGO04a], some cases exist when it is desired to specify further non-determinism. There, transitions are specified to be *blockable*. If a blockable transition is triggered, it may fire or it may be un-triggered (blocked) nevertheless. Opposite behavior is specified by *enforceable* transitions: An enforceable transition may be fired although it is not triggered due to time guard and I/O-guard. In order to restrict enforced firing of transitions, a time constant called *minimal inter enforceable time* T^{MIET} is specified. Whenever a transition has been enforced, the next one may not be enforced before this time passed by.

Figure A.11: a) Blockable and b) enforceable transitions

Figure A.11 shows the mapping of blockable and enforceable transitions respectively to standard hybrid reconfiguration charts and hierarchical states. Figure A.11a shows that a new boolean flag is introduced in the source location of the blockable transition. This flag is non-deterministically set either to true or to false. If the blockable transition's guard g evaluates to true and if the I/O-guard is fulfilled, the flag determines if the transition fires, as the guard is enriched to $g \wedge x$ in the mapping.

Mapping the enforceable transition is done similar: In this case, a second transition with the same action is created that fires dependent on the flag x. This transition obtains the highest priority. It resets a clock t_{enf} when it fires. It is only triggered when the valuation of this clock, which has been reset to zero when any transition was enforced the last time, is greater or equal the T^{MIET} time constant.

A.5   Integration with Compositional Modelchecking

In Section 2.2.2, we introduced real-time coordination patterns. They have been defined in [GTB$^+$03] like in Definition 26.

Definition 26 *A* pattern P *is a 4-tuple* $(\mathcal{M}, \Psi, \phi, M^P)$ *with a set* $\mathcal{M}$ *of automata* M_1, $\ldots$, M_k *for each role, a set* Ψ *of invariants* ψ_1, $\ldots$, ψ_k *for each role, the pattern constraint* ϕ, *and the connector automaton* M^P.

For multiple patterns $P_1, \ldots, P_n$ we refer to their constraints as ϕ_i^P and connector automata as M_i^P. Let $C = (S, M^C, P, prop)$ be a component realizing pattern's roles $M_1^r, \ldots, M_h^r$. We derive the component role invariant ψ^C by simply combining the related role invariants $(\psi_1 \wedge \cdots \wedge \psi_h)$. For multiple components $C_1, \ldots, C_m$ we refer to their overall component behavior as M_j^C and invariant as ψ_j^C.

Our approach assumes that the required system can be built by a number of components and patterns which overlap at their ports resp. roles (see Figure 3.1). This can be formally defined as follows:

Definition 27 *A system* $\mathcal{S}$ *is a triple* $(\mathcal{P}, \mathcal{C}, map)$ *with a set* $\mathcal{P}$ *of patterns* $P_1, \ldots P_n$, *a set* $\mathcal{C}$ *of components* $C_1, \ldots, C_m$, *and a bijective mapping map which assigns to each component port the related unique pattern role. The syntactical correctness of such a system requires that all related automata* $M_1^P, \ldots, M_n^P, M_1^C, \ldots, M_m^C$ *are connected accordingly by map such that all roles are realized by the component ports.*

Thus, we can build arbitrary complex combinations of shuttle components in our example. They are connected via the ConvoyCoordination pattern using multiple instances which are accordingly adjusted to permit their composition (renaming of signals etc.). Therefore, instead of n patterns and m components, we will usually only have n' and m' different patterns resp. components within a single system ($n' \le n$ and $m' \le m$).

Pattern Verification   As described in Section 2.3.1, we verify whether the behavioral requirement holds for a pattern. If the requirement holds and if the pattern does not contain any deadlocks, the pattern is named *correct*. The special symbol δ is used to denote that a *deadlock* (a state without any outgoing transition) can be reached. $M \models \neg \delta$ thus denotes that M does not contain any deadlocks.

Definition 28 *Formally, a pattern* $P = (\mathcal{M}, \Psi, \phi, M^P)$ *with a set* $\mathcal{M}$ *of automata* M_1, ..., M_k *is a* correct pattern *iff:*

$$M_1 \| \ldots \| M_k \| M^P \models \phi \wedge \neg \delta \tag{A.16}$$

This can be verified using a real-time modelchecker which first builds the model $M_1 \| \ldots \| M_k \| M^P$ and then checks whether the constraint $\phi \wedge \neg \delta$ holds.

For proving the correctness of all n patterns (n' different ones) of a system, we will have n' checks in $O(\exp(k))$, where k is the maximal number of roles per pattern. We can guarantee a fixed upper bound for k for arbitrary n, because the number of roles per pattern will not further increase when more components and patterns are added. Thus, the required verification becomes possible when the state space of each single pattern is not too large.

Component Verification

Definition 29 *A component* $C = (S, M^C, P, prop)$ *which refines the automata* M_1, ..., M_h *is a* correct component *if holds:*

$$\left(M^C \sqsubseteq (M_1 \| \ldots \| M_h) \right) \quad and \quad \left(M^C \models \psi^C \wedge \neg \delta \right) \tag{A.17}$$

Again, we can use a real-time modelchecker to prove $\psi^C \wedge \neg \delta$ for M^C. To ensure that M^C refines each of the role protocols associated to its ports, we propose to use syntactical refinement rules instead of an explicit verification step (see [GH06]).

Proving the correctness of all m components (m' different ones) requires m' checks in $O(\exp(h))$, where h is the maximal number of roles per component. Like in the case of patterns, usually a fixed upper bound for h exists in our domain.

System Verification   Due to the compositional nature of our approach, an additional step to perform verification for the overall system after its composition is not required. We define our notion of a semantically correct system in Definition 30.

Definition 30 *For* $\mathcal{S} = (\mathcal{P}, \mathcal{C}, map)$ *with a set* $\mathcal{P}$ *of patterns* $P_1, \ldots P_n$, *a set* $\mathcal{C}$ *of components* $C_1, \ldots, C_m$, *semantical correctness* holds iff the pattern constraints ϕ_i^P and component invariants ψ_j^C also hold for the system itself:

$$M_1^P \| \ldots \| M_n^P \| M_1^C \| \ldots \| M_m^C \models \phi_{C_1}^P \wedge \cdots \wedge \phi_n^P \wedge \neg \delta \ and \tag{A.18}$$
$$M_1^P \| \ldots \| M_n^P \| M_1^C \| \ldots \| M_m^C \models \psi_1^C \wedge \cdots \wedge \psi_m^C. \tag{A.19}$$

In Figure 3.1 we depicted the different models built for verification. Common modular approaches result in a disjoint decomposition of the system. In our approach, however, we have overlapping models where the specified role protocols of each pattern and parallel operating protocol refinement of the components refer to the same port. These sets of ports and roles are employed as maximal non-deterministic context for the components as well as guaranteed behavior of each pattern role. For more details about the compositional verification approach see [GTB+03, Gie03].

Appendix B

Partitioning Algorithm

In Section 3.2.2, we described how to abstract a configuration by its reduced graph. The algorithm, informally introduced in Section 3.2.2, has been defined formally in [BGGO04b]. This formalization is presented in this appendix.

We describe a basic continuous component by an acyclic graph. A single node is characterized by input, output, and state variables and a set of expressions with a left-hand-side variable and a right-hand-side expression with references to other variables. We derive an acyclic expression graph $G = (N, E)$ with node set N and edge set $E \subseteq N \times N$, where for each $n \in N$ and the related expression $v := \ldots v' \ldots$ holds that for each variable v' the expression refers to in the right-hand-side, an edge $(n', n) \in E$ exists with n' the node related to variable v'.

For an acyclic graph $G = (N, E)$, we have the following additionally defined terms:

- $d_{out}((N, E), n) := |\{n' \in N | (n, n') \in E\}|$ the out-degree of node n,

- $d_{in}((N, E), n) := |\{n' \in N | (n', n) \in E\}|$ the in-degree of node n,

- $N_{out} \subseteq N$ the subset of output nodes with $\forall n \in N_{out}$ holds $d_{out}((N, e), n) = 0$,

- $N_{in} \subseteq N$ the subset of input nodes with $\forall n \in N_{in}$ holds $d_{in}((N, E), n) = 0$, and

- $N_{state} \subseteq N$ the subset of nodes which represent the internal state of the node.

The partitioning problem for a given acyclic expression graph $G = (N, E)$ of a node is how to determine a minimum number of partitions $N_1, \ldots, N_n \subseteq N$ such that:

1. $N = N_1 \cup \cdots \cup N_n$ and $\forall i \neq j \ N_i \cap N_j = \emptyset$,

2. the derived graph $G_p = (N_p, E_p)$ with $N_p = \{N_1, \ldots, N_n\}$ and $E_p = \{(N_i, N_j) | i \neq j \land i, j = 1, \ldots, n \land \exists n' \in N_i \land n'' \in N_j : (n', n'') \in E\}$ is acyclic, and

3. for any context graph $G' = (N', E')$ with $(N \cap N') \subseteq (N_{in} \cup N_{out})$ and $G'' = (N'', E'')$ with $N'' = N \cup N'$ and $E'' = E \cup E'$ an acyclic graph holds that the related derived graph the partitioning build by $N_1, \ldots, N_n$ and each node of $N' - N$ is also an acyclic graph (cf. [OGBG04]).

Such a minimal partitioning is computed by means of the following algorithm that obtains an acyclic expression graph and returns its reduced graph:

```
node_partitioning((N,E)) begin
  Din  :  N  →  ℘(Nin ∪ Nstate); // input dependencies
  Iout :  N  →  ℘(Nout ∪ Nstate); // influenced outputs
  L    :  N  →  ℘(Nin); // related input nodes
  c    :  N  →  ℕ; // visited successors

  // forward traversal to compute all input dependencies
  F := Nin ∪ Nstate;
  forall n ∈ F do Din[n] := { n }; done
  forall n ∈ N do c[n] := 0; done

  while ( F ≠ ∅ ) do
    forall (n ∈ F ) do
      forall n' ∈ N with (n,n') ∈ E do
        c[n'] := c[n'] + 1;
        if c[n'] == din((N, E), n') then
          Din[n'] := ⋃(n'',n')∈ E Din[n''];
          if (n' ∉ Nstate ∪ Nout) then
            F := F ∪ {n'};
          fi
        fi
      done
      F := F − {n};
    done
  done

  // backward traversal to compute all influenced outputs
  F := Nout ∪ Nstate;
  forall n ∈ F do Iout[n] := { n }; done
  forall n ∈ N do c[n] := 0; done

  while ( F ≠ ∅ ) do
    forall n ∈ F  do
      forall n' ∈ N with (n',n) ∈ E do
        c[n'] := c[n'] + 1;
        if c[n'] == dout((N, E), n') then
          Iout[n'] := ⋃(n',n'')∈ E Iout[n''];
          if (n' ∉ Nstate ∪ Nin) then
            F := F ∪ {n'};
          fi
        fi
      done
      F := F − {n};
    done
  done

  // compute S and ND nodes
  N' := N;
```

```
forall n ∈ N do
  // n is an element of the S-node
  if (I_out[n] ⊆ N_state) then
    L[n] := 'S';
    N' := N' - {n};
  else
    // n is an element of the ND-node
    if (D_in[n] ⊆ N_state) then
      L[n] := 'ND';
      N' := N' - {n};
    fi
  fi
done


// backward traversal to compute L
// L[n] set of related input nodes
E' := E ∩ (N' × N');
F := N_out ∩ N';
forall n ∈ F do L[n] := D_in[n] ∩ N'; done
forall n ∈ N do c[n] := 0; done

while ( F ≠ ∅ ) do
  forall n ∈ F do
    forall n' ∈ N' with (n',n) ∈ E' do
      c[n'] := c[n'] + 1;
      if c[n'] == d_out((N', E'),n') then
        L[n'] := ∩_{(n',n'')∈ E'} L[n''];
        F := F ∪ {n'};
      fi
    done
    F := F - {n};
  done
done


// n and n' are in the same superordinated node
// iff L[n] = L[n']
forall n ∈ N do N_sup^{L[n]} := ∅; done
forall n ∈ N do
  N_sup^{L[n]} := N_sup^{L[n]} ∪ {n};
done
N_sup = ∅; //the set of all superordinated nodes
forall n ∈ N do
  if (N_sub^{L[n]} ∉ N_sub)
    N_sub = N_sub ∪ {N_sub^{L[n]}};
  fi
done


// compute all input dependencies for the superordinated nodes
E_sup = ∅;
forall (n_sup ∈ N_sup) do
  forall n ∈ n_sup with (n',n)∈ E and n' ∈ n'_sup ∈ N_sup do
```

```
        if ((n_sup, n'_sup) ∉ E_sup)
            E_sup = E_sup ∪ {(n_sup, n'_sup)};
        fi
    done
  done

  return (N_sup, E_sup);
end
```

Appendix C

Elementary Operations

Table C.1 shows the elementary operations, that are part of the platform model (PM). They are the basis for the WCET determination of story patterns and story diagrams, as described in Section 4.2.3. The worst-case execution times have been determined on an Intel Pentium 4 system with 2.4 GHz by testing.

Elementary Operation	WCET
BIND_LINK_TO_ONE	20 ηsec
BIND_OPTIONAL_TO_ONE	20 ηsec
CHECK_LINK_TO_ONE	30 ηsec
CHECK_OPTIONAL_LINK_TO_ONE	30 ηsec
CHECK_NEGATIVE_LINK_TO_ONE	30 ηsec
CHECK_NEGATIVE_NODE_TO_ONE	30 ηsec
CHECK_SINGLE_NEGATIVE_NODE_TO_ONE	30 ηsec
CREATE_LINK_TO_ONE	20 ηsec
DESTROY_LINK_TO_ONE	20 ηsec
BIND_LINK_TO_MANY	10 ηsec
BIND_OPTIONAL_TO_MANY	10 ηsec
CHECK_LINK_TO_MANY	40 ηsec
CHECK_OPTIONAL_LINK_TO_MANY	50 ηsec
CHECK_NEGATIVE_LINK_TO_MANY	50 ηsec
CHECK_NEGATIVE_NODE_TO_MANY	50 ηsec
CHECK_SINGLE_NEGATIVE_NODE_TO_MANY	50 ηsec
CREATE_LINK_TO_MANY	30 ηsec
DESTORY_LINK_TO_MANY	40 ηsec
BIND_MULTILINK_DIRECT	100 ηsec
BIND_MULTILINK_INDIRECT	100 ηsec
BIND_MULTILINK_INDEX	160 ηsec
BIND_MULTILINK_FIRST	60 ηsec
BIND_MULTILINK_LAST	60 ηsec
CHECK_MULTILINK_DIRECT	90 ηsec
CHECK_MULTILINK_INDIRECT	90 ηsec
CHECK_MULTILINK_INDEX	160 ηsec
CHECK_MULTILINK_FIRST	60 ηsec
CHECK_MULTILINK_LAST	80 ηsec
CHECK_ISOMORPHISM	20 ηsec
CREATE_OBJECT	20 ηsec
DESTROY_OBJECT	30 ηsec
SET_ITERATOR_WITH_METHODCALL_ITERATOROF	40 ηsec
INITIALIZE_ATTRIBUTE_WITH_NULL	10 ηsec
INITIALIZE_ITERATOR	30 ηsec
INITIALIZE_BOOL_VALUE	1860 ηsec
SET_BOOL_VALUE	1890 ηsec
DO_BREAK_WHILE	20 ηsec

Table C.1: Elementary Operations and their WCETs

Appendix D

WCET Determination & Optimization of Story Patterns

In Section 4.2.3, we introduced informally the *story graph* in order to determine optimal matching sequences for story patterns and their WCETs. In this appendix, we first introduce the elements from the story pattern definition from [Zün02] which are required in the remainder of this appendix. Then, we use these elements to define our story graph formally and to relate it to its corresponding story pattern. Finally, we present how to determine and to optimize a story patterns WCET.

A story pattern grr is formally defined as $\mathsf{grr} = (\mathsf{LG}, \mathsf{RG})$ with $\mathsf{LG} = (N_{\mathsf{LG}}, E_{\mathsf{LG}}, l_{\mathsf{LG}}, a_{\mathsf{LG}})$ the *left graph* and $\mathsf{RG} = (N_{\mathsf{RG}}, E_{\mathsf{RG}}, l_{\mathsf{RG}}, a_{\mathsf{RG}})$ the *right graph*. l_{LG} and l_{RG} respectively are node labeling functions, a_{LG} and a_{RG} respectively are attribute value functions. For further information, we refer to [Zün02]. $N_{\mathsf{grr}} := N_{LG} \cup N_{RG}$ are the nodes of the story pattern and $E_{\mathsf{grr}} := E_{LG} \cup E_{RG}$ are the edges. In the following, we will just refer to N_{grr} and E_{grr}.

Formal definition of a story Graph   A formal definition of the *story graph* is given in Definition 31.[1]

Definition 31 *A story graph G is a tuple $G = (V, E)$ with V the set of nodes and $E \subseteq (V \times V \times \mathbb{N}^3 \times \mathbb{N} \times \wp(E_{\mathsf{grr}}) \times T)$ the set of edges.* $T = \{$ BindNormal, BindOptional, CheckIsomorphism, CheckLink, CheckAttribute, CheckConstraint, CheckNegativeLink, CheckNegativeNode$\}$ *is the set of edge types of the story graph. An edge $e = (s, t, w, c, L, \mathsf{type}) \in E$ consists of the following elements:*

- *$s \in V$ is the source node,*

- *$t \in V$ is the target node,*

- *$w = A_{tt} = (w_f, w_d, c_a)$ is a triple we call AnalysedTypeTime. It includes all timing information required to compute the WCET for an implementation of matching the edge e.*

---

[1] $\wp(A)$ denotes the power set of A.

- $c \in \mathbb{N}$ *is the maximum number of iterations that is required for binding the edge* e.

- $L = \{e_{\text{grr}1}, \ldots, e_{\text{grr}n}\} \subseteq E_{\text{grr}}$ *is a set of story pattern edges that are associated with the story graph edge* e.

- type $\in T$ *is the type of the edge* e.

Deriving a story graph from a story pattern   When deriving a story graph $G = (V, E)$ from a story pattern grr with node set N_{grr} and edge set E_{grr}, we simply use the story pattern nodes as story graph nodes: $V := N_{\text{grr}}$. The story graph edges are derived from the story pattern edges: For each story pattern edge $e_{\text{grr}} \in E_{\text{grr}}$, we create at least one story graph edge $e = (s, t, w, c, L, \text{type}) \in E$, conform to the rules given in Section 4.2.3. In L, we store the corresponding story pattern edges. Usually L contains exactly one story pattern edge ($|L| = 1$), but if the story graph edge is of type CheckNegativeNode, multiple story pattern edges are associated with it (cf. Section 4.2.3 or [BGST05, Sei05]). L does not influence WCET computation, but it provides information required for implementation issues. Note that it holds $|V| = |N_{\text{grr}}|$ and $|E| \geq |E_{\text{grr}}|$.

An AnalysedTypeTime $w = A_{tt} = (w_f, w_d, c_a)$ contains run-time information of the implementation that we provide. w_f is a fixed execution time that occurs due to a code fragment before starting a possible loop. w_d is the execution time for a single loop iteration. The values for w_f and w_d are derived from the elementary operations that are part of the platform model. The number of iterations is stored in c_a that results from the exactly defined multiplicities of the related association in the related class diagram introduced in Section 2.2.3. Note the distinction between c_a and c: They are equal ($c_a = c$), except for story graph edges with type $= \{\text{CheckNegativeNode}\}$. In this case $c = 1$ and c_a is derived from the defined exact multiplicity of the related association.

WCET of a matching sequence for a story pattern   Following the rules, outlined in Section 4.2.3, leads to a matching sequence S for the story pattern. This matching sequence is an n-tuple of story graph edges and thus, it has the form as defined in Definition 32.

Definition 32 *Let* $G = (V, E)$ *be the story graph of the story pattern* grr. *A matching sequence* S *has the form* $S = (e_1, \ldots, e_n)$ *with* $e_i = (s_i, t_i, w_i, c_i, L_i, \text{type}_i) \in E$.

As explained in [Sei05], the WCET of such a matching sequence S is given by Definition 33.

Definition 33 *Let* $C(S)$ *be the WCET for a matching sequence* S *of a story graph* G *with* $S = (e_1, \ldots, e_n)$, $e_i = (s_i, t_i, w_i, c_i, L_i, \text{type}_i)$, *and* $w_i = (w_{fi}, w_{di}, c_{ai})$. *Then* $C(S) = \sum_{i=1}^{n} \left[(w_{fi} + w_{di} \cdot c_{ai}) \cdot \left(\prod_{j=0}^{i-1} c_j \right) \right] + pC(G, S)$ *with* $c_0 := 1$.

The function $pC(G, S)$ returns a run-time that is caused by code fragments that do not affect the run-time of the related matching sequence related to S. These code fragments are executed before or after performing the matching. For example, instance and reference deletion takes place after successful matching.

Searching the optimal matching sequence Although the order of choosing the edges of a story graph is restricted by the selection rules, usually multiple different matching sequences exist. The algorithm from Figure D.1, taken from [BGST05], is applied to obtain the optimal matching sequence (i.e. the one that leads to a minimal WCET).

1: $s \leftarrow$ Defined WCET of the engineer
2: $AS \leftarrow ApproximatedSolution(G)$
3: $k \leftarrow C(AS) \vee$ defined upper bound of the engineer
4: $minimum \leftarrow \emptyset$
5: $L \leftarrow \emptyset \wedge S.valid = true$
6: **function** OPTIMALSOLUTION(G, S)
7:     Sort all edges from $i = 1...n$ ascending by $w_{fi} + (w_{di} \cdot c_{ai})$
8:     **if** (Not all edges $e_i \in E$ in G marked) $\wedge$ (Edges still reachable) $\wedge$ ($S.valid = true$) **then**
9:         **for** All reachable edges $e_i \in E$ in G **do**
10:            $G' = (V', E') \leftarrow G = (V, E)$
11:            $L' \leftarrow L \circ e_i$
12:            Process all necessary markings $e_i' \in E'$ of G'
13:            **if** $C(L') < k$ **then**
14:                $OptimalSolution(G', L')$
15:            **else**
16:                $S'.valid \leftarrow false$
17:            **end if**
18:        **end for**
19:        **if** still edges e_i available **then**
20:            $S.valid \leftarrow false$
21:        **end if**
22:    **end if**
23:    **if** L.valid = true **then**
24:        $minimum \leftarrow L$
25:        $k \leftarrow C(minimum)$
26:    **end if**
27:    **if** $k \leq s$ **then**
28:        Terminate
29:    **end if**
30: **end function**

Figure D.1: Algorithm for $min(C(S))$ determination

This algorithm requires a function ApproximatedSolution. This function implements the heuristic algorithm that is used to obtain a first approximated solution. This algorithm, also taken from [BGST05], is shown in Figure D.2.

1: **function** APPROXIMATEDSOLUTION(G)
2:     $S \leftarrow \emptyset$
3:     Sort all edges from $i = 1...n$ ascending by $w_{fi} + (w_{di} \cdot c_{ai})$
4:     **for** Not all edges e_i in G are marked **do**
5:         **for** Unmarked edges reachable **do**
6:             Choose possible edge e_i from $S(G)$ with smallest $w_{fi} + (w_{di} \cdot c_{ai})$
7:             $S \leftarrow S \circ e_i$
8:         **end for**
9:     **end for**
10:    $return(L)$
11: **end function**

Figure D.2: Algorithm to determine a first matching sequence

Appendix E

Profile Synthesis Algorithm

In Section 4.2.5, we presented our algorithm to derive profiles from the extended models, which have been introduced in Section 3.2.5. The algorithm, which has originally been defined formally in [BGGO04a], is presented in this appendix.

Let $G = (N, T)$ denote the related graph with nodes N representing the states of the statechart and $T \subseteq N \times N$ its transitions. We additionally distinguish the subset T_r, T_b, and T_e of required, blockable, and enforceable transitions with $T = T_r \cup T_b$ and $T_r \cap T_b = \emptyset$. Any subgraph (N', T') with $N' \subseteq N$ and $T' \subseteq T \cap N' \times N'$ could be a possible profile.

The quality of each state $n \in N$ is denoted by $q : N \to \mathbb{R}$ and for a group of states $N' \subseteq N$ we use $q(N') := \max\{q(n) | n \in N'\}$. The quality of a profile is given by the maximum of all contained state's qualities $(q((N,T)) = q(N))$. The required amount for all m resources of each state and transition is accordingly assigned by the function $r : (N \cup T) \to \mathbb{R}^m$. For a subgraph (N', T'), we use the element-wise cost maxima as costs $(r((N', T')) := \max(\{(r_1, \ldots, r_m) | \forall i \in [1 : m] \; \exists x \in N' \cup T' : r(x) = (x_1, \ldots, x_i, \ldots, x_m) \wedge x_i = r_i\})$.[1]

Optimal Permanent Profiles

The profile framework usually expects that an application is able to stay within the assigned profile permanently. For such permanent profiles of an application, we require that the related subgraph is closed with respect to required transitions.

Definition 34 *A profile* (N', T') *is* permanent *iff forall required edges* $(n, n') \in T_r \cap N' \times N$ *holds* $n' \in N'$.

We further denote with $[(N', T')]$ the largest subgraph of (N', T') which is closed with respect to required transitions. It can be computed as the largest fix-point of the function C on profiles defined as $C((N', T')) := (N'', T'')$ with $N'' = \{n \in N' | \forall (n, n') \in T_r : n' \in N'\}$ and $T'' = T' \cap (N'' \times N'')$. The set of permanent profiles is further closed under union and intersection.

The number of profiles can be exponential in the number of states (which might itself be rather large). Thus, we are not interested in computing all possible profiles but only *optimal* ones. Informally, a profile is optimal when no other profile contains it which offers a higher or equal quality for the same or less costs. We formalize optimality in the following definition:

Definition 35 *A permanent profile* (N', T') *is optimal iff no other permanent profile* (N'', T'') *exists with:*

$$(N', T') \quad \subset \quad (N'', T'') \tag{E.1}$$

$$r((N', T')) \quad \geq \quad r((N'', T'')) \tag{E.2}$$

$$q((N', T')) \quad \leq \quad q((N'', T'')) \tag{E.3}$$

The conditions E.1, E.2, and E.3 respectively describe that no larger profile with equal or less costs exists which has the same or higher quality. As the quality is implied by set containment, we can simply skip condition E.3. Also condition E.2 can be made more strict, as a larger set of nodes and transitions can by definition only be as cheap as the contained one but not cheaper. Thus, we have:

$$(N', T') \quad \subset \quad (N'', T'') \tag{E.4}$$

$$r((N', T')) \quad = \quad r((N'', T'')). \tag{E.5}$$

If such a profile (N'', T'') exists, we further say that (N'', T'') dominates (N', T'). The full graph (N, T) is an optimal one by definition as condition E.4 cannot be fulfilled by any other profile. To compute optimal profiles efficiently, we use the following idea.

Lemma 1 *For a given optimal profile* (N', T') *with costs* $k = r((N', T'))$, *we can construct an optimal profile* $(N_{k'}, T_{k'})$ *for any* $k' \leq k$ *with maximal* $r((N_{k'}, T_{k'})) \leq k'$ *as follows:*

- $N'' = N' - \{n \in N' | r(n) > k'\}$,

- $T'' = T' - \{t \in T' | r(t) > k'\}$, *and*

- $(N_{k'}, T_{k'}) = [(N'', T'')]$.

Proof 3 *Assuming a profile* (N''', T''') *exists which fulfills conditions E.4 and E.5 w.r.t. the profile* $(N_{k'}, T_{k'})$ *constructed as outlined above, we have* $k'' = r((N''', T'''))$ *and* $(N''', T''') \supset (N_{k'}, T_{k'})$. *It must hold* $(N''', T''') \subseteq (N', T')$, *because otherwise* $(N''', T''') \cup (N', T')$ *dominates* (N', T') *and, thus,* (N', T') *would not be optimal.*

Thus, an element $x \in (N''' \cup T''') - (N_{k'} \cup T_{k'})$ *must exist, as otherwise the assumed profile would not dominate* $(N_{k'}, T_{k'})$. *For* $x \in (N' \cup T') - (N'' \cup T'')$ *we can conclude that* $r(x) > k'$ *and, thus,* $r((N''', T''')) > k'$ *which contradicts our assumption. For* $x \in (N'' \cup T'') - (N_{k'} \cup T_{k'})$ *we can conclude that* (N''', T''') *is not permanent which also contradicts our assumption. Thus, finally no such profile* (N''', T''') *which dominates* $(N_{k'}, T_{k'})$ *can exist and thus the profile* $(N_{k'}, T_{k'})$ *is an optimal one.*

As no $(N''', T''') \supset (N_{k'}, T_{k'})$ *can exist,* $k''' = r((N_{k'}, T_{k'}))$ *is always maximal with respect to the upper bound* k'.

Therefore, we compute the optimal profile for a given $k' \in \mathbb{R}^m$ by simply starting with the full graph and applying the outlined steps. Hierarchical and orthogonal states are respected as described in [Sch05b].

Besides optimality of permanent profiles, a controlled transition between two profiles is required to allow the framework to enforce a switch between these two profiles. Using the set of enforceable transitions T_e, we can formally define whether the framework can enforce the transition from one profile to another.

Definition 36 *A profile* (N', T') *is* reachable *from a profile* (N'', T'') *iff forall* $n \in N'' - N'$ *exists* $(n, n') \in T_e$ *with* $n' \in N'$. *We write* $(N'', T'') \rightarrow_e (N', T')$.

For the relation between optimal profiles and reachability, we can prove the following Lemma 2, which ensures that each time a non-optimal profile is reachable although the larger optimal profile is reachable. Thus, we can restrict our attention to optional profiles when reachability is considered.

Lemma 2 *For profiles* (N', T'), (N'', T''), *and* (N''', T''') *with* $(N', T') \subseteq (N'', T'')$ *holds*

$$(N''', T''') \rightarrow_e (N', T') \Rightarrow (N''', T''') \rightarrow_e (N'', T'')$$

Proof 4 *Follows directly from Definition 36, as* $N''' - N' \supseteq N''' - N''$.

Temporary Profiles

Let T_r^{MIET} be the set of uncontrolled steps which are the possible series of steps which can occur within the time bound T^{MIET} and T_e the controlled transitions. For a temporary profile, we thus only require that a related core profile exists which ensures that for any application of a composed edge from T_r^{MIET} the profile is not left.

Definition 37 *For a profile* (N', T') *and its* core (N'', T''), *it must hold that forall edges* $(n, n') \in T_r^{MIET} \cap N'' \times N$ *holds* $n' \in N'$.

To compute the largest core (N'', T'') of (N', T') with respect to T_r^{MIET}, we can compute $N'' = \{n \in N' | \forall (n, n') \in T_r^{MIET} : n' \in N'\}$ and $T'' = T \cap (N'' \times N'')$. We write $[(N', T')]^{MIET}$ to denote this maximal core. Analogously, we can compute the largest profile (N', T') for a given core (N'', T'') with respect to T_r^{MIET} as $N' = \{n \in N | \forall (n, n') \in T_r^{MIET} : n \in N''\}$ and $T' = T \cap (N' \times N')$. We write $](N', T')[^{MIET}$ to denote this maximal profile for a given core. The problem to realize a transition between two optimal profiles relates to the problem of finding a series of temporary profiles (*attractor*) with respect to T_e the controlled transitions.

Definition 38 *A series of profiles* $\{(N_i, T_i) | i \in \mathbb{N}\}$ *is an* attractor *for the profile* (N'', T'') *with respect to the controller transitions* T_e *and the uncontrolled transitions* T_r^{MIET} *iff for all* $n \in N_{i+1}$ *and* $(n, n') \in T_r^{MIET}$ *exists* $(n', n'') \in T_e$ *with* $n'' \in N_i$ *and* $(N_0, T_0) = (N'', T'')$.

We have to construct an attractor for the target profile (N'', T'') such that a path backwards to our start profile (N', T') exists: We compute the *attractor* starting with the target profile. By looking for additional states of the current profile where any possible uncontrolled step can be continued in such a manner that the current profile is reached, we compute the next profile. If the extension leads to a profile which includes the source profile, we are done. Otherwise no indirect connection can be established.

Using T_r^{MIET}, we can thus compute the *attractor* of (N'', T'') as follows:

1. Initially set $N_0 = N''$ and $T_0 = T''$.

2. Compute $N'_{i+1} = N_i \cup \{n \in N - N_i | \exists (n, n') \in T_e \wedge n' \in N_i\}$ and $T'_{i+1} = T \cap (N'_{i+1} \times N'_{i+1})$ from (N_i, T_i).

3. Compute the core $(N''_{i+1}, T''_{i+1}) = [(N'_{i+1}, T'_{i+1})]^{MIET}$ of (N'_{i+1}, T'_{i+1}) and determine the next profile (N_{i+1}, T_{i+1}) by $N_{i+1} = N''_{i+1} \cup N_i$ and $T_{i+1} = T \cap (N_{i+1} \times N_{i+1})$.

4. Repeat with step 2 until the start profile (N', T') is included $((N_{i+1}, T_{i+1}) \supseteq (N', T'))$ or the expansion has terminated $((N_{i+1}, T_{i+1}) = (N_i, T_i))$.

By construction, we always have $(N_{i+1}, T_{i+1}) \supseteq (N_i, T_i)$. Thus, the profiles of the attractor $\{(N_i, T_i) | i \in \mathbb{N}\}$ are monotonously increasing but not necessarily strict monotonous increasing. For each step $i \in [2 : p]$ we further write $(N_i, T_i) \rightarrow_{r,e} (N_{i-1}, T_{i-1})$ as it holds:

$$(N_i, T_i) \rightarrow_r^{MIET}](N_i, T_i)[^{MIET} \rightarrow_e (N_{i-1}, T_{i-1}).$$

If no $(N_i, T_i) \supseteq (N', T')$ has been found, in fact no possible sequence of temporary profiles leads from (N', T') to (N'', T''). Otherwise, if we have found a profile (N_p, T_p) which contains (N', T'), we can construct such a sequence using the computed profiles of the attractor in opposite ordering

$$(N', T') \supseteq (N_p, T_p) \rightarrow_{r,e} \cdots \rightarrow_{r,e} (N_0, T_0) = (N'', T'').$$

Compute Profile Graph

For a resource function $r : (N \cup T) \rightarrow \mathbb{R}^m$, no unique ordering of the elements with respect to resource requirements is possible and, thus, we have a partially ordered set of profiles, which in the worst-case contains exponentially many optimal profiles. Thus, we propose to partition the m dimensional space using a proper set K of upper resource limits which is derived as follows: (1) determine for each dimension the minima and maxima $(\min_i = \min(\{r_i(x) | x \in N \cup T\})$ and $\max_i = \max(\{r_i(x) | x \in N \cup T\}))$, (2) determine a number of steps $s_i \geq 1$ for each dimension, and (3) chose K as $K_1 \times \cdots \times K_m$ with $K_i = \{c | \exists j \in [0 : s_i] : c = \min_i + (\max_i - \min_i)/s_i * j\}$.

As every use of the algorithm, which is sketched in Lemma 1, will cost at most $|N| + |T|$ steps, computing all optimal profiles is then in $O(|K| * (|N| + |T|))$. The computation of the maximal $|K|$ profiles with at most $|K|^2$ direct transitions is in $O(|K|^2 * (|N| + |T|))$.

For the indirect connections via temporary profiles, we require $O(|N| + |T|)^2$ for computing the attractors and, thus, the algorithm to compute them is in $O(|K|^2 * (|N| + |T|)^2)$. Thus, we have an overall algorithmic effort, which is in $O(|K|^2 * (|N| + |T|)^2 + |K|^3)$.

Appendix F

Hybrid Component Exchange Format

As mentioned in Chapter 5, the CAE tool CAMeL-View and the CASE tool Fujaba have been extended to export and import hybrid components. The XML exchange format is defined by the following DTD:

```
<!ELEMENT Component (SourceCode, CompStateDependentPorts,
    SubComponentNames, ContPorts, Nodes, ConstructorInformation, Private)>

  <!ATTLIST Component
      tool (CAMeL | Fujaba) #REQUIRED
      type (isHybrid | isComponent | isBasisBlock | isHcs) #REQUIRED
      name CDATA #REQUIRED>

<!ELEMENT SourceCode (CPPHeaderSourceCode+, CPPSourceCode+,
Checksum+)>

<!ELEMENT CPPHeaderSourceCode>

  <!ATTLIST CPPHeaderSourceCode fileName CDATA #REQUIRED>

<!ELEMENT CPPSourceCode>

  <!ATTLIST CPPSourceCode fileName CDATA #REQUIRED>

<!ELEMENT Checksum(#CDATA)>

<!ELEMENT CompStateDependentPorts (State*)>

<!ELEMENT State (Node*)>

  <!ATTLIST State name CDATA #REQUIRED >
```

```
<!ELEMENT Node (PortCont*, Node*)>

  <!ATTLIST Node
          type   CDATA #REQUIRED
          nodeID CDATA #REQUIRED>

<!ELEMENT ContPort (mathClass*, size*, unit*, default*)>

  <!ATTLIST ContPort
          type (in | out | parameter) #REQUIRED
          PortID CDATA #REQUIRED>

<!ELEMENT mathClass(#CDATA)> <!ELEMENT size(#CDATA)>

<!ELEMENT unit(#CDATA)> <!ELEMENT default(#CDATA)>

<!ELEMENT SubComponentNames (SubComponentName*)>

<!ELEMENT SubComponentName>

  <!ATTLIST SubComponentName
          name        CDATA #REQUIRED
          fileName    CDATA #REQUIRED>

<!ELEMENT ContPorts (ContPort*)>

<!ELEMENT Nodes (NodePortDependence*)>

<!ELEMENT NodePortDependence (Port* , SubNode*)>

  <!ATTLIST NodePortDependence
          type (isD | isS | isND) #REQUIRED
          nodeID        CDATA #REQUIRED>

<!ELEMENT Port>
  <!ATTLIST Port portID CDATA #REQUIRED>

<!ELEMENT SubNode (Block)>

  <!ATTLIST SubNode nodeID CDATA #REQUIRED>

<!ELEMENT Block>
```

```
<!ATTLIST Block name CDATA #REQUIRED>

<!ELEMENT ConstructorInformation (noOfContInputPorts,
                                  noOfContOutputPorts ,
                                  noOfContParamPorts,
                                  noOfSubComponents)>

<!ELEMENT noOfContInputPorts (#CDATA)>

<!ELEMENT noOfContOutputPorts (#CDATA)>

<!ELEMENT noOfContParamPorts (#CDATA)>

<!ELEMENT noOfSubcomponents (#CDATA)>

<!ELEMENT Private>

  <!ATTLIST Private xmls CDATA #REQUIRED>

<!ELEMENT Private(OdssClassName, DSLSourceCode, Conditions*)>

<!ELEMENT OdssClassName (#CDATA)>

<!ELEMENT DSLSourceCode (#CDATA)>

<!ELEMENT Conditions (Condition*)>

<!ELEMENT Condition (sourceComponent, sourcePortID, destComponent,
destPortID)>

  <!ATTLIST Condition type (inputCondition     | outputCondition |
            parameterCondition | coupleCondition) #REQUIRED>

<!ELEMENT sourceComponent (#CDATA)>

<!ELEMENT sourcePortID (#CDATA)>

<!ELEMENT destComponent (#CDATA)>

<!ELEMENT destPortID (#CDATA)>
```